D1590688

Judicial Conflict
and Consensus

Judicial Conflict and Consensus

Behavioral Studies of American Appellate Courts

Edited by
SHELDON GOLDMAN
and **CHARLES M. LAMB**

THE UNIVERSITY PRESS OF KENTUCKY

Scholarly publisher for the Commonwealth,
serving Bellarmine College, Berea College, Centre
College of Kentucky, Eastern Kentucky University,
The Filson Club, Georgetown College, Kentucky
Historical Society, Kentucky State University,
Morehead State University, Murray State University,
Northern Kentucky University, Transylvania University,
University of Kentucky, University of Louisville,
and Western Kentucky University.

Editorial and Sales Offices: Lexington, Kentucky 40506-0024

Library of Congress Cataloging in Publication Data

Main entry under title:

Judicial conflict and consensus.

Includes index.
1. Judicial process—United States.
2. Appellate courts—United States. I. Goldman,
Sheldon. II. Lamb, Charles M.
KF8775.J82 1986   347.73'242   85-17937
ISBN 0-8131-1554-X   347.3073

In memory of
Joseph Tanenhaus
and Harold Chase

Contents

Tables and Figures

TABLES

FIGURES

Preface

Our purpose in assembling the pieces prepared for this volume was to bring together some of the best researchers and latest research on judicial behavior generally centered on the theme of conflict and consensus on appellate courts in America. It is our hope that this concentrated dose of studies on judicial behavior can illuminate both what we know and need to know about how appellate courts function. If the cumulative effect of the studies published here accomplishes that objective, we will consider this undertaking a success. By focusing on three court levels it is also our aim that this book makes a contribution to comparative judicial behavior within the American political landscape.

As editors we thank the contributors to this volume for agreeing to participate and for their cooperation. The reader should understand that it was necessary to impose page lengths on the authors and that were it not for this restriction, more elaborate argument or more detailed analysis would have been offered by many of the authors.

We have sought to provide in the Prologue a broader portrait of the contents in the context of the research problem of conflict and consensus on appellate courts. In the Epilogue we seek to tie together the contributions of the individual chapters to judicial decision-making theory, comparative judicial behavior, and implications for future research.

We are grateful to those who facilitated the creation of special panels devoted to judicial conflict and consensus at the annual meetings of the American Political Science Association (1982), Southern Political Science Association (1982), and Midwest Political Science Association (1983) at which early versions of the substantive chapters were first presented.

Prologue

SHELDON GOLDMAN and
CHARLES M. LAMB

Judges who serve on most collegial courts in the United States are believed by students of courts to aim for decisional consensus. Indeed, evidence suggests a continual quest to reduce conflict through holding conferences, circulating draft opinions and memorandums, and conducting private meetings between individual judges or groups of judges.[1] On some courts the expectation is that judges will suppress dissenting opinions because of the perceived advantages of judicial unanimity. A unanimous decision can usually expect a friendlier reception from other courts, politicians, lawyers, the media, and even the general public than a divided one. When judges speak with one voice, it suggests that they have reached the "right" decision, which may be particularly crucial if it has major implications beyond the immediate dispute. It reinforces the judicial myth that there is always an objective legal solution which is dictated by the law and principles of legal reasoning. The avoidance of overt dissension may be imperative to mobilize political and public support behind new or controversial court policy and ultimately to obtain compliance.[2]

Yet consensual decision making serves another key function in addition to promoting support for and compliance with judicial policy. That function is to avoid or minimize conflict among judges with different values and attitudes, especially judges serving on the same appellate courts. Of course, accommodation, compromise, and cohesion are not always possible on collegial courts. In resolving disputes emerging from American society, internal disagreements frequently arise over constitutional or statutory questions. As Justice Oliver Wendell Holmes, Jr., said about the Supreme Court, "we are very quiet there, but it is the quiet of a storm center."[3] Nor should we expect appellate court judges to agree easily in most cases. As Justice Tom C.

Clark once observed: "Differences of opinion must be expected on legal questions as on other subjects. . . . The history of progress is filled with many pages of disagreement. Why, therefore, . . . expect 'the most influential men . . . on the bench . . . trained in different philosophy and matured in a different climate' to have the same thoughts and views? They don't and they won't."[4] Judges thus are often required to invest a great deal of time and energy hammering out agreements so as to avoid public disagreement. Too much conflict may become institutionally dysfunctional. When consenting to unanimous decisions, judges may be placing institutional considerations above personal preferences. Unanimity thus underscores the individual judge's fidelity to the group (the judicial institution) because no judge is seen as deviating from group norms. All act as one.

To understand judicial politics and behavior, therefore, we must recognize that conflict accompanies the passionate nature of many disputes brought to appellate courts and that such conflict directly affects the decision-making process. If a reasonable degree of consensus is not reached through amicable give-and-take, judicial decision making can become substantially prolonged and backlogs of cases can accumulate as the energies of judges become diverted by the writing of concurrences and dissents. Moreover, judges may subsequently develop overt or covert ill will toward the colleagues with whom they disagree, which may take such diverse forms as open hostility and personal antagonism to forbearance but cloaked disaccord.[5] One reality of judicial decision making is that regardless of the institutional factors promoting consensus, conflict is inevitable in some cases that are debated behind closed conference doors. Disagreement is typically hidden from the public; it is resolved to the extent possible before appellate courts publicly announce their decisions. Yet dissent on collegial courts provides clear evidence that conflict occurs and is not always amenable to resolution.

Our purpose in this book is to explore the type, frequency, intensity, and especially the causes and phenomena related to conflict and consensus at the three principal levels of appellate courts in America. We hope that the studies presented in this volume will stimulate further research on these questions. Part I focuses on the U.S. Supreme Court, Part II on the U.S. courts of appeals, and Part III on the state courts of last resort. The book is aimed at a diverse audience: students and scholars in political science, social psychology, and law. We do not seek to identify and examine conflict and consensus through traditional legal analysis of case law.[6] Rather, we have brought together twelve studies written for this book which focus on judicial behavior from a common conceptual perspective. The chapters discuss conflict and consensus on American collegial courts and are concerned with description, theory, and explanation of judicial behavior.

It is fair to ask why we want to know more about judicial conflict and consensus. Let us suggest several reasons at the outset. First, such knowledge may promote an understanding of American collegial courts as legal policy-making institutions. Appellate courts are legal institutions as reflected in, for example, the procedures and reasoning processes their members use in making decisions. By refining and extending precedent, or by striking out on new paths of doctrine, collegial courts function as legal policy makers, whether by interpreting constitutions or statutes. In so doing, appellate judges frequently disagree over which precedents should be applied and how, what the new legal policy actually means, or the extremes to which it may be pushed. Judges clash over how the law should be construed, which tells us much about how courts function as legal bodies. For example, if judges are willing to overrule prior decisions not because they can objectively demonstrate that precedents have been eroded or are no longer relevant for the category of dispute for which they were originally designed but based on the judges' own policy preferences in the guise of their personal reading of the Constitution or statutes, then the enormous emphasis placed on *stare decisis* as a cornerstone of the legal process is clearly shaken.

Second, appellate courts are political institutions with substantial power, and examination of conflict on courts may tell us about a variety of ways in which that power is or can be exercised. Appellate courts may strike down the actions of other branches of government, and a large body of literature suggests that courts have significant impacts on the political system, as in questions of civil rights, the rights of persons accused of crimes, reapportionment, obscenity, church-state relations, and the like.[7] Moreover, as policy makers within small groups, appellate judges behave much like politicians, although they are divorced from party politics. They attempt to influence the decisions of their colleagues through persuasion, negotiation, and bargaining.[8] Opinions may often end up being politically negotiated statements of policy. In making policy, judges often disagree over how politically charged issues should be decided and how far a court's policy should extend. But like politicians, judges may be willing to bargain for a court policy that is generally consistent with, but weaker than, their own views rather than refuse to compromise and thus let an important decision go in the opposite direction. The study of conflict on courts also suggests which issues are most divisive within the political, social, and economic systems. As Justice Robert H. Jackson has written: "Conflicts which have divided the Justices always mirror a conflict which pervades society. In fact, it may be said that the Supreme Court conference chamber is the forum where each fundamental cause has had its most determined and understanding championship. The student of our times will nowhere find the deeper conflicts of American political philosophy and economic policy more authentically and intelligently portrayed than in the opinions and dissents of the members of the Supreme Court."[9]

The study of judicial conflict and consensus is important for a third reason: it may tell us about the internal operations of courts and give us clues as to what occurs behind closed doors. Conflict is easily discernible in institutions whose decision-making processes are largely open to public scrutiny, such as the United States Congress. Secrecy envelops the judiciary's deliberative process, however, and rarely do dissenting or concurring opinions reveal what actually has taken place in judicial chambers or conference rooms. Dissenting opinions instead overwhelmingly take issue with the final decisions and the logic of the court majority. To understand how judges in fact function in a small group, it is important to look beyond the consensual image that courts seek to advance.

Fourth, an understanding of conflict and consensus may enhance our knowledge of the individual attitudes and values of judges.[10] Numerous studies relying on cumulative scaling or other analyses of judges' votes have suggested the basic civil liberty and economic attitudes of judges on the U.S. Supreme Court and the U.S. courts of appeals.[11] By such analysis we gain insight into how judges' attitudes and values help to shape specific patterns of conflict and consensus on different courts.

A fifth reason for our interest in conflict and consensus is that such studies may improve our understanding of the concept of judicial role, that is, how judges perceive they should behave in their official capacities.[12] Two of the most fundamental role conceptions are whether judges should be "activists" or should abide by the tenets of restraint.[13] That judges have different role conceptions, however, does not necessarily mean that their values and attitudes are equally divergent. Justice Louis D. Brandeis was an advocate of restraint during the heyday of the laissez-faire Court in the early 1930s, but he was perhaps just as liberal in certain areas of civil liberties as some of the activists of the Warren Court.[14] Conflict caused by judges' divergent role conceptions may therefore be quite different from conflict over values and attitudes.

Finally, patterns of judicial conflict and consensus may allow us to draw inferences about the exercise of leadership on courts.[15] Important decisions are not reached with ease in a small group composed of strong-willed individuals. Such decisions require a balance of forceful and effective leadership, especially if a court is to speak with one voice and to stand as a unit in the aftermath as subsequent litigation seeks to clarify the new policy made. Research has illustrated, for instance, the phenomenon of social leadership on the U.S. Supreme Court which is manifested by a concern with reducing tension within the group and promoting harmonious personal relationships. The phenomenon of task leadership, on the other hand, is concerned with expediting and efficiently performing the function of deciding and handing down decisions. When both forms of leadership are effectively performed, consensus is often achieved. It has been found that the chief justice is in the best position to exercise both forms of leadership. One well-documented example occurred with Chief Justice Charles Evans Hughes.[16] These concepts of social and task leadership have also been applied to the roles played by chief justices of state courts of last resort.[17]

In short, we are interested in conflict and consensus on appellate courts for a variety of reasons, some of which are pursued in the studies in this volume. But we underscore that our concern in this book is with the behavior of judges, not the logical progression of legal arguments proffered by judges to rationalize the policies they make. The studies in this volume should be valuable not only for their substantive contribution to our understanding of the behavioral dimensions of conflict and consensus; they should also be of heuristic value and indicate some directions future research might profitably take. We now turn to several observations concerning the principal approach relied upon in the forthcoming chapters: that dealing with the quantitative measurement of conflict and consensus as revealed through judges' voting behavior.

QUANTITATIVE ANALYSIS OF
CONFLICT AND CONSENSUS

Some of the major contributions to the study of judicial conflict and consensus have been revealed through the use of small group analysis.[18] This approach to examining judicial decision making typically involves exploring interpersonal relationships on courts as revealed by such data sources as the private papers of deceased judges. Given the important findings of small group analysis, why do the chapters in this book rely mainly on voting statistics to examine judicial conflict and consensus? After all, as Walter F. Murphy argued, because judges vote alike does not necessarily mean that "their votes are the result of interaction; standing alone, voting records tell very little about the force or direction of any interpersonal influence that may exist."[19]

Our response is that the chapters in this volume go beyond questions of judicial interaction and influence. And even when these topics are addressed, one cannot rule out the possibility that if judges vote together, they also work together with greater harmony than do judges who possess very different values and attitudes. Not only does this conclusion accord with common sense, but there is little evidence in the literature of judges with similar attitudes and values maintaining conflictual relationships as defined in this book. More to the point, however, is that a major difficulty with sole reliance on traditional small group analysis is that its source material and scholarly analysis are subjective. Furthermore, there is a fundamental problem with data collection in that many judges do not keep detailed notes of the deliberations in court conferences or accounts of individual interactions with their colleagues. Even when they do, we cannot assume that judges' personal papers constitute full and objective reports of the internal dynamics of judicial decision making.

Other major hurdles are associated with attempting small group analysis. Many appellate judges do not donate their personal papers to libraries for public inspection. Some who do carefully edit or "launder" their papers or restrict access so that confidential behind-the-scenes involvements between judges on, or even off, a court are not revealed, sometimes for many decades, sometimes never.[20] Moreover, the convention among judges has been that personal papers will not be made public until all those with whom they served are no longer on the bench, thereby frustrating the analysis of conflict and consensus until long after the life of a particular court. Even when a judge's papers are opened to the public, there are practical problems of time and expense associated with travel to cities throughout the nation where the papers are housed. Although some Supreme Court justices have conveniently donated their papers to the Library of Congress, others have not. And if one wishes to examine the papers of judges who served on the U.S. courts of appeals or state supreme courts, the problem of the lack of a central location for research is greatly exacerbated. Interviewing present or past judges also has drawbacks. Even if the researcher is granted interviews, judges may not be candid in answering questions concerning conflict on their courts. For all these reasons, much can be said for careful investigation of conflict and consensus by analysis of contemporary voting behavior.

Empirical examination of judicial conflict and consensus may thus provide a valuable supplement to the findings of small group analysis. Empirical studies normally assume and have even tested and found that differences between judges' attitudes and values are a primary cause of sustained disagreement.[21] Dissent informs the public that conflict exists on a court, and conflict suggests that legitimate conflicting paths to decision were open to the judges. By contrast, judicial consensus may in at least some cases indicate the presence of no substantial decisional leeway; the law's application may be relatively clear and routine. The traditional theory underlying judicial conflict research has assumed that concurring votes and opinions are not evidence of major conflict, even though concurring judges frequently express in their opinions noteworthy reservations about specific aspects of the court majority's policy. More recently students of judicial behavior have detected latent conflict even in unanimously decided cases.[22] In any event, all of this research suggests that, at a minimum, conflict will appear in nonrandom voting patterns and that through such studies we gain some insight into the dynamics of the small judicial group.

Consonant with these assumptions, judicial conflict has usually been operationally defined in terms of voting disagreement. If judges vote on opposite sides of issues in nonunanimous cases, conflict is evident. Divided cases tell us that judges "are operating on different assumptions, that their inarticulate major premises are dissimilar, that their value systems are differently constructed and weighted, that their political, economic, and social views contrast in important respects."[23] Voting agreement by an entire court is usually defined as consensus,

unless one adopts the newer approach of inferring latent conflict in
certain unanimous decisions on the basis of previous analysis of attitudes and values.

Bloc analysis, usually based on factor analysis or an approxima-
tion such as McQuitty Elementary Factor Analysis,[24] has traditionally
been a principal methodology used to detect conflict and consensus on
appellate courts.[25] Bloc analysis reveals the extent of voting agreement
and disagreement among members of collegial courts. It is a technique
for ordering voting data from matrices that depict relationships in
judicial voting patterns. C. Herman Pritchett first used the basic principles of bloc analysis in the 1940s and 1950s to examine voting behavior
on the Supreme Court.[26] Subsequently, bloc voting has been shown to
exist on the U.S. courts of appeals[27] and state supreme courts.[28] The
method has been developed by Glendon Schubert[29] and John D.
Sprague.[30] But as is made clear in the following chapters, several other
statistical methods for analyzing various facets of conflict and consensus are also relevant.

A substantial amount of quantitative research has been conducted
on judicial conflict and consensus, and a brief survey of some of that
literature is appropriate and instructive at this point. In *The Roosevelt
Court,* Pritchett discovered that between the 1930 and 1946 terms
conflict on the U.S. Supreme Court varied from 11 to 64 percent of its
opinions, with the Court each year between 1943 and 1946 handing
down more split decisions than unanimous ones.[31] Extending Pritchett's findings from the 1946 through the 1962 terms, Schubert
discovered that an average of 54 percent of all the Court's decisions
were nonunanimous.[32] Additionally, since 1949 the *Harvard Law
Review* has published Supreme Court statistics, and since 1966 in
particular it has annually reported rates of dissent on the Court for the
preceding term. These data demonstrate that dissent rates in full
opinions since the 1965 term have ranged from a high of 81.1 percent
for the 1970 term to a low of 56.1 percent for the 1965 term.[33] Conflict
on the Supreme Court was therefore clearly prominent during the 1970s
and usually greater than what Pritchett and Schubert had found for
earlier terms.

In striking contrast to the high percentage of Supreme Court cases
decided nonunanimously, rates of dissent on the U.S. courts of appeals
typically range from 2 percent or less on some courts to no more than
about 16 percent on others. Between fiscal years 1962 and 1964, the

highest percentage of nonunanimous decisions was 15.5 percent on the District of Columbia Circuit followed by 11.5 percent and 11.4 percent on the Second and Fifth Circuits respectively. On the other circuits, nonunanimous decisions occurred in less than 6 percent of all cases.[34] In addition, it has been found that rates of dissent on the appeals courts tend to change only slightly over time. Compared to fiscal years 1962–64, between 1965 and 1971 the dissent rate on the District of Columbia Circuit dipped to 13.2 percent, while the rate of conflict on the Fourth Circuit increased slightly from 5.9 percent to 7.6 percent.[35]

Disagreement occurs on most state courts of last resort in less than 10 percent of all cases, although for a few courts and years it has been found at the 40 or 50 percent rate. In 1916, the dissent rate on thirty-one of the forty-eight state supreme courts was less than 10 percent, but it was as high as 36.5 percent in Nebraska and 34.1 percent in New York. By 1941, the dissent rate was below 10 percent in only twenty-three states and was above 30 percent in Idaho, New Jersey, and Utah. In 1966, the dissent rate on the supreme courts of Michigan, New York, and Pennsylvania was over 40 percent, and dissent occurred in less than 10 percent of all cases decided by the supreme courts of twenty-nine other states.[36] By 1972, the dissent rate on Michigan's supreme court had climbed to 56.2 percent, but it had declined to 29.7 percent in Pennsylvania and 38.4 percent in New York. The average dissent rate on all state supreme courts was 12.6 percent in 1966, as compared to 15.1 percent in 1972.[37] As with the U.S. courts of appeals, then, a high level of conflict is rare on state supreme courts, and the degree of conflict may be stable or unstable longitudinally, depending on the particular court and the time period under consideration.

These statistics raise the obvious question of why conflict is typically so much higher on the U.S. Supreme Court than on the other major appellate courts.[38] Part of the explanation is that other appellate courts tend to siphon off less controversial issues. "Hard cases" and "tough questions," which provoke dissent, also are often appealed to the Supreme Court regardless of whether a unanimous decision was announced by a U.S. court of appeals or a state supreme court. This, of course, occurs because the Supreme Court, as the most authoritative judicial body in the nation, has considerable control over its appellate docket. Since a higher percentage of controversial cases may ultimately be selected to appear on the docket of the Supreme Court than normally come to other appellate courts, a higher level of dissent on the Supreme

Court can be expected. The Supreme Court is also the appellate court most likely to overrule precedent involving the federal Constitution or federal law, so again one would expect a higher rate of disagreement than on other collegial courts.[39]

Some research suggests that consensus on lower appellate courts is explained to a large degree by institutional variables. Since the Supreme Court always sits *en banc,* there is a greater statistical chance of one of nine Supreme Court justices dissenting than one of three judges, as on a typical appeals court panel.[40] Through interviews with appeals court judges, five factors have been identified as contributing to consensus as a folkway on those courts: at least a surface adherence to *stare decisis,* the shared value (at least in the abstract) of "rendering justice," the desire to win the respect of other judges and the legal community with well-crafted and reasoned written opinions and decisions, the shared value of being accommodating during judicial conferences, and the desire to maintain amicable personal relations among colleagues.[41] These factors may be equally important in promoting consensus on state supreme courts. For instance, the observance of *stare decisis,* especially when U.S. Supreme Court decisions are applicable, involves role perceptions, and Henry R. Glick has suggested that most state supreme court justices view their roles as being "law-interpreters" and "pragmatists," not as "law-makers."[42]

It is also possible that judges on the U.S. courts of appeals and state supreme courts make a greater attempt to disguise or suppress conflict than do justices of the Supreme Court.[43] After all, the Supreme Court may be more likely to accept appeals and embarrass lower court judges by overruling them if a high degree of conflict characterizes the lower court record or if a particularly persuasive dissent has been written below. Or Supreme Court justices may simply not be willing to wait as long, or to try as hard, to reach unanimity in some cases as are judges on other courts, especially since Supreme Court justices do not face the possibility of being rebuked by a higher court overturning their decisions. These, then, are some likely explanations for the Supreme Court's extremely high rate of dissent when compared to other collegial courts, although surely other reasons exist.

Finally, some attention should be devoted here not only to the causes but to the effects of judicial conflict and consensus, although the following chapters typically focus on causes rather than consequences. Consensus on appellate courts primarily seems to have the effect of lubricating the judicial decision-making process and of making courts appear to be legal institutions as opposed to political ones.[44] Conflict, on the other hand, seems to have more effects.[45] On what may appear to be the negative side, dissensus encourages the filing of additional appeals,[46] increases uncertainty about what the law really means,[47] and requires that a dissenting judge's colleagues in the majority spend more time carefully writing majority opinions and responding to the dissenters' arguments.[48] On the positive side, however, conflict in the form of dissents does not necessarily threaten the likelihood of compliance by lower courts,[49] it reduces cognitive dissonance,[50] and it provides a means whereby frustrated judges may voice their personal views.[51]

AN OVERVIEW OF THE STUDIES IN THIS BOOK

Lawrence Baum's 1983 assessment of the field of judicial politics concurred with C. Herman Pritchett's suggestion to "let a hundred flowers bloom."[52] That is a partial goal in this collection of studies, although they are all behaviorally oriented with emphasis on judges' voting. Most of the studies assess causes and characteristics of conflict and its variation over time. The contributors rely on several different approaches for examining judicial conflict and consensus in the three major levels of American appellate courts. They combine a mixture of description, theory, and explanation in macro and microlevel analyses, at times in unique ways, to verify prior research and to provide new insights into conflict and consensus on collegial courts. In the Epilogue of this volume, the studies are directly related to each other in terms of theory, comparative institutional behavior, and lines of future research that they suggest.

David J. Danelski develops a model in Chapter 1 containing several variables that potentially affect Supreme Court conflict and its resolution. These variables include the values and role expectations of the justices, perceptions of issues, different forms of leadership in the small group, and personality. Relying on Justice William O. Douglas's docket books for four terms and the private papers of eight justices, Danelski demonstrates how conflict and consensus may be shaped and altered by these variables from the time of the conference vote to the time of the final decision. In discussing task, social, and policy leadership, he also suggests how concurring and dissenting behavior affects the Court as a small group. In Chapter 2, S. Sidney Ulmer conducts a macrolevel exploratory investigation of dissent rates by chief justices of the Supreme Court. Finding considerable variation over time in dissent rates by the eleven chief justices from John Marshall to Warren Burger, Ulmer develops five models to identify variables that may explain such behavior. These variables include age at appointment, number of years served, prior judicial or legislative experience, external political pressure by Congress on the Court, complexity of cases, frequency of appointments, and appointing president. Edward V. Heck's general focus in Chapter 3 is the effect of new Supreme Court appointments on conflictual and consensual voting patterns; he examines all justices' participation rates with the Court majority for each natural court from the 1953 to the 1981 terms. Exploring whether a new appointment will lead to greater consensus, Heck tests four hypotheses: that the justice nearest the Court's center is normally a member of its largest bloc, that the chief justice is usually close to the Court's "center of gravity" so he can exercise leadership opportunities, that freshmen justices gravitate to the Court's center, and that the justice most frequently agreeing with the newest Court member will have a high level of consensus with the majority. Harold J. Spaeth and Michael F. Altfeld in Chapter 4 conduct a microlevel analysis of Justice Felix Frankfurter's years on the Warren Court in cases involving the regulation of business and labor. They illuminate a clear instance of substantial disparity between a justice's purported role conception and his voting and opinion behavior. Additionally, they shed light on general trends of voting conflict and consensus among the justices of the Warren Court in four subsets of labor and business cases.

The first study in Part II on the United States courts of appeals is by Donald R. Songer. Exploring conflict and consensus in all courts of appeals from 1953 through 1975 in criminal justice and labor relations cases, Songer initially examines longitudinal variations in rates of dissent across courts. Then, in an attempt to test hypotheses most often used by students of the Supreme Court, the author looks at the effect of ten hypothetical factors that generally involve the influence on dissent of the legal culture, organizational and institutional characteristics, and the sociopolitical system. Chapter 6, by Justin J. Green, extends a line of research that emerged in the mid-1970s concerning whether low dissent rates on the courts of appeals hide disagreement in unanimous decisions. His study has three foci. Green first explains the theory behind such research. Second, he discusses recent structural and operational changes in the courts of appeals that may affect decision making in these small groups (for example, the creation of new courts, increases in the number of judges, and changes in court rules and internal procedures). Then, to verify prior findings and test whether some of the above changes in structure and operations have had an effect, he updates his previous work on conflictual voting behavior in unanimous appeals court panels by examining all published criminal decisions handed down by the courts of appeals during 1980. In Chapter 7, Stephen L. Wasby investigates agreement and disgreement in the U.S. Court of Appeals for the Ninth Circuit among active-duty as well as "extra" court members, such as senior circuit judges, active-duty and senior district judges, and visiting judges from outside the circuit. Interviews with Ninth Circuit judges provide some insights into disagreement, but emphasis is placed on voting by different combinations of three-judge panels from 1970 through 1975. Wasby analyzes variation in disagreement between different categories of judges over the six-year period in published and unpublished opinions and relates voting by judges in these categories to decisions reversing or affirming to determine whether some judges pay greater deference to lower courts. By contrast, Charles M. Lamb presents in Chapter 8 a microlevel analysis of conflict in the D.C. Circuit during Warren Burger's tenure (1956–69). The D.C. Circuit was selected because very high levels of voting conflict in criminal justice decisions occurred during these fourteen years. Principal areas of focus include voting conflict when the court reversed rather than affirmed the lower court; the relationship between magnitude of voting conflict, time required to reach final decisions, and volume of court outputs; the relationship between background traits and conflict among individual judges; and voting agreement between Burger and his colleagues over time and in five major criminal justice issues.

Part III on state supreme courts is introduced by a macrolevel study by Henry R. Glick and George W. Pruet, Jr. They investigate levels and causes of dissent in the fifty state supreme courts for selected years between 1916 and 1981. Glick and Pruet first seek to determine how levels of state supreme court conflict have varied longitudinally. They then analyze in greater detail the influence of environmental and structural variables on levels of conflict. These variables include states' social and economic complexity (for example, urbanization and percentage of private and criminal litigation), political complexity (such as state expenditures and two-party competition), and the complexity of state court structure (for example, number of judges and presence of intermediate appellate courts). Chapter 10, by Victor E. Flango, Craig R. Ducat, and R. Neal McKnight, explores the concept of judicial leadership through opinion assignment as an aspect of conflict and consensus on state supreme courts. Initially the authors discuss the different ways in which opinions are assigned in state courts of last resort and the theoretical link between opinion assignment and judicial leadership. Then, through several approaches, they empirically analyze over a number of years majority and minority leadership in the supreme courts of Michigan and Pennsylvania, which use rotational and chief justice assignment procedures, respectively. By contrast, John A. Stookey's study in Chapter 11 seeks to explain through time-series analysis the historical evolution of dissent in the Arizona Supreme Court. He approaches the task by testing the docket composition theory—that changes in conflict are a function of the types of issues decided by a court. Using voting data from 1913 through 1976 for the Arizona Supreme Court, Stookey examines the hypothesis that level of dissent increases as a higher percent of public law cases are decided, as opposed to cases involving criminal and private law issues. Secondarily, the author looks for empirical support in other structural variables (such as number of judges and the existence of an intermediate appellate court) and in the justice composition theory—that dissent is a function of ideological, background, and role conception heterogeneity among judges on a court. Finally, in Chapter 12, Robert L. Dudley examines conflict and consensus from the vantage point of agenda setting and coalition building. The focus involves votes on access and the merits for the California Supreme Court between early 1973 and early 1980. Since some California Supreme Court rules and procedures for accepting cases for review are similar to those of the U.S. Supreme Court, the data provide an opportunity to test some ideas developed by students of the nation's highest court. Dudley's investigation draws on this literature and emphasizes vote distributions in petitions for review and cases decided on the merits, the relationship between justices' votes to grant review and to reverse the lower court, and whether justices vote to hear cases to reverse lower court errors.

1. See, for example, Lawrence Baum, *The Supreme Court,* 2d ed. (Washington, D.C.: Congressional Quarterly, Inc., 1985), pp. 152-53; Edward N. Beiser, "The Rhode Island Supreme Court: A Well-Integrated Political System," *Law and Society Review* 8 (1974): 167-86; Henry Robert Glick and Kenneth N. Vines, *State Court Systems* (Englewood Cliffs, N.J.: Prentice-Hall, 1973), pp. 77-82; J. Woodford Howard, Jr., *Mr. Justice Murphy: A Political Biography* (Princeton: Princeton University Press, 1968); Alpheus Thomas Mason, *Harlan Fiske Stone: Pillar of the Law* (New York: Viking, 1956); Walter F. Murphy, *Elements of Judicial Strategy* (Chicago: University of Chicago Press, 1964); Steven A. Peterson, "Dissent in American Courts," *Journal of Politics* 43 (1981): 412-34; Stephen L. Wasby, *The Supreme Court in the Federal Judicial System,* 2nd ed. (New York: Holt, Rinehart and Winston, 1984), pp. 180-88.

2. This seems to be true, for example, with regard to *Brown v. Board of Education,* 347 U.S. 483 (1954). See S. Sidney Ulmer, "Earl Warren and the *Brown* Decision," *Journal of Politics* 33 (1971): 689-702. In general, see Charles A. Johnson and Bradley C. Canon, *Judicial Policies: Implementation and Impact* (Washington, D.C.: Congressional Quarterly, Inc., 1984).

3. Oliver Wendell Holmes, Jr., *Collected Legal Papers* (New York: Harcourt, 1920), p. 292.

4. Tom C. Clark, "Internal Operation of the United States Supreme Court," *American Judicature Society Journal* 43 (1959): 51. Justice Clark was citing E. Smyth Gambrell.

5. See, for example, Murphy, *Elements of Judicial Strategy,* pp. 55, 173-75; Gerald T. Dunne, "Justices Hugo Black and Robert Jackson: The Great Feud," *St. Louis University Law Journal* 19 (1975): 465-87; Kenneth N. Vines and Herbert Jacob, "State Courts and Public Policy," in Herbert Jacob and Kenneth N. Vines, eds., *Politics in the American States: A Comparative Analysis,* 3d ed. (Boston: Little, Brown, 1976), p. 265.

6. For a prime illustration of the case analysis method for describing conflict and consensus, see Wallace Mendelson, *Justices Black and Frankfurter: Conflict on the Court,* 2d ed. (Chicago: University of Chicago Press, 1966).

7. See, for example, Theodore L. Becker and Malcolm M. Feeley, eds., *The Impact of Supreme Court Decisions: Empirical Studies,* 2d ed. (New York: Oxford University Press, 1973); Sheldon Goldman and Austin Sarat, eds., *American Court Systems: Readings in Judicial Process and Behavior* (San Francisco: W. H. Freeman, 1978), pp. 546-648; Johnson and Canon, *Judicial Policies;* Stephen L. Wasby, *The Impact of the United States Supreme Court: Some Perspectives* (Homewood, Ill.: Dorsey, 1970).

8. See, for example, Murphy, *Elements of Judicial Strategy,* chap. 3; David J. Danelski, "The Influence of the Chief Justice in the Decisional Process of the Supreme Court," in Goldman and Sarat, *American Court Systems,* pp. 506-19. For a more popular description of these phenomena, see Bob Woodward and Scott Armstrong, *The Brethren: Inside the Supreme Court* (New York: Simon and Schuster, 1979).

9. Robert H. Jackson, *The Struggle for Judicial Supremacy: A Study in American*

Power Politics (New York: Knopf, 1941), p. 312. Overlapping the views of Justice Jackson, Justice William J. Brennan has also emphasized that divisiveness on the Supreme Court is a function of conflict in American society. In 1963, he noted: "How conflicts . . . ought to be resolved constantly troubles our whole society. There should be no surprise, then, that how properly to resolve them often produces sharp divisions within the Court itself. When problems are so fundamental, the claims of the competing interests are often nicely balanced and close divisions are almost inevitable" (William J. Brennan, "Inside View of the High Court," *New York Times Magazine*, October 6, 1963, p. 100).

10. David J. Danelski, "Conflict and Its Resolution in the Supreme Court," *Journal of Conflict Resolution* 11 (1967): 73-76; see also Glendon Schubert, *The Judicial Mind: The Attitudes and Ideologies of Supreme Court Justices, 1946-1963* (Evanston: Northwestern University Press, 1965).

11. See, for example, the research cited in Glendon Schubert, "Judicial Process and Behavior, 1963-1971," in James A. Robinson, ed., *Political Science Annual: An International Review*, 3 (Indianapolis: Bobbs-Merrill, 1972), 228-31; and the research cited in Sheldon Goldman, "Voting Behavior on the United States Courts of Appeals Revisited," *American Political Science Review* 69 (1975): 491-506.

12. Danelski, "Conflict," pp. 76-79.

13. See, for example, Stephen C. Halpern and Charles M. Lamb, eds., *Supreme Court Activism and Restraint* (Lexington, Mass.: Lexington Books, 1982); James L. Gibson, "Judges' Role Orientations, Attitudes, and Decisions: An Interactive Model," *American Political Science Review* 72 (1978): 911-24.

14. Alpheus Thomas Mason, *Brandeis: A Free Man's Life* (New York: Viking, 1946); Sheldon Goldman, "In Defense of Justice: Some Thoughts on Reading Professor Mendelson's 'Mr. Justice Douglas and Government by Judiciary,' " *Journal of Politics* 39 (1977): 150.

15. Danelski, "Conflict," pp. 79-82.

16. Danelski, "The Influence," p. 511.

17. Craig R. Ducat and Victor E. Flango, *Leadership in State Supreme Courts: Roles of the Chief Justice*, Sage Professional Papers in American Politics, 04-030 (Beverly Hills: Sage, 1976).

18. See, for example, Danelski, "The Influence"; Murphy, *Elements of Judicial Strategy*; S. Sidney Ulmer, *Courts as Small and Not So Small Groups* (New York: General Learning Press, 1971).

19. Walter F. Murphy, "Courts as Small Groups," *Harvard Law Review* 79 (1966): 1566.

20. See, for example, Bruce Allen Murphy, *The Brandeis/Frankfurter Connection: The Secret Political Activities of Two Supreme Court Justices* (New York: Oxford University Press, 1982).

21. See, for example, Sheldon Goldman and Thomas P. Jahnige, *The Federal Courts as a Political System*, 3d ed. (New York: Harper & Row, 1985), pp. 137-46; S. Sidney Ulmer, "Toward a Theory of Sub-Group Formation in the United States Supreme Court," *Journal of Politics* 27 (1965): 133-52.

22. Burton M. Atkins and Justin J. Green, "Consensus on the United States Courts of Appeals: Illusion or Reality?" *American Journal of Political Science* 20 (1976): 735-48; Donald R. Songer, "Consensual and Nonconsensual Decisions in Unanimous Opinions of the United States Courts of Appeals," *American Journal of Political Science* 26 (1982): 225-39.

23. C. Herman Pritchett, *The Roosevelt Court: A Study of Judicial Politics and Values, 1937-1947* (New York: Macmillan, 1948), p. xii. See also Sheldon Goldman, "Conflict and Consensus in the United States Courts of Appeals," *Wisconsin Law Review* (1968): 463; Glick and Vines, *State Court Systems*, pp. 77-82; Richard J. Richardson and Kenneth N. Vines, *The Politics of Federal Courts: Lower Courts in the United States* (Boston: Little, Brown, 1970), p. 138; Vines and Jacob, "State Courts and Public Policy," pp. 260-61.

24. Louis L. McQuitty, "Elementary Factor Analysis," *Psychological Reports* 9 (1961): 71-78.

25. See, for example, Burton M. Atkins, "Decision-Making Rules and Judicial Strategy on the United States Courts of Appeals," *Western Political Quarterly* 25 (1972): 633-35; Sheldon Goldman, "Conflict on the U.S. Courts of Appeals 1965-1971: A Quantitative Analysis," *University of Cincinnati Law Review* 42 (1973): 645-52. Cf. John D. Sprague, *Voting Patterns of the United States Supreme Court: Cases in Federalism, 1889-1959* (Indianapolis: Bobbs-Merrill, 1968).

26. C. Herman Pritchett, "Divisions of Opinion among Justices on the U.S. Supreme Court, 1939-1941," *American Political Science Review* 35 (1941): 890-98; C. Herman Pritchett, *Roosevelt Court*, pp. 23-45, 89-90, 129-32, 161-66, 189-92, 208, 239-63; C. Herman Pritchett, *Civil Liberties and the Vinson Court* (Chicago: University of Chicago Press, 1954), pp. 20-22, 177-85, 188-92, 224-26.

27. See, for example, Atkins, "Decision-Making Rules," pp. 633-35; Goldman, "Conflict on the U.S. Courts," pp. 646-53; Charles M. Lamb, "Warren Burger and the Insanity Defense—Judicial Philosophy and Voting Behavior on a U.S. Court of Appeals," *American University Law Review* 24 (1974): 123-24.

28. See the discussion in Jacob and Vines, "State Courts and Public Policy," pp. 264-65.

29. Glendon Schubert, *Quantitative Analysis of Judicial Behavior* (Glencoe, Ill.: Free Press, 1959), chap. 3.

30. Sprague, *Voting Patterns*, pp. 31-40.

31. Pritchett, *Roosevelt Court*, p. 25. For discussions of the frequency of dissent in the Supreme Court before 1930, see Joel B. Grossman and Richard S. Wells, *Constitutional Law and Judicial Policy Making*, 2d ed. (New York: Wiley, 1980), pp. 230-34; Stephen C. Halpern and Kenneth N. Vines, "Institutional Disunity, the Judges' Bill and the Role of the U.S. Supreme Court," *Western Political Quarterly* 30 (1977): 471-83.

32. Schubert, *Judicial Mind*, p. 45.

33. See "The Supreme Court: _____ Term," in the November issue of the *Harvard Law Review* for each year since 1966. If summary judgments are included, the proportion of decisions with dissent decreases markedly.

34. Goldman,"Conflict and Consensus," pp. 463-64.

35. Goldman, "Voting Behavior," p. 493.

36. Glick and Vines, *State Court Systems*, p. 79.

37. Vines and Jacob, "State Courts and Public Policy," p. 261; see also Robert J. Sickels, "The Illusion of Judicial Consensus: Zoning Decisions in the Maryland Court of Appeals," *American Political Science Review* 59 (1965): 100-104.

38. See generally J. Woodford Howard, Jr., *Courts of Appeals in the Federal Judicial System: A Study of the Second, Fifth, and District of Columbia Circuits* (Princeton: Princeton University Press, 1981), pp. 193-94; Peterson, "Dissent in American Courts."

39. See, for example, Howard Ball, "Careless Justice: The United States Supreme Court's Shopping Center Opinions," *Polity* 11 (1978): 200-228.

40. Justin J. Green and Burton M. Atkins, "Designated Judges: How Well Do They Perform?" *Judicature* 61 (1978): 368; Richard J. Richardson and Kenneth N. Vines, "Review, Dissent and the Appellate Process: A Political Interpretation," *Journal of Politics* 29 (1967): 611.

41. Goldman, "Conflict and Consensus," pp. 476-80.

42. Henry Robert Glick, *Supreme Courts in State Politics: An Investigation of the Judicial Role* (New York: Basic Books, 1971), chap. 2.

43. With regard to state supreme courts, see Vines and Jacob, "State Courts and Public Policy," p. 261.

44. Goldman, "Conflict and Consensus," pp. 476-80.

45. See generally Peterson, "Dissent in American Courts," pp. 425-33.

46. Gregory J. Rathjen, "Lawyers and the Appellate Choice," *American Politics Quarterly* 6 (1978): 397-401.

47. Goldman and Jahnige, *The Federal Courts as a Political System*, p. 197.

48. Marvin Schick, *Learned Hand's Court* (Baltimore: Johns Hopkins Press, 1970), pp. 312-27; Elliot E. Slotnick, "Judicial Career Patterns and Majority Opinion Assignment on the Supreme Court," *Journal of Politics* 41 (1979): 640-48.

49. Charles A. Johnson, "Lower Court Reactions to Supreme Court Decisions: A Quantitative Examination," *American Journal of Political Science* 23 (1979): 792-804.

50. Gregory J. Rathjen, "An Analysis of Separate Opinion Writing Behavior as Dissonance Reduction," *American Politics Quarterly* 2 (1974): 393-411.

51. S. Sidney Ulmer, "Social Backgrounds as an Indicator to the Votes of Supreme Court Justices in Criminal Cases: 1947-1956 Terms," *American Journal of Political Science* 18 (1973): 588.

52. Lawrence Baum, "Judicial Politics: Still a Distinctive Field," in Ada W. Finifter, ed., *Political Science: The State of the Discipline* (Washington, D.C.: American Political Science Association, 1983), pp. 191, 207.

I
The United States
Supreme Court

1

Causes and Consequences of Conflict and Its Resolution in the Supreme Court

DAVID J. DANELSKI

This study is to a large extent exploratory, but it also reexamines some familiar terrain, builds on the work of a number of scholars, and tests as well as raises hypotheses. It is a broad attempt to explain judicial behavior by considering together two important questions in decision-making and impact research: what are the causes and what are the consequences (particularly the policy consequences) of conflict and its resolution in the Supreme Court?

CAUSES OF CONFLICT AND ITS RESOLUTION

Conflict in the Supreme Court is disagreement among the justices expressed in conference discussions, remarks from the bench, intra-Court communications, votes, and opinions. From a policy perspective, votes and opinions in nonunanimous cases are the most important indicators of conflict. Voting behavior is usually dichotomous: justices vote to affirm or reverse, grant or deny, remand or not remand, and so on. Opinion behavior often reflects the extent and intensity of disagreement. Typically the most intense response is writing a dissenting opinion. Other responses are joining dissenting opinions, dissenting without opinion, writing concurring opinions, joining concurring opinions, and concurring without opinion. By contrast, conflict resolution in the Supreme Court is the achievement of agreement after the expression of disagreement. The best example is a unanimous decision and opinion after a divided vote in conference.

Judicial decision-making theory is obviously relevant in explaining conflict and its resolution in the Supreme Court. Although the literature

Figure 1.1. Supreme Court Decision-Making Model

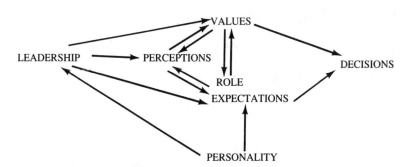

on the subject is massive, no single, comprehensive theory of decision making has yet emerged. The major variables for such a theory, however, are generally known.[1] They are portrayed hypothetically in the model shown in Figure 1.1.

The justices' values and role expectations in the model are interacting, multidimensional variables; thus dimensional differences, such as differences in intensity, as well as differences in values and role expectations, must be taken into account in explaining conflict in the Court.[2] Role expectations affect the expression of conflict both directly and indirectly. The expectation of acquiescence in majority decisions in cases that do not involve important legal principles usually operates directly to limit dissent. Expectations of judicial restraint and precedent adherence, however, usually limit dissent indirectly by avoiding value conflicts leading to divisions in the Court. Similarly, leadership expectations that the chief justice will reconcile differences among justices usually limit dissents indirectly.[3]

The justices' perceptions are important variables in the model because they interact with both values and role expectations. Perceptions of issues determine which values and role expectations operate in cases, and high saliency of specific values and role expectations make for greater readiness to perceive issues in terms of those values and role expectations. Although there is usually considerable perceptual overlap as to issues in cases, justices sometimes perceive the same stimuli in cases differently, and those differences in perceptions often cause conflict.[4]

Leadership—both task and social—usually resolves conflicts, but when there is serious competition for task leadership, and social leadership is inadequate to relieve the resulting group tensions, conflict tends to increase.[5] Leadership is also important because the values, role expectations, and perceptions of persuasive justices weigh more heavily than those of other justices in determining the outcome of cases. Thus if there is great disparity in the values or role expectations of leading competitors for task leadership, conflict related to these values and role expectations is likely to be exacerbated.[6]

Personality affects leadership and role expectations. Justices with moderately aggressive or detached personalities are most likely to exercise task leadership, and those with moderately compliant or self-effacing personalities are most likely to exercise social leadership.[7] Justices who are assertive and also warm, caring, and tactful are most likely to exercise both task and social leadership. Furthermore, there is evidence that justices with a high sense of self-esteem tend to hold activist role expectations and that those with a low sense of self-esteem tend to hold restraintist role expectations.[8]

In an effort to explore further and test the above explanation of conflict and its resolution in the Supreme Court, the following hypotheses will be considered: (1) Differences in values, role expectations, and perceptions cause conflict. (2) Adequacy of task and social leadership affects conflict and its resolution. (3) Personality is related to leadership and thus affects conflict and its resolution.

Data to explore and test the above hypotheses were drawn principally from three sources: (1) Justice William O. Douglas's docket books for the 1939, 1940, 1942, and 1943 terms, the last two terms of Charles Evans Hughes's chief justiceship, and the second and third terms of Harlan Fiske Stone's chief justiceship; (2) the Court's official reports for the 1939–1944 terms; and (3) the private papers of Hughes, Stone, Douglas, Hugo L. Black, Stanley F. Reed, Felix Frankfurter, Frank Murphy, and Wiley B. Rutledge. Douglas's docket books, which are located at the Library of Congress, contain conference votes, opinion assignments, and other official actions taken by the Court. Only justices may be present at conferences; thus Douglas personally recorded all the conference votes in his docket books.

Values, Role Expectations, and Perceptions. The principal data for the following analysis are thirty-one civil liberties decisions by the Supreme Court between February 1943, following Rutledge's appointment to the Court, and the end of the 1943 term in June 1944 in which at least one justice cast a dissenting or pass vote in conference. The analysis proceeded in a series of steps.

The first step was an attempt to scale the conference votes in the thirty-one decisions as shown in Douglas's docket books. The attempt failed to disclose unidimensionality; the coefficient of reproducibility for the attempted scale was .80. This finding is consistent with the model shown in Figure 1.1, which hypothesizes a multicausal explanation of decision making.

The second step was an attempt to scale the reported votes in the same thirty-one decisions. Again the attempt failed to disclose unidimensionality; the coefficient of reproducibility for the attempted scale was .86.

The third step was a content analysis of all opinions in the thirty-one decisions for the purpose of separating decisions in which votes appeared to turn on role expectations—activism-restraint or precedent adherence—from the rest of the decisions. Only two decisions could be classified as containing votes that turned on precedent-adherence expectations. One was *Smith* v. *Allwright,* in which Owen J. Roberts argued in dissent that his colleagues had departed from precedent.[9] The other was *United States* v. *Saylor,* in which Douglas, writing for himself, Black, and Reed, argued in dissent that the precedent relied upon by the majority did not bind it.[10] Both decisions were eliminated from this analysis.[11] Of the twenty-nine remaining decisions, thirteen contained votes that appeared to turn on activism-restraint expectations. These thirteen decisions determined the outcome of twenty-one cases.

The fourth step was an attempt to scale the votes in both the thirteen activism-restraint decisions and the sixteen residual decisions. The votes in both sets of decisions formed scales with coefficients of reproducibility of .90. The scales are shown in Figures 1.2 and 1.3.[12] They are consistent with the hypothesis that activism-restraint expectations and values underlie the votes portrayed.

The fifth step was an analysis of all dissenting opinions in civil liberties decisions during the 1941 through 1944 terms. Opinions in which dissenting justices articulated expectations of either activism or restraint were separated from the rest of the opinions, and the justices were given activism-restraint scores: $+1$ for each activist dissenting opinion and -1 for each restraintist dissenting opinion. Those scores were the basis for the activism-restraint dissenting opinion scale shown

Figure 1.2. Activism-Restraint Voting Scale

Justices

	Mu	Ru	Bl	Do	St	Ja	Ro	Fr	Re	
Hirabayashi v. *U.S.*	⊟	−	−	−	−	−	−	−	−	0-9
Yasui v. *U.S.*	⊟	−	−	−	−	−	−	−	−	0-9
Falbo v. *U.S.*	+	−	−	−	−	−	−	−	−	1-8
Prince v. *Mass.*	+	−	−	−	−	−	−	−	−	1-8
Yakus v. *U.S.*	+	⊞	−	⊟	−	−	⊞	−	−	3-6
Mortensen v. *U.S.*	+	+	−	−	−	+	+	+	−	5-4
Murdock v. *Penn.*[a]	+	+	+	+	+	−	−	−	−	5-4
Jones v. *Opelika*[b]	+	+	+	+	+	−	−	−	−	5-4
Martin v. *Struthers*	+	+	⊕	+	+	−	−	−	−	5-4
Follett v. *McCormick*	+	+	+	+	+	−	−	−	+	6-3
Ashcraft v. *Tenn.*	+	+	+	+	+	⊖	−	−	+	6-3
W. Va. Bd. of Ed. v. *Barnette*	+	+	+	+	+	+	−	−	−	6-3
Pollock v. *Williams*	⊕	⊕	+	+	⊖	+	+	+	⊖	7-2

	Mu	Ru	Bl	Do	St	Ja	Ro	Fr	Re
Totals[c]	11-0	9-2	7-4	7-4	6-5	3-8	3-8	2-9	2-9
Scale Position	11	9	7	7	7	2	1	1	0
Scale Scores	1.00	.64	.27	.27	.27	−.64	−.82	−.82	−1.00

$R = 1 - \frac{7}{81} = .91$ $S = 1 - \frac{7}{25} = .72$

[a]Eight cases counted as one decision.

[b]Three cases counted as one decision.

[c]All computations based on nonunanimous reported decisions.

Key: + = vote consistent with activism expectations
 − = vote consistent with restraint expectations
 ○ = vote change; opposite vote in conference
 □ = pass vote in conference

Figure 1.3. Residual Voting Scale

	Mu	Bl	Ru	Do	Re	Ja	Ro	Fr	St	
U.S. v. Laudani	⊖	−	−	−	−	−	−	−	−	0-9
Buchalter v. N.Y.	*	−	−	⊖	−	−	−	−	−	0-8
U.S. v. Mitchell	−	+	−	−	−	−	−	−	−	1-8
U.S. v. Gaskin	+	−	−	−	−	⊖	−	−	⊖	1-8
U.S. v. Lepowitch	*	−	−	−	−	−	+	−	−	1-7
Snowden v. Hughes	+	−	−	+	−	−	−	−	−	2-7
Galloway v. U.S.	+	+	−	+	⊖	−	−	−	−	3-6
Lyons v. Okla.	+	+	⊕	⊟	−	−	−	−	−	3-6
U.S. v. Dotterweich	+	−	+	−	+	−	+	−	−	4-5
Hartzel v. U.S.	+	+	+	−	−	−	+	−	+	5-4
Feldman v. U.S.	*	+	+	⊞	−	*	−	−	−	3-4
Scheiderman v. U.S.	+	+	+	+	+	*	−	−	−	5-3
U.S. v. Ballard	⊕	+	+	⊕	+	⊕	−	−	⊖	6-3
Roberts v. U.S.	+	⊕	⊕	⊕	−	⊕	⊕	−	−	6-3
Bartchy v. U.S.	+	+	+	+	+	+	−	+	−	7-2
Billings v. Truesdell	+	+	+	+	+	+	−	+	+	8-1

Totals[a]   11-1 10-4 9-5 8-6 5-9 4-8 4-10 2-12 2-12

Scale Position   13   10   9   6   5   4½   3   2   1

Scale Scores   .86   .43 .29 −.14 −.29 −.36 −.57 −.71 −.86

$R = 1 - 9/87 = .90$ $S = 1 - 12/33 = .63$

[a]All computations based on nonunanimous reported decisions.

Key: + = vote consistent with civil liberties outcome
       − = vote not consistent with civil liberties outcome
       * = nonparticipation
       ○ = vote change; opposite vote in conference
       □ = pass vote in conference

Table 1.1. Dissenting Opinion Analysis in Civil Liberties
Decisions, 1941-1944 Terms

Justices	Activism-Restraint Dissenting Opinions		Residual Dissenting Opinions	
			Civil Liberties Outcomes	
	Activism-Restraint	Score	Pro-Con	Score
Murphy	3-0	3	10-1	9
Rutledge	1-0	1.5[a]	2-0	3[a]
Black	1-0	1	7-1	6
Douglas	1-0	1	2-1	1
Stone	1-3	−2	2-4	−2
Roberts	0-2	−2	2-1	1
Jackson	0-3	−3	2-0	2
Reed	0-5	−5	1-3	−2
Frankfurter	0-5	−5	2-4	−2

[a]Rutledge's score is adjusted because he served only two and a half of the four terms covered in the analysis.

in Table 1.1. The justices were then given scores on their commitment to civil liberties in the residual decisions: +1 for each dissenting opinion supporting a civil liberties outcome and −1 for each dissenting opinion opposing a civil liberties outcome. Those scores were the basis of the residual dissenting opinion scale shown in Table 1.1.[13]

The sixth step was Spearman rank-correlation analysis of the four scales in Figures 1.2 and 1.3 and Table 1.1. The result of the analysis, given in Table 1.2, shows that role expectations and values are significantly correlated, largely because of the behavior of the four activists— Murphy, Rutledge, Black, and Douglas—whose votes and dissenting opinions in activism-restraint decisions reflected their values in much the same way they did in other civil liberties decisions and whose general consistency of ranking in relation to each other in the scales (Murphy at the top, Douglas at or tied for the fourth position, and Rutledge or Black in between) also reflected the levels of their commitment to civil liberties. If those activists had not been on the Court and statistical composites of Stone, Jackson, Roberts, Reed, and Frankfurter had sat in their places, the three weakest relationships in the table—AR(V)-R(V), AR(V)-R(DO), and AR(DO)-R(V)—would decrease to the point that they would not be significant at the .05 level. The remaining three relationships, however, would remain signifi-

Table 1.2. Spearman Rank-Correlation Analysis of Voting and
Dissenting Opinion Scales

	AR(V)	R(V)	AR(DO)	R(DO)
AR(V)	–			
R(V)	.60	–		
AR(DO)	.92	.73	–	
R(DO)	.73	.85	.80	–

AR(V)   Activism-Restraint Voting Scale (Figure 1.2)
R(V)   Residual Voting Scale (Figure 1.3)
AR(DO)   Activism-Restraint Dissenting Opinion Scale (Table 1.1)
R(DO)   Residual Dissenting Opinion Scale (Table 1.1)

Significance level (one-tailed test)
    .60   .05 level
    .78   .01 level

cant—AR(V)-AR(DO) at the .01 level and R(V)-R(DO) and AR (DO)-
R(DO) at the .05 level.[14] These findings are consistent with the
hypotheses that (1) role expectations account at least for the votes of the
restraintists in the decisions in the activism-restraint voting scale, (2)
values account for the votes of both activists and restraintists in the
residual voting scale, and (3) activism-restraint expectations and commitment to civil liberties values are to some extent related. Hence it is
not surprising that Murphy, an arch-civil libertarian, was also an arch-
activist, for his commitment to civil liberties values overwhelmed any
commitment he had to judicial restraint.[15] Nor is it surprising that
Frankfurter, the self-proclaimed spokesman for judicial restraint, more
than occasionally voted on the basis of his values.[16] Like those of his
colleagues, Frankfurter's votes indicated in Figure 1.2 are consistent
with a value explanation just as those indicated in Figure 1.1 are
consistent with a role-orientation explanation. Further, the finding that
activism-restraint expectations and civil liberties value commitments
are to some extent related suggests that interaction of values and role
expectations in justices such as Frankfurter may result in restraint
justifications of votes that turn at least partly on values. In view of that,
and also because the activists' votes—those of Murphy, Black,
Rutledge, and Douglas—clearly appear to turn on liberal values,
Figure 1.1 is perhaps best interpreted as showing that votes turn on the
interaction of role expectations and values. To a lesser extent that
interpretation probably applies to Figure 1.2, but because no justice

articulated restraint expectations in the decisions portrayed in that figure, the conclusion is necessarily speculative.

The seventh step was an attempt to measure the extent to which differences in perceptions cause conflict in the Court. The voting scales in Figures 1.2 and 1.3 were used to identify decisions that appeared to turn on disparities of perceptions, that is, those that contained two or more inconsistent votes. There were three such decisions—*Mortensen* in the activism-restraint voting scale and *Dotterweich* and *Hartzel* in the residual voting scale. Examination of conference notes and intra-Court correspondence revealed that justices deciding those cases perceived the issues differently. In *Mortensen,* conflict appeared to turn more on differences in perceptions of the reach of the Mann Act than on role expectations.[17] In *Dotterweich,* the minority perceived a civil liberties issue, but the majority did not. Roberts's remarks in the conference illustrate the minority's perception. "I take a different view," he said. "This is a criminal statute & we should ask the legislature with great definiteness to point out what guilt hinges on."[18] In *Hartzel,* Murphy saw the issue as one of free speech while Stone saw it as concerning sufficiency of evidence.[19] Thus in those three cases, perceptual differences appear to account for inconsistent votes, and in *Mortensen* and *Dotterweich* they also appear to account for conflict among the justices.[20]

The eighth and final step in this analysis explored post-conference vote changes in relation to the scale patterns in Figures 1.2 and 1.3. There are at least three competing hypotheses that might explain the vote changes: (1) Acquiescence expectations cause justices to change their dissenting votes to majority votes. (2) Post-conference activity—discussions with colleagues and law clerks, writing and circulation of opinions, criticisms and comments on opinions—leads to more generally shared perceptions of issues and thus causes greater agreement. (3) Post-conference activity sharpens perceptions of issues in relation to the justices' values and role expectations and thus causes them to change votes that are inconsistent with their overall voting patterns. Vote changes shown in Figures 1.2 and 1.3 support all three hypotheses, but support for the third hypothesis is somewhat greater than for the other two. Two of the twenty-eight vote changes (including pass votes) support none of the hypotheses, for they are inconsistent dissenting votes. Twenty of the remaining twenty-six vote changes support each hypothesis, for they are majority votes that fit scale patterns. The remaining six votes support only the third hypothesis, for they are dissenting votes that fit the scale patterns. Thus sharpened perception of issues may either increase or decrease conflict.[21]

This eight-step analysis leads to the conclusion that Supreme Court decisions turn primarily on the interaction of values and role expectations. Hence differences in commitments to values and role expectations often cause conflict, and, to a lesser extent, so do differences in perceptions. Conflict resolution then turns, for the most part, on the reconciliation of those differences—in short, on leadership.

Leadership and Personality. Unsuccessful attempts at task leadership cause conflict and tension, which, if unrelieved by social leadership behavior, negatively affect decision making in the Court. Successful task and social leadership attempts, on the other hand, usually result in conflict resolution. Thus leadership ability is related to conflict and its resolution in the Court. An earlier study based on the justices' papers showed that conflict was lowest when task leadership was performed primarily by a single member of the Court—Willis Van Devanter in the 1920s and Hughes in the 1930s—and social leadership was performed sufficiently to satisfy the emotional conditions for collegial, productive, satisfying decision making. William Howard Taft was more than adequate as the Court's social leader in the 1920s, and Hughes was at least adequate in the role in the 1930s. Stone, however, lacked the leadership skills of Taft and Hughes, and soon after Stone was promoted to the chief justiceship, persons who knew him well predicted he would have difficulties in leading the Court. In the Stone Court, there was competition for task leadership, inadequate social leadership, a decline in collegiality, and an increase in conflict.[22] These findings were the result of qualitative analysis of several justices' papers, particularly those of Taft, Hughes, and Stone, for docket books recording conference voting behavior for that period were not yet available. The present availability of Douglas's docket books permits quantitative analysis of leadership in the Hughes and Stone Courts.

The Douglas docket books contain data that can be used to measure leadership in the period between the conference vote and announcement of decisions in open Court. A justice's leadership score can be calculated by summing all dissenting and pass votes in conference that later became majority votes in cases assigned to that justice for opinion and then dividing the sum obtained by the total number of conference

Table 1.3. Leadership Scores

Justice	1939 and 1940 Terms		1942 and 1943 Terms	
	Score	N	Score	N
Hughes	.91	21		
McReynolds	.40	10		
Stone	.59	73	.52	31
Roberts	.58	38	.35	46
Black	.88	41	.53	71
Reed	.32	28	.33	36
Frankfurter	.25	64	.14	51
Douglas	.52	63	.46	83
Murphy	.57	21	.47	30
Jackson			.52	54
Rutledge			.50	22

Leadership score $= \dfrac{d + p}{N}$ where d is a dissenting vote and p a pass vote in conference that later became a majority vote in a decision assigned to a justice for opinion. N is the total number of dissenting and pass votes in conference in all decisions assigned for opinion to that justice.

dissenting and pass votes in those cases. The score thus obtained is essentially a measure of task leadership, for usually vote changes turn on the persuasiveness of the opinions circulated. The measure, however, contains some elements of social leadership, for vote changes sometimes involve negotiation, expectations of reciprocity, and even considerations of friendship. In addition, expectations of acquiescence underlie some vote changes.

Table 1.3 shows the leadership scores for the Hughes Court during the 1939 and 1940 terms and for the Stone Court during the 1942 and 1943 terms. The scores confirm what is known about Hughes's and Black's leadership ability.[23] The leadership scores for the 1942 and 1943 terms also reflect competition for leadership in the Stone Court. Black, however, was a more successful leader during that period than his score suggests. During the 1942 and 1943 terms, Frankfurter, Stone, and Roberts seldom followed his lead, but Douglas, Murphy, Rutledge, Reed, and Jackson often changed their votes to join his opinions.[24] Black's leadership score for those justices averages slightly more than .70, compared with his overall leadership score for the Court of .53. His opinion in *Roberts* v. *United States,* a case in the 1943 term involving the interpretation of the Federal Probation Act, illustrates his persuasive powers.[25] In conference the vote was 8–1, with Murphy casting the sole vote for the criminal defendant. Black, who had been assigned to write for the Court, decided soon after he began work on the opinion that the majority had erred. Instead of bringing the case back to the conference, he circulated an opinion sustaining the opposite result. Murphy, having voted that way in conference, of course, immediately joined the opinion, as did Douglas, Rutledge, Jackson, and Roberts, thus reversing the original conference vote.[26]

Stone's leadership scores for both periods are relatively high, which is not surprising, for he was a respected legal craftsman. His leadership problems were not in writing persuasive opinions but in conference discussion. His presentation of cases as chief justice tended to be rambling, and in conference he did not remain above the fray so that he might later be in a position to reconcile differences among his colleagues.[27] Had he been as effective in conference discussion and post-conference negotiation as he was in opinion-writing, he would have been a formidable leader of his Court.

Frankfurter's low leadership scores—the lowest among all justices for both periods—also are not surprising. It was not that Frankfurter made no attempts to lead. Douglas said Frankfurter was one of the three most active proselytizers on the Court, the other two being Black and Stone. Douglas went on to write that Frankfurter pushed his views "every waking hour. . . . Up and down the halls he went, pleading, needling, nudging, probing. He never stopped trying to change the votes on a case until the decision came down."[28] Frankfurter sought to lead, but he often failed, and, according to H. N. Hirsch, he failed because of his narcissistic personality. Frankfurter, Hirsch wrote, had a grandiose self-image as a leader, and when some of his colleagues rejected his early attempts at leadership, he responded with arrogance and vindictiveness, which undermined his later attempts.[29] Other analyses also support the conclusion that Frankfurter's personality stood in the way of effective leadership. Alan A. Stone, after noting Frankfurter's vanity, arrogance, apparent sense of superiority, and condescending attitude toward his colleagues, wrote: "I imagine that, while sitting around the conference table week after week, Frankfurter's fellow Justices must have sensed his uneven human qualities, his awesome intellectual gifts, and his emotional immaturity. Perhaps this awareness had something to do with his inability to persuade his colleagues. Power in a group of peers is distributed by just such intangible human perceptions."[30]

Stone's lack of success as a social leader in the 1940s also appears to have been related to his personality. Adequate proof of this proposition requires at least a psychobiographical study like Hirsch's of Frankfurter. Alpheus T. Mason's biography, however, provides considerable evidence on Stone's personality, which appears to have been similar to Taft's but with some flawed edges. Stone was a warm, gregarious man who might have been an adequate social leader, but, according to Mason and others, he was also a vain, sensitive man whose ego was easily bruised, who sometimes responded to criticism sarcastically, and who did not hide his low opinion of the abilities of some of his colleagues.[31]

Just as personality helps to explain leadership failures, it also helps to explain leadership successes. A previous study concluded that Hughes's moderately detached personality was related to his ability to act as both task and social leader, and Black's moderately aggressive personality was related to his task leadership in the 1940s.[32] Neither of those conclusions, however, was based on intensive psychobiographical analysis or quantitative analysis.

Although quantitative measures of personality are yet to be developed for justices whose work has passed into history,[33] the effects of their personalities on decision making through such mediating variables as leadership can be measured. Increases in dissent during the Stone Court appear to be at least partly attributable to a failure of social leadership, which in turn appears related not only to Stone's personality but also to the personalities of his colleagues. The dramatic rise of dissent during Stone's chief justiceship, when social leadership was inadequate, does not prove the latter caused the former, for other variables may also have been at work. Because inadequate performance of social leadership results in decreased collegiality and satisfaction in the Court, it would seem that when those conditions are present, acquiescence in majority opinions would decrease and reported dissent would increase correspondingly. To test this hypothesis, a basis for empirical comparison—a period in which social leadership was at least minimally adequate—is necessary. The 1939 and 1940 terms of the Hughes Court provide such a basis for measuring effects of inadequate social leadership during the Stone Court. For purposes of the test, acquiescence was measured by dividing the sum of a justice's dissenting conference votes that later became majority votes by the sum of all dissenting conference votes cast by that justice. Acquiescence scores

Table 1.4. Acquiescence Scores

Justice	1939 and 1940 Terms		1942 and 1943 Terms	
	Score	N	Score	N
Hughes	.22	49		
McReynolds	.40	67		
Stone	.45	20	.26	42
Roberts	.35	83	.32	103
Black	.32	28	.30	61
Reed	.69	27	.44	63
Frankfurter	.64	11	.20	54
Douglas	.32	28	.24	59
Murphy'	.42	12	.33	68
Jackson			.30	56
Rutledge			.25	24

Acquiescence score $= \frac{dc}{N}$ where dc is a dissenting vote in conference later changed to a majority vote and N is the total number of votes in conference for each justice.

for each period are shown in Table 1.4. Consistent with the hypothesis, acquiescence fell from 38 percent in the Hughes Court to 28 percent in the Stone Court, reflecting a rate of decrease in acquiescence of slightly more than 25 percent.

The foregoing analysis provides quantitative confirmation of previous findings concerning the importance of task and social leadership in decision making and conflict resolution in the Court. It also shows that personality affects both decision making and conflict resolution, but the relationship between personality and leadership still requires quantitative confirmation.

CONSEQUENCES OF CONFLICT
AND ITS RESOLUTION

Conflict in the Supreme Court has both positive and negative consequences. It makes for alertness, clarifies issues, raises alternative approaches, and tests the intensity of justices' commitments to given positions, but when it gets out of hand—becoming highly emotional and antagonistic—decision making tends to be uncollegial, inefficient, and unsatisfying. At such times, concurring and dissenting behavior tends to escalate, and often the result is public criticism.[34]

Most of the consequences of conflict resolution are positive. Conflict opens emotional wounds; resolution binds them. One result of conflict resolution is satisfaction and efficiency in the Court. Another result is legitimation of public policy, for greater unity in the Court's decisions reinforces the myth of law's certainty.[35] But, as Hughes said, conflict resolution at the expense of deeply held convictions or to avoid policy issues that require decision leaves conflict smoldering and creates future problems in the Court.[36]

Justices prize the right to express their individual positions on issues. They see concurring and dissenting behavior as useful in achieving their policy goals in the Court, and they assume that the publication of their individual views will affect the future development of law and policy. It is by no means clear that their assumptions are correct, but the assumptions, nonetheless, raise important testable hypotheses.

In addition to the data used in the first part of this study, data were collected from the *U.S. Reports* that had been identified by using *Shepard's United States Citator.* All cases in the 1942 term containing concurring opinions two or more pages in length were Shepardized, and all cases citing those concurring opinions were analyzed. *Shepard's United States Citator* was also used to determine which cases decided during the 1939–1943 terms had been overruled, and then the overruling cases were examined to determine the part played by the original dissenting opinions in the overrulings. That analysis was expanded, and comparable data were collected for all cases overruled by the Supreme Court from the 1958 through the 1980 terms.

Concurring Behavior. Concurring opinions rarely become opinions of the Court. For the four terms considered in this study, Douglas's papers revealed only one such instance—*Dickinson Industrial Site* v. *Cowan*—a bankruptcy case in the 1939 term in which Douglas's concurring opinion supplanted Reed's opinion for the Court.[37]

Concurring votes and opinions are far more likely to affect the content of Court opinions than to supplant them. An example is *Anderson National Bank* v. *Luckett,* which Stone had assigned to himself for opinion.[38] Most of his colleagues praised the opinion he had circulated, but Black, troubled by it, wrote Stone: "I regret my inability to accept all of your opinion in this case. What troubles me is the discussion of 'substantive due process' and the use of the 'unreasonable or arbitrary' criterion to determine procedural due process. These features of the opinion have historical implications that I do not wish to see perpetuated. It may be that you could not eliminate those statements without too much interference with your train of argument. If you cannot, will you please note that I concur in the result and in all of the opinion except the statements in Part I with reference to due process."[39] Stone made the revisions Black requested.

Attempts to influence the content of Court opinions are not always successful. An illustration is Douglas's attempt to influence Stone's opinion for the Court in *Hirabayashi* v. *United States*.[40] "I am anxious to go as far as I can reasonably to meet the views of my associates," Stone wrote to Douglas, "but it seems to me that if I accepted your suggestions very little structure of my opinion would be left, and that I should lose most of my adherents. It seems to me, therefore, that it would be wiser for me to stand by the substance of my opinion and for you to express your views in your concurring opinion as you have already done." Douglas followed Stone's suggestion.[41]

It appears that concurring opinions play a small role at best in the future development of law and policy. The first step in testing that hypothesis was the identification of all concurring opinions two pages or more in length delivered during the 1942 term. There were thirteen such opinions in eleven cases.[42] A research assistant then Shepardized the opinions to determine whether they had been cited in later Supreme Court opinions. Seven concurring opinions had never been cited. The remaining six had been cited only nine times. In six of the nine instances, they had been mentioned only by their own authors and always in dissenting or concurring opinions.[43] In the remaining three instances, the citations were even less significant.[44]

This analysis suggests two conclusions. First, concurring behavior sometimes has significant consequences in the Court's decisional process by influencing the content of majority opinions. Second, concurring behavior seems to play a small role in the development of law and policy. The latter conclusion is necessarily tentative because it is based on examination of only thirteen concurring opinions in one Court term.

Dissenting Behavior. One of the most important consequences of dissenting behavior in the decisional process is reversal of a conference vote prior to final decision. A dramatic example is *Martin* v. *Struthers*, which involved the constitutionality of an industrial town's anti-door-bell-ringing ordinance as applied to the Jehovah's Witnesses.[45] Failing by a single vote to muster a majority in conference, Stone wrote a powerful dissenting opinion in which he said, "The ordinance is a bald and unqualified suppression of the communication of ideas." In face of that dissenting opinion and one by Murphy, Black, who had been assigned to write for the Court, reversed himself, scrapped his opinion, and wrote an opinion sustaining the opposite result.[46]

The exact number of reversals resulting from dissenters' persuasive efforts is difficult to ascertain, for some reversals occur because opinion-writers change their minds for other reasons; sometimes the opinions "won't write," or, as the justices come to perceive the issues more clearly, they realize they cannot support their original positions. Black's switch in *Roberts* v. *United States*, discussed earlier, is an example of the latter. Douglas's docket books indicate seven such reversals in the 1939 and 1940 terms and ten in the 1942 and 1943 terms.

Just as concurring votes and opinions sometimes influence the content of majority opinions, so do dissenting votes and opinions. The papers of the justices are replete with instances of bargaining in which the price of acquiescence is change in a majority opinion.[47] But justices usually write dissenting opinions with the idea that they will be published and someday influence the decision of similar cases and provide the basis for overruling the cases in which they wrote the dissenting opinions. The justices of the late Hughes and early Stone Courts had good reason to believe that their dissenting views might someday be vindicated, for between 1939 and 1944 they had overruled twenty-four precedents, and future Courts would most likely deal similarly with the decisions with which they disagreed. Four cases decided during the 1939, 1940, 1942, and 1943 terms were later overruled, as were three cases decided in the intervening 1941 term. Those seven decisions are shown in Table 1.5.

Except for the *Gobitis* overruling, all of the decisions listed in Table 1.5 stood for more than a generation. And except for *More* and *Gobitis*, all had been closely divided decisions. The closeness of the vote in five of the seven cases suggests that prescient dissenters discern the policy direction of the law earlier than their colleagues and thus mark certain precedents as candidates for overruling. Nonetheless, a precedent determined by even a single vote is still a precedent and ordinarily will not be overruled until a substantial amount of time has passed.

In the six nonunanimous decisions listed in Table 1.5, dissenting opinions had significant consequences for the development of law and

Table 1.5. Overruled Cases Decided in the 1939-1943 Terms

Cases	Term Decided	Reported Vote	Term Overruled	Terms Valid
Gobitis v. *Minersville School Dist.*	1939	8-1	1942	3
More v. *Ill. Central Ry.*	1940	9-0	1971	31
Reitz v. *Mealey*	1941	5-4	1970	29
Betts v. *Brady*	1941	6-3	1962	21
Goldman v. *United States*	1941	5-3	1967	26
Magnolia Petroleum Co. v. *Hunt*	1943	5-4	1979	36
Hazel-Atlas Glass v. *Hartford-Empire*	1943	5-4	1976	34

policy. In overruling two cases—*Gobitis* and *Reitz*—the Court explicitly cited the preceding dissenting opinions as the basis for its decisions. In overruling three other cases—*Betts, Goldman,* and *Magnolia*—the Court relied upon the ideas expressed in the previous dissenting opinions. And although the Court overruled *Hazel-Atlas* on other grounds, it mentioned the previous dissent.

A data base of seven cases is a slender reed upon which to rest even a tentative explanation. Thus the data base of overruled decisions was expanded in Table 1.6 to include all overrulings for twenty-three terms—1958 through 1980. Fifty-seven decisions were overruled during that period. Forty-four were divided decisions, and the vast majority of them—thirty—were closely divided, that is, 5–4, 5–3, 5–2, or 6–3 decisions. Although twelve of the overruled precedents stood for less than ten years, the average life of a decision in the group was 19.6 years. This suggests that time, changing circumstances, and intervening decisions on related issues erode precedent, and that is to some extent correct, for in eight of the forty-one divided cases shown in Table 1.6 in which justices wrote dissenting opinions (19.5 percent), those were the reasons the Court gave in overruling them. But for thirty-one of the divided cases with dissenting opinions (75.6 percent), the Court explicitly cited previous dissenting opinions as the basis for overruling or based its overruling on the ideas expressed in the previous dissenting opinions (see Tables 1.6 and 1.7). This finding provides some support for the hypothesis that dissenting opinions have important consequences for the development of constitutional and legal policy.[48]

Because some justices write more frequently and persuasively in dissent than their colleagues, their dissenting opinions have greater

Table 1.6. The Consequences of Dissent: Overruling and Overruled Decisions, 1958-1980 Terms

Overruling Decision	Term	Vote	Overruled Decision	Term	Vote	Terms Valid	Category
James v. *United States* 366 U.S. 213	1960	6-3	*Commissioner* v. *Wilcox* 327 U.S. 404	1945	7-1	15	C
Mapp v. *Ohio* 367 U.S. 643	1960	5-4	*Wolf* v. *Colorado* 338 U.S. 25	1948	6-3	12	B
Construction & General Laborers' Union v. *Curry* 371 U.S. 542	1962	8-1	*Montgomery Building & Construction Trades Council* v. *Ledbetter Erection Co.* 344 U.S. 178	1952	7-2	10	D
Gideon v. *Wainwright* 372 U.S. 335	1962	7-1	*Betts* v. *Brady* 316 U.S. 455	1941	6-3	21	B
Fay v. *Noia* 372 U.S. 391	1962	6-3	*Darr* v. *Burford* 339 U.S. 200	1949	5-3	13	B
Murphy v. *Waterfront Commission of New York* 378 U.S. 52	1963	5-4	*United States* v. *Murdock* 284 U.S. 141	1931	9-0	32	E
Jackson v. *Denno* 378 U.S. 368	1963	5-4	*Stein* v. *New York* 346 U.S. 156	1952	6-3	11	A
Pointer v. *Texas* 380 U.S. 400	1964	7-2	*West* v. *Louisiana* 194 U.S. 258	1903	8-1	61	E
Swift & Co. v. *Wickham* 382 U.S. 111	1965	6-3	*Kesler* v. *Department of Public Safety* 369 U.S. 153	1961	6-3	4	C
Harris v. *United States* 382 U.S. 162	1965	5-4	*Brown* v. *United States* 359 U.S. 41	1958	5-4	7	A
Harper v. *Virginia State Board of Education* 383 U.S. 663	1965	6-3	*Breedlove* v. *Suttles* 302 U.S. 277	1937	9-0	28	E
Miranda v. *Arizona* 384 U.S. 436	1965	5-4	*Crooker* v. *California* 357 U.S. 433	1957	5-4	8	A
			Cicenia v. *LaGay* 357 U.S. 504	1957	5-3	8	B
Spevack v. *Klein* 385 U.S. 511	1966	5-4	*Cohen* v. *Hurley* 366 U.S. 117	1960	5-4	6	A
Afroyim v. *Rusk* 387 U.S. 253	1966	5-4	*Perez* v. *Brownell* 356 U.S. 44	1957	5-4	9	A
Camara v. *Municipal Court of San Francisco* 387 U.S. 523	1966	6-3	*Frank* v. *Maryland* 359 U.S. 360	1958	5-4	8	B

Continued on next page

Table 1.6, continued

Overruling Decision	Term	Vote	Overruled Decision	Term	Vote	Terms Valid	Category
Curtis Publishing Co. v. *Butts* 388 U.S. 130	1966	5-4	*Garrison* v. *Louisiana* 379 U.S. 64	1964	9-0	2	E
Katz v. *United States* 389 U.S. 347	1967	7-1	*Olmstead* v. *United States* 277 U.S. 438	1927	5-4	40	B
			Goldman v. *United States* 316 U.S. 129	1941	5-3	26	B
Marchetti v. *United States* 390 U.S. 39	1967	7-1	*United States* v. *Kahriger* 345 U.S. 22	1952	6-3	15	B
			Lewis v. *United States* 348 U.S. 419	1954	6-3	13	B
Peyton v. *Rowe* 391 U.S. 54	1967	9-0	*McNally* v. *Hill* 293 U.S. 131	1934	9-0	33	E
Bruton v. *United States* 391 U.S. 123	1967	6-2	*Delli Paoli* v. *United States* 352 U.S. 232	1956	5-4	11	A
Carafas v. *LaVallee* 391 U.S. 234	1967	8-0	*Parker* v. *Ellis* 362 U.S. 574	1959	5-4	8	A
Jones v. *Alfred H. Mayer* 392 U.S. 409	1967	7-2	*Hodges* v. *United States* 203 U.S. 1	1906	7-2	61	A
Moore v. *Ogilvie* 394 U.S. 814	1968	7-2	*MacDougall* v. *Green* 335 U.S. 281	1948	6-3	20	B
Brandenburg v. *Ohio* 395 U.S. 444	1968	9-0	*Whitney* v. *California* 274 U.S. 357	1926	9-0	42	E
Chimel v. *California* 395 U.S. 752	1968	7-2	*Harris* v. *United States* 331 U.S. 145	1946	5-4	22	B
			United States v. *Rabinowitz* 339 U.S. 56	1949	5-3	19	A
Benton v. *Maryland* 395 U.S. 784	1968	6-3	*Palko* v. *Connecticut* 302 U.S. 319	1937	8-1	31	E
Boys Markets Inc. v. *Retail Clerks Union* 398 U.S. 235	1969	6-2	*Sinclair Refining Co.* v. *Atkinson* 370 U.S. 195	1961	5-3	8	A
Moragne v. *States Marine Lines* 398 U.S. 375	1969	8-0	*The Harrisburg* 119 U.S. 199	1886	9-0	83	E
Blonder-Tongue Laboratories Inc. v. *University of Illinois Foundation* 402 U.S. 313	1970	9-0	*Triplett* v. *Lowell* 297 U.S. 638	1935	9-0	35	E

Table 1.6, continued

Overruling Decision	Term	Vote	Overruled Decision	Term	Vote	Terms Valid	Cat-egory
Perez v. *Campbell* 402 U.S. 637	1970	5-4	*Reitz* v. *Mealey* 314 U.S. 33	1941	5-4	29	A
Dunn v. *Blumstein* 405 U.S. 330	1971	6-1	*Pope* v. *Williams* 193 U.S. 621	1903	9-0	68	E
Andrews v. *Louisville &* *Nashville Railroad Co.* 406 U.S. 320	1971	7-1	*More* v. *Illinois Central* *Railroad Co.* 312 U.S. 630	1940	9-0	31	E
Lehnhausen v. *Lake* *Shore Auto Parts Co.* 410 U.S. 356	1972	9-0	*Quaker City Cab Co.* v. *Pennsylvania* 277 U.S. 389	1927	7-2	45	D
North Dakota State *Board of Pharmacy* v. *Snyder's Drug Stores Inc.* 414 U.S. 156	1973	9-0	*Liggett Co.* v. *Baldridge* 278 U.S. 105	1928	7-2	45	D
Michelin Tire Corp. v. *Wages* 423 U.S. 276	1975	8-0	*Low* v. *Austin* 80 U.S. 29	1871	9-0	104	E
Dove v. *United States* 423 U.S. 325	1975	8-1	*Durham* v. *United States* 401 U.S. 481	1970	5-4	5	B
National League of Cities v. *Usery* 426 U.S. 833	1975	6-3	*Maryland* v. *Wirtz* 392 U.S. 183	1967	6-2	8	A
International Association *of Machinists Aerospace* *Workers* v. *Wisconsin* *Employment Relations* *Commission* 427 U.S. 132	1975	6-3	*International Union,* *U.A.W.* v. *Wisconsin* *Employment Relations* *Board* 336 U.S. 245	1948	5-4	27	D
New Orleans v. *Dukes* 427 U.S. 297	1975	8-0	*Morey* v. *Doud* 354 U.S. 457	1956	6-3	19	A
Standard Oil Co. v. *United States* 429 U.S. 17	1976	8-0	*In re Potts* 166 U.S. 263	1896	9-0	80	E
			Hazel-Atlas Glass Co. v. *Hartford-Empire Co.* 322 U.S. 238	1943	5-4	33	D
Craig v. *Boren* 429 U.S. 190	1976	7-2	*Goesaert* v. *Cleary* 335 U.S. 464	1948	6-3	28	D
Oregon ex rel State Land *Board* v. *Corvallis Sand* *& Gravel Co.* 429 U.S. 363	1976	6-3	*Bonelli Cattle Co.* v. *Arizona* 414 U.S. 313	1973	7-1	3	A

Continued on next page

Table 1.6, continued

Overruling Decision	Term	Vote	Overruled Decision	Term	Vote	Terms Valid	Category
Complete Auto Transit, Inc. v. *Brady* 430 U.S. 274	1976	9-0	*Spector Motor Service, Inc.* v. *O'Connor* 340 U.S. 602	1950	6-3	26	B
Continental T.V., Inc. v. *GTE Sylvania, Inc.* 433 U.S. 36	1976	6-2	*United States* v. *Arnold, Schwinn & Co.* 388 U.S. 365	1966	7-0	10	E
Shaffer v. *Heitner* 433 U.S. 186	1976	7-1	*Pennoyer* v. *Neff* 95 U.S. 714	1877	8-1	99	D
			Harris v. *Balk* 198 U.S. 215	1904	7-2	72	D
Department of Revenue v. *Association of Washington Stevedoring Cos.* 435 U.S. 734	1977	8-0	*Puget Sound Stevedoring Co.* v. *Tax Commission* 302 U.S. 90	1937	9-0	42	E
			Joseph v. *Carter & Weekes Stevedoring Co.* 330 U.S. 422	1946	5-4	33	B
Monell v. *Department of Social Services* 436 U.S. 658	977	7-2	*Monroe* v. *Pape* 365 U.S. 167	1960	8-1	17	A
Hughes v. *Oklahoma* 441 U.S. 322	1978	7-2	*Geer* v. *Connecticut* 161 U.S. 519	1895	5-2	83	A
United States v. *Salvucci* 448 U.S. 83	1979	7-2	*Jones* v. *United States* 362 U.S. 257	1959	8-1	20	E
Thomas v. *Washington Gas Light Co.* 448 U.S. 261	1979	7-2	*Magnolia Petroleum Co.* v. *Hunt* 320 U.S. 430	1943	5-4	36	B

Key for "Category" column:
A: dissenting opinion explicitly cited as the basis for the overruling decision
B: ideas expressed in the dissenting opinion clearly used as the basis for the overruling decision
C: decision overruled for reasons not contained in the dissenting opinion
D: decision overruled because of intervening cases or passage of time cited as a justification for the overruling decision
E: no dissent or no dissenting opinion written in the overruled decision

Table 1.7. Uses of Dissenting Opinions in Overruling Decisions, 1958-1980 Terms

	N	Percent	Adjusted Percentage[a]
(A) Dissenting opinion as basis of overruling decision	16	28.1	39.0
(B) Ideas in dissenting opinion basis of overruling decision	15	26.3	36.6
(C) Decision overruled for reasons not contained in dissenting opinion	2	3.5	4.9
(D) Decision overruled because of intervening cases or erosion of time	8	14.0	19.5
(E) No dissenting opinion in the decision overruled	16	28.1	—
Totals	57	100.0	100.0

[a]Percentage of total excluding (E)

consequences for future decision making. In the twenty-three years covered in Table 1.6, the dissenting opinions of five justices—Frank-furter, Douglas, Warren, Black, and Murphy—appeared to be the basis of three-fourths of overruled cases in Categories A and B. Influence of individual dissenting behavior is clearest in cases in which the Court specifically cited a prior dissenting opinion in overruling a precedent. In the sixteen overruled cases in Category A, Frankfurter wrote dissent-ing opinions in five, Douglas in four, and Warren in three. One overrul-ing case cited both Douglas's and Warren's dissenting opinions in the case overruled; thus these three justices appeared to have influenced the overruling of eleven of the sixteen cases. No other justice wrote more than one dissenting opinion in cases in Category A. The influence of individual dissenting behavior on overruling precedents is less clear in cases in Category B for two reasons: first, similarity of reasoning in dissenting opinions and overruling opinions is the basis for inferring influence; second, more than one justice wrote dissenting opinions in several of the overruled cases. Nonetheless, it is clear that the dissent-ing opinions of four justices—Frankfurter, Douglas, Black, and Mur-phy—provided the rationale for overruling twelve of the fifteen cases in Category B. No other justice wrote more than one dissenting opinion in that category.

The phenomenon described above appears to be a form of policy leadership. Justices who fail in their attempts at task leadership in the decisional process appeal in dissenting opinions, as Hughes once said, "to the brooding spirit of the law, to the intelligence of a future day," hoping their views will someday become law.[49] All justices do that, but Frankfurter and Douglas had an impact on future policy far exceeding that of any of their colleagues, for between them they wrote more dissenting opinions in cases in Categories A and B than the rest of the justices combined.

This analysis suggests two conclusions. First, dissenting behavior sometimes has significant policy consequences prior to decision because dissenters persuade majority justices to change their votes, and, even if they do not, their behavior sometimes influences the content of majority opinions. Second, dissenting opinions have significant policy consequences for the future development of the law and policy by calling attention to questionable precedents and by persuasively arguing that they should be overruled.

Conflict and its resolution in the Supreme Court is a human process that has significant policy consequences. Disagreement over values and role expectations is at the core of the conflict, and that disagreement exists not just in the Court but in society as well. Activism makes for change; restraint makes for stability. For law to live and yet fulfill its function of guiding behavior, both change and stability are necessary. The debate in the Court over the appropriate amount of activism and restraint occurs in the context of a rational decision-making process in which the justices' values and role expectations are central. Those values and role expectations cannot be easily changed, but the justices' perceptions of issues, which are related to both, can be changed by deliberation, discussion, and leadership. Attempts at task and social leadership contribute to both conflict and its resolution, and the justices' personalities either help or hinder them in the process. But leadership goes beyond the tasks of decision and maintaining the Court as an effective decision-making group. There is also policy leadership, which is often reflected in majority opinions, but it can be exercised also in dissenting opinions that successfully persuade long after they are written and in many cases long after their writers have left the Court. Hence conflict is useful in the quest for workable policy just as conflict resolution is useful in legitimating such policy.

I appreciate the research assistance of Richard A. Nagareda and Rebecca J. Danelski for this chapter.

1. See David J. Danelski, "Conflict and Its Resolution in the Supreme Court," *Journal of Conflict Resolution* 11 (1967): 71-86, and James L. Gibson, "From Simplicity to Complexity: The Development of Theory in the Study of Judicial Behavior," *Political Behavior* 5 (1983): 7-49.

2. See David J. Danelski, "Values as Variables in Judicial Decision-Making: Notes toward a Theory," *Vanderbilt Law Review* 19 (1966): 721-40. "Values" refers to the ideological component of judicial decision making. Some scholars, such as Glendon Schubert, use the term "attitudes" to refer to that component. See Schubert, *The Judicial Mind: The Attitudes and Ideologies of Supreme Court Justices, 1946-1963* (Evanston: Northwestern University Press, 1965); cf. C. Herman Pritchett, *The Roosevelt Court: A Study in Judicial Politics and Values, 1937-1947* (New York: Macmillan, 1948). Pritchett was the first scholar to hypothesize that the interaction of values and role expectations explains Supreme Court decision making. See Pritchett, *Civil Liberties and the Vinson Court* (Chicago: University of Chicago Press, 1954), pp. 187-88.

3. See David J. Danelski, "The Influence of the Chief Justice in the Decisional Process of the Supreme Court," in Sheldon Goldman and Austin Sarat, eds., *American Court Systems: Readings in Judicial Process and Behavior* (San Francisco: W. H. Freeman, 1978), p. 516.

4. See Danelski, "Values as Variables," pp. 737-38; J. Woodford Howard, Jr., "On the Fluidity of Judicial Choice," *American Political Science Review* 62 (1968): 43-56.

5. Danelski, "The Influence," pp. 509-13.

6. Danelski, "Conflict and Its Resolution," p. 80.

7. Ibid., pp. 82-84.

8. James L. Gibson, "Personality and Elite Political Behavior: The Influence of Self Esteem in Judicial Decision Making," *Journal of Politics* 43 (1981): 104-25.

9. 321 U.S. 649 (1944).

10. 322 U.S. 385 (1944).

11. Analysis of the voting behavior in *Smith* and *Saylor* suggests that both values and role expectations were the bases of those decisions. Murphy's conference notes in *Saylor* indicate that Roberts's, Frankfurter's, and Jackson's votes turned on precedent-adherence expectations. Jackson's values and role expectations conflicted. He said he preferred decentralized control of elections but would abide by precedent. Black's comments indicated rather clearly that his vote turned on his values. "I came out the other way," Murphy recorded Black as saying. "I start out with the idea the Moseley case is law. I would have joined Lamar in dissent in Moseley. . . . I don't like a statute as general as this to send a man to a penitentiary." Conference notes, nos. 716-17, 1943 term, May 2, 1944, Frank Murphy Papers, Bentley Historical Library, University of Michigan.

12. For an explanation of scale analysis of judicial votes, see Schubert, *Judicial Mind*, pp. 75-81.

13. The analysis shown in Table 1.1 is an attempt to solve in a manageable way the problem of circularity in scale analysis. See Joseph Tanenhaus, "The Cumulative Scaling of Judicial Decisions," *Harvard Law Review* 79 (1966): 1583-94. The analysis is based on the assumption that justices who are strongly role-oriented or value-oriented will write dissenting opinions expressing those orientations more frequently than will their colleagues. The analysis yields an ordered metric that is essentially an independent measure of role and value orientations. The data for the analysis come from a period—the 1941 through 1944 terms—when eight of the nine justices listed in Figures 1.1 and 1.2 sat together and thus responded to the same stimuli by writing or not writing dissenting opinions in civil liberties cases. Although this fact strengthens the analysis, the scale scores are only rough measures of the justices' role and value commitments. This exploratory methodological effort has implications beyond scale analysis of judicial votes, for it provides a basis for using regression analysis to test the relationships between values and role expectations and decisions.

14. A simulated nine-justice Court that is statistically a composite of Stone, Jackson, Roberts, Reed, and Frankfurter was created for purposes of Spearman rank-correlation analysis by dividing the sum of the squared differences in ranks of the five justices in each scale by five and then multiplying by nine. The standard formula for computing Spearman rank-correlation coefficients was then used.

15. A note by Murphy to Stone concerning his vote in *Bridges* v. *California* provides an illustration. "Conscience and judgment," wrote Murphy, "are inseparable, and the former allows no choice." Murphy to Stone, May 29, 1941, Murphy Papers. Similarly, Murphy told Frankfurter in a discussion of *Schneiderman* v. *United States*: "My instincts are satisfied . . . but not my understanding of the law. . . . I think the Chief has the better of the law in this case, but the faith of my whole life is wrapped up in support of Liberty." Quoted by Frankfurter in Joseph Lash, ed., *From the Diaries of Felix Frankfurter* (New York: Norton, 1975), p. 259.

16. Learned Hand's observation about Frankfurter's commitment to judicial restraint is revealing. "Well, of course," Hand said in his oral history memoir, "Frankfurter has a very passionate nature, and that is rather an initial handicap for a judge. Not if . . . he has the faculty of adding to it supreme self-restraint. But Felix hasn't supreme self-restraint. He has learned a great deal of it, but he hasn't it." Hand Memoir, Columbia Oral History Project, Columbia University. Douglas recalled that "no one poured his emotions more completely into decisions [than Frankfurter], while professing just the opposite." William O. Douglas, *The Court Years, 1939-1975* (New York: Random House, 1980), p. 34. Jackson acknowledged that he found the exercise of judicial restraint difficult. "You try to approach each case," he recalled in his oral history memoir at Columbia University, "without predilections or prejudgments, but sometimes that's difficult."

17. Murphy referred specifically to the majority's perception of the Mann Act's purpose. See *Mortensen*, 322 U.S. at 377. Why Stone made an issue of lack of restraint in a statutory interpretation case is puzzling, particularly when restraintists Frankfurter, Roberts, and Jackson did not agree with him. Perhaps Murphy's value-laden rhetoric in the majority's opinion (for example, "petitioners are entitled to have just and fair

treatment under the law") provoked Stone's restraintist response. Frankfurter had no difficulty agreeing with Murphy's opinion as published and in fact influenced its content. "You are very obliging," wrote Frankfurter on the back of Murphy's opinion, "and have, from my point of view, much tightened your opinion and saved the moral you wanted to preach." Murphy's revisions of the opinion, however, cost him Black's vote. Undated notes, *Mortensen* file, Murphy Papers.

18. Conference notes, *U.S.* v. *Dotterweich,* 1943 term, October 19, 1943, Murphy Papers.

19. Stone to Murphy, June 1, 1944, Harlan Fiske Stone Papers, Library of Congress. Murphy apparently viewed his decision as a value choice. On June 17, 1944, he wrote Senator Burton K. Wheeler: "I appreciated receiving your very kind letter concerning the Court's decision in the *Hartzel* case. . . . I enjoyed hearing from you again and knowing that you approved my stand in this case." Murphy Papers. Murphy's values of freedom and patriotism were in conflict in *Hartzel,* and he sought to resolve the conflict with an extraordinary suggestion to Frankfurter. According to Frankfurter, Murphy came to him and said that it was wrong to reverse Hartzel's conviction and urged Frankfurter to get another vote for affirmance. "Well," said Frankfurter, "haven't you a vote—wouldn't that make five of us?" "Oh, but you know me," Murphy replied. "I want to be for free speech and I want to write a dissenting opinion in that case. But I think it is wrong to reverse the conviction." Frankfurter to Learned Hand, February 13, 1958, Felix Frankfurter Papers, Library of Congress.

20. If there had not been differences of perceptions in *Mortensen, Dotterweich,* and *Hartzel,* presumably there would have been no inconsistent votes in those decisions in the scales in Figures 1.2 and 1.3. In that case, the coefficients of reproducibility for the scales would be respectively .95 and .96.

21. Replication of the eighth step of the analysis for civil liberties decisions by the Supreme Court during the 1957 term provides even stronger support for the third hypothesis. In the decisions shown in Schubert's C Scale for the 1957 term in *The Judicial Mind,* Harold H. Burton's docket book for that term at the Library of Congress indicates twenty-two vote changes, including changes of pass votes. Twenty-one of the twenty-two vote changes support the third hypothesis, but only nine of the twenty-two vote changes support the first and second hypotheses.

22. Danelski, "The Influence," pp. 510-13. On October 12, 1941, Augustus N. Hand wrote to Hughes that Stone "never seemed . . . a sure bet as a leader because of a certain inability to express himself orally and to maintain a position in a discussion." Charles Evans Hughes Papers, Library of Congress. In his oral history memoir at Columbia University, Jackson said that it was a "fact that Stone was not able to lead his Court." Douglas predicted when Stone became chief justice that unless he changed, the Court's atmosphere would be unhappy and uncongenial. Douglas to Black, June 22, 1941, Hugo L. Black Papers, Library of Congress.

23. Danelski, "The Influence," pp. 511-12.

24. In view of the later Black-Jackson feud, Black's ability to persuade Jackson may seem surprising. When Jackson first came to the Court, however, relations between him and Black were good. Jackson recalls in his oral history memoir: "There were a

good many cases at first in which I went along with Black. I agreed with some of his viewpoints. But the methods of this group [Black, Douglas, Murphy, and Rutledge] were pretty hard for Stone or me to take." Earlier in the memoir Jackson said: "It wasn't long after I came on the Court that I realized that Justice Black felt he was entitled to be leader of the New Deal group on the Court." Columbia Oral History Project.

25. 320 U.S. 264 (1943).

26. Black to Members of the Conference, November 6, 1943, Douglas Papers.

27. Danelski, "The Influence," pp. 512-13, 517.

28. Douglas, *Court Years*, pp. 18, 21-22.

29. H. N. Hirsch, *The Enigma of Felix Frankfurter* (New York: Basic Books, 1981).

30. Alan A. Stone, review of *The Enigma of Felix Frankfurter, Harvard Law Review* 95 (1981): 365.

31. Alpheus Thomas Mason, *Harlan Fiske Stone: Pillar of the Law* (New York: Viking, 1956), pp. 334-35, 339, 602-3, 613-14, 792-93; Harlan B. Phillips, ed., *Felix Frankfurter Reminisces* (New York: Reynal, 1960), p. 221; Phillip B. Kurland, review of *Harlan Fiske Stone, Harvard Law Review* 70 (1957): 1321-22.

32. Danelski, "Conflict and Its Resolution," pp. 83-84.

33. Such measures are not beyond researchers' reach. Obvious sources of data for empirical personality analysis are the justices' law clerks.

34. See Mason, *Harlan Fiske Stone*, pp. 607-12.

35. See Jerome Frank, *Law and The Modern Mind* (New York: Brentano, 1930), chap. 1.

36. Charles Evans Hughes, *The Supreme Court of the United States* (New York: Columbia University Press, 1928), p. 67.

37. 309 U.S. 382 (1940).

38. 321 U.S. 233 (1944).

39. Black to Stone, February 23, 1944, Stone Papers.

40. 320 U.S. 81 (1943).

41. Stone to Douglas, June 4, 1943, Stone Papers.

42. The eleven cases were *Hirabayashi* v. *U.S.*, 320 U.S. 81 (1943) (Douglas and Murphy); *Ecker* v. *Western R. R. Corp.*, 318 U.S. 448 (1943) (Roberts); *Williams* v. *North Carolina*, 317 U.S. 287 (1942) (Frankfurter); *United States ex rel. Marcus* v. *Hess*, 317 U.S. 537 (1942) (Frankfurter); *Tiller* v. *Atlantic Coast Line Ry. Co.*, 318 U.S. 54 (1943) (Frankfurter); *Reconstruction Finance Corp.* v. *Bankers Trust Co.*, 318 U.S. 163 (1943) (Douglas); *Penn Dairies* v. *Milk Control Comm.*, 318 U.S. 261 (1943) (Murphy); *Creek County* v. *Seber*, 318 U.S. 705 (1943) (Rutledge); *Martin* v. *Struthers*, 319 U.S. 141 (1943) (Murphy); *Douglas* v. *Jeannette*, 319 U.S. 157 (1943) (Jackson); and *Schneiderman* v. *U.S.*, 320 U.S. 118 (1943) (Douglas and Rutledge).

43. The six opinions cited were Frankfurter's in *Williams* and *Hess*, Murphy's in *Penn Dairies*, Rutledge's and Douglas's in *Schneiderman*, and Jackson's in *Douglas*.

44. See *Sutton* v. *Leib*, 342 U.S. at 404; *Carlson* v. *Landon* 342 U.S. at 536; and *Miranda* v. *Arizona*, 384 U.S. at 526.

45. 319 U.S. 141 (1943).

46. Black's original opinion for the Court and Stone's dissenting opinion are in the *Martin* v. *Struthers* file, 1942 term, Stone Papers.

47. See Walter F. Murphy, *Elements of Judicial Strategy* (Chicago: University of Chicago Press, 1964), pp. 43-74.

48. See S. Sidney Ulmer, "An Empirical Analysis of Selected Aspects of Law-making of the Supreme Court of the United States," *Journal of Public Law* 8 (1959): 414-36, which suggested this analysis.

49. Hughes, *Supreme Court,* p. 68.

2

Exploring the Dissent
Patterns of the Chief Justices:
John Marshall to Warren Burger

S. SIDNEY ULMER

Felix Frankfurter once bemoaned the fact that "layman are constantly troubled, even as are lawyers . . . about division on the Court." But why, he asked, "should anyone expect nine men . . . all to have the same thoughts and views. . . . No one expects such harmony . . . among physicists, let alone among professors of sociology or history."[1] According to Frankfurter, the media are largely responsible for such concerns in the public. Just as newspapers are more likely to publish stories about divorces than about marriages, divisions in the Court—the conflict among the justices in nonunanimous cases—make headlines.

Conflict within the Supreme Court, however, is distinguishable from conflict that is reported to the public. As Frankfurter suggests, the justices, in the process of deciding cases, may be expected to bring differing perspectives to the legal and factual issues they face. The initial disagreements that their different views produce, however, may be suppressed by merely changing a dissenting vote to a majority vote once the decision is final.[2] If all justices join the majority, no division is reported to the public and the value of projecting institutional solidarity is served. When, on the other hand, a dissenting justice allows his disagreement with his colleagues to be reported, he must do so because he believes that public knowledge of the conflict is more important than projecting the fiction of consensus. Obviously, all justices now subscribe to the latter view in some cases.

As for physicists, sociologists, and historians, Frankfurter's analysis is somewhat inapt. Neither the public nor the legal profession gets excited when such specialists disagree. Conflict in the Supreme Court, however, is said to have readily identifiable consequences[3] and, when in dissent, has been variously damned. Frankfurter has remarked on the candor of the dissenter—a "luxury" he thought not available to the majority justices.[4] Benjamin Cardozo put the point more dramatically by describing dissenters as "irresponsible."[5] Oliver Wendell Holmes and John Marshall would dissent if the matter was of sufficient importance, but neither felt comfortable in the role and would sometimes apologize for casting a dissenting vote.[6]

Others have expressed the view that dissent diminishes the image of monolithic solidarity, which allegedly enhances respect for the Court and obedience to its mandates.[7] Danelski has shown that dissenting opinions occasionally shape majority opinions.[8] Certainly the expression of dissent carries implications for the decision-making model chosen to explain Court actions. The model adopted by Justice Roberts in *U.S.* v. *Butler*[9] implies objective decision making that leaves no room for dissent. Unanimous decisions, by contrast, would be difficult to square with the decisional models favored by such disparate parties as Richard Nixon and the judicial behavioralists.[10] When there is doubt about the Court's objectivity, litigation may be encouraged and losing parties may be emboldened to resist complying with Supreme Court mandates and precedents. As a consequence, the Court on occasion makes concerted efforts to reach unanimity in cases involving important social policy making.[11]

In this chapter, I adopt a limited focus on conflict in the Court, presenting an exploratory analysis conducted at a macro level. My purpose is to provide some background relevant to, and to stimulate thinking about, the conflict of chief justices with their Courts. Therefore, I reach no theoretical conclusions but do suggest ideas and hypotheses for further investigation. The focus of my interest is the dissent behavior of chief justices. It may be assumed that chief justices have the same reasons as associate justices for avoiding excessive conflict in the Court—to protect the Court qua institution. But they also have some unique reasons for discouraging conflict in their Courts and avoiding the dissenting position generally in casting their individual votes.

It has been suggested that the magnitude of conflict in the Court is, to some extent, a measure of leadership skills exhibited by the chief justice. Danelski reports that the low production of the Stone Court was associated with a good deal of unbridled and unfriendly conflict among the justices. Greater production in the Hughes Court, on the other hand, was associated with Hughes's devoted attention to avoiding conflict.

A chief justice may have other reasons for avoiding dissent. When voting with the majority, a chief decides who shall write the opinion "for the Court" and therefore has a particularly good reason for avoiding the role of dissenter. The writer of an opinion largely determines the grounds of decision, its future use as precedent, and the extent to which the public will approve of it. In choosing what to say and how to say it, the opinion-writer may contribute to holding or enlarging a majority and, in general, to the development of legal rules and social policy. By choosing the writer, the chief justice indirectly influences this process in a highly significant manner.

For all these reasons, the preferences of the chief justices might be assumed to rank as follows: (1) to have all cases decided unanimously, (2) to vote with the majority in all nonunanimous cases, (3) to cast a dissenting vote in some nonunanimous cases, or (4) to cast a dissenting vote in all nonunanimous cases.

The first choice is impossible, given a collegial court as large as nine members and the acceptability accorded the right to dissent. The second implies a chief justice without a mind of his own, devoid of a philosophy that guides his decision making or lacking confidence in interpretation that permits him to disagree with his colleagues. Obviously, this is not to be expected and it is not found. The fourth possibility implies a chief justice completely out of touch with the development of law and policy in his Court as well as the absence of the respect, deference, and acceptance of viewpoint normally accorded the most inept chief justice on occasion. Such a possibility is quickly dismissed. Thus preference number three is to be expected—the question being simply: how often does the chief justice dissent?

That a chief justice would give up the advantages accruing to him when he is in the majority position—as they all do from time to time—is a phenomenon worthy of study. This chapter asks whether this giving up is a variable across Courts for individual chief justices. If significant variation is discovered, an exploration of some associated predictors will be in order.

CONFLICT IN THE COURT

The chief justices examined in this section are all those who have completed their service on the Court and cast at least one dissenting

Table 2.1. Supreme Courts and Chief Justices Compared by Dissent Rate

Chief Justice	I N of Cases[a]	II N of Nonunanimous Cases[a]	III Chief Justice Dissents	$\frac{II}{I}$	$\frac{III}{I}$	$\frac{III}{II}$
John Marshall	1,187	87	7	.0732	.0058	.0804
Roger B. Taney	1,708	257	38	.1504	.0222	.1478
Salmon P. Chase	1,109	140	33	.1262	.0297	.2357
Morrison R. Waite	2,642	301	45	.1139	.0170	.1495
Melville W. Fuller	4,866	752	113	.1545	.0232	.1502
Edward D. White	2,541	313	39	.1231	.0153	.1246
William H. Taft	1,708	180	16	.1053	.0093	.0888
Charles E. Hughes	2,050	347	46	.1692	.0224	.1325
Harlan F. Stone	704	342	95	.4857	.1349	.2777
Fred M. Vinson	723	542	90	.7496	.1244	.1660
Earl Warren	1,772	1,220	215	.6884	.1213	.1762

[a]Opinion cases only, defined as cases accompanied by a written opinion—*per curiam* or signed. An opinion, for purposes of identification, is required to be at least one paragraph in length and to express something beyond mere concurring, dissenting, or majority vote.

vote during their tenure. (Chief Justice Burger's dissent behavior is examined briefly later in this chapter.) Since I was unable to find a dissenting vote for Chief Justices John Jay, John Rutledge, and Oliver Ellsworth, this examination is limited to all chief justices from John Marshall through Earl Warren. For these eleven Courts, an overall conflict rate has been determined, that is, the number of nonunanimous opinion cases decided as a percentage of all opinion cases in which chief justices participated. Table 2.1 lists the chief justices in order of service. For each Court, the raw data and percentages for level of conflict and the dissent rates for each of the eleven chief justices individually are given. Column 5 shows that conflict in the Court has varied from a low of 7.32 percent to a high of 74.96 percent. A visual presentation of the change in rate across eleven Courts is provided in Figure 2.1.

If cases without conflict were viewed as a tentative indicator of leadership, administrative skills, or both, a leadership ranking from high to low would be as follows: Marshall (92.7 percent), Taft (89.4), Waite (88.6), White (87.7), Chase (87.3), Taney (84.9), Fuller (84.5), Hughes (83.1), Stone (51.4), Warren (31.1), and Vinson (25). Yet

Figure 2.1. Percentage of Nonunanimous Cases in the U.S. Supreme
Court, Marshall through Warren

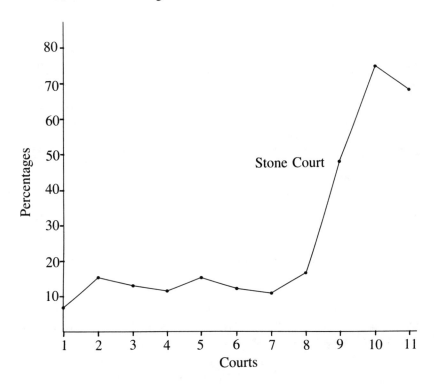

without further analysis, these inferences may be misleading. With the
exception of Hughes, we have little evidence demonstrating that the
respective chief justices were necessarily the task leaders in their
Courts. Thus it may be questionable to rank Marshall (who went out of
his way to stifle dissent) as a more skillful leader than the other chiefs.
The ranking might be more acceptable if ability to stifle dissent is
viewed as a component of leadership.

Other factors that could account for variation in conflict rate would
include change in the attitudes of the justices toward dissent or expressing dissent, the varying complexity of cases being decided, and interpersonal feuding in the Court. There is no adequate way to measure
change in attitudes toward dissent or levels of personal conflict across

eleven different Courts, although several observations about the Stone Court can be offered.

The Stone Court retained six members of the Hughes Court until its final term, when Justice Harold H. Burton was appointed. It is unlikely that these six justices dramatically changed their attitudes toward the propriety of expressing dissent in the five years of the Stone Court, during which time the dissent rate was never less than 35 percent. In the years of the Hughes Court, by contrast, the mean rate of conflict was 16.9 percent and the dissent rate exceeded 35 percent in only one of twelve terms. Thus it is improbable that the attitudes of the Stone Court justices toward dissent differed markedly from those of earlier justices.

One might plausibly think that the cases decided by the Supreme Court vary in complexity. The more complex (or "hard") the case, the smaller the probability that unanimity will be obtained. Dissent is, in part, a function of complexity.[12] Greatest conflict occurs when the Court decides a case by a 5–4 vote. Thus there should be a correlation between 5–4 cases and overall conflict rate. In fact, the Pearson r for that relationship is .845 ($r^2 = .714$). This correlation does not rule out the leadership hypothesis or other hypothetical explanations. But the dissent rate increased in four of the last five Courts examined before declining slightly in the Warren Court. Moreover, beginning with the Marshall Court, the rate of 5–4 decisions has increased with each Court—with two exceptions. The Waite Court shows a lower rate than the Chase Court and the Taft Court a lower rate than the White Court. Otherwise, each Court has a higher percentage of 5–4 decisions than its predecessor.

All this is consistent with the proposition that the cases have become more complex as we have moved through recent Courts. It is also consistent with the suggestion by Stephen C. Halpern and Kenneth N. Vines that recent Courts have evidenced greater disunity as they have increased their influence on the selection of cases for plenary review.[13]

The leadership hypothesis remains an alternative explanation for the variation observed in conflict rate. There is no probative evidence, however, for the notion that Hughes was a less effective leader than Taft and Vinson less effective than Stone. Indeed, Danelski's evidence in Chapter 1 points in a contrary direction. One possible working hypothesis, then, is that conflict variation in the Court is, inter alia, a function of complexity in cases and interpersonal relations.

Figure 2.2. Percentage of Dissenting Votes Cast by Chief Justices, Marshall through Warren

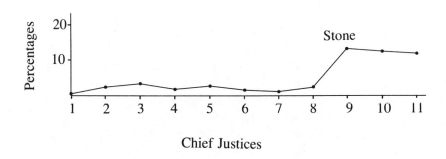

Chief Justices

CHIEF JUSTICES IN DISSENT

When the chief justice becomes the focus of analysis, the question is somewhat different. We wish to know whether the dissent rates for the chiefs vary across Courts and, if so, their antecedents. Table 2.1 shows that the dissent rate for John Marshall was less than 1 percent of all cases decided. Other chiefs, however, show rates varying from 1 to 13 percent. The justices differ also in the nonunanimous cases. The differences are particularly marked for Marshall and Taft, who dissented in only 8 and 9 percent of the nonunanimous cases decided in their Courts. Stone, again, is an exception because he dissented in a larger proportion of nonunanimous cases than any other chief justice. But the differences here do not begin to match those examined earlier. Salmon P. Chase is almost at the level of Stone; and Vinson and Warren are at a level that is roughly 60 percent that of Stone.

Figure 2.2 shows the curve for dissent rates of eleven chief justices in all cases in which they participated. It is clear that Stone dissented significantly more often than all the chief justices preceding him and at a rate comparable to those for Vinson and Warren. When change in dissent rate is considered, however, Stone is an aberrational dissenter among all chief justices. Nevertheless, there are ups and downs in the pattern, indicating that dissent among chief justices is a legitimate variable. Our challenge is to account for that variation with one or more explanatory factors.

My exploratory analysis of this variation uses the alternative model approach.[14] Instead of directly stating and testing a theory, four limited models are presented, each of which is backed by a particular bit of theoretical reasoning. The reasoning in any or all cases is not necessarily profound, but all the models reflect some degree of plausibility and therefore cannot be rejected out of hand. Since this is an exploratory investigation, the point is to identify concepts and variables that seem to have potential as explanatory factors and those that seem to lack such potential. Such knowledge can be a useful guide for further research.

The analysis proceeds by regressing the dissent rate of the chief justices on the predictors specified in the four models. If the regression coefficients are not significant at the .05 level for any particular model, we can infer that the model holds little promise for future research. A contrary finding, however, should lead to further efforts to understand why chief justices dissent at varying career rates across Courts.

Model 1. The first model to be tested is experiential. It suggests that the greater the man's experience in life or as chief justice, the greater will be his ability as chief justice to marshal his majorities—to avoid the dissenter's role.[15] The indicators to this criterion are age at appointment and years served in the Court as chief justice. The empirical hypothesis to be tested is that those who are appointed to the Court at later ages and who serve as chief for longer periods of time will have lower dissent rates over their careers than those who are younger at appointment and those who serve as chief for shorter time spans. The regression equation is dissent rate $(DR) = a - bX + cY + e$, where X is age at appointment, Y is years served as chief, and e is the error term. With this equation, DR was found to equal $-3.88 + .182X + .141Y$. For this equation, the regression coefficients are not significant at .05, the sign of the age coefficient is contrary to that specified in the model, the adjusted R^2 is .113,[16] and F is significant at .40. These results suggest that dissent rate is not a function of experience in life or as chief justice.

Model 2. The second model is also experiential, but it is less general than Model 1. Model 2 suggests that experience in official decision-making roles before coming to the Court equips a chief justice to deal more effectively with his colleagues once he gets there. I suggest that prior service on a bench or in a legislative body is pertinent,[17] though certainly not inclusive. If bench service is represented by X and legislative service by Y, $DR = a + bX + cY + e$. Calculating the appropriate values, we get $DR = .295 + 3.81X - .419Y + e$. None of these coefficients is significant at .05, the sign for legislative service is misspecified, the adjusted R^2 is .045, and F is significant at .54. Thus the regression results are not consistent with the hypothesis either when the predictors are used singly or jointly. In short, dissent rate is not explained by prior decisional experience as a judge or legislator.

Model 3. A third model may be taken from the literature dealing with the realignment of political power or electoral realignments in the period 1800–1968. According to Richard Funston, there have been four realignment periods and five stable periods in this time span.[18] It has been hypothesized, though not established, that the Supreme Court is more likely to declare acts of Congress unconstitutional—that is, to exercise greater power—during realignment periods than during stable periods. If this is true, one might expect chief justices to exert greater control over their Courts during stable periods. This hypothesis follows from Stuart S. Nagel's observation that high dissent in the Supreme Court correlates with frequency of congressional attack on the Court through the introduction of bills tending to curb the Court.[19] In a stable period, congressional pressure would constitute a more viable threat to a high-dissenting Court, thereby making it easier for a chief justice to get unanimity or larger majorities.

Model 3 assumes that $DR = a + bX + e$, where X is the dummy variable: realignment/nonrealignment period. The regression equation is $DR = .699 + .029X + e$. Although the signs are, for the first time, as specified and adjusted R^2 is .298, the coefficient for the dummy variable is not significant at .05 and F is significant at .28. Thus variation in chief justices' dissent rate cannot be attributed to variation in congressional pressure on the Court.

Model 4. Model 4 is a limited environmental disruption model. Political scientists have demonstrated that the internal environment of the Court can cause changes in the voting patterns of the justices.[20] The internal development of the "counter dissent" in the early 1940s is a case in point. Hugo Black's attack on Frankfurter in *F.P.C.* v. *Hope Natural Gas Co.*[21] illustrates a practice still widely followed—the use of the dissent or a concurrence, not to appeal to the brooding spirit of the law but as an attack on the intelligence, knowledge, analytical skills, or good faith of one or more other justices. (For a recent example, one need only examine William H. Rehnquist's dissent in *United Steelworkers* v. *Weber*.)[22] The feuding between Black and Frankfurter frequently caught up the other justices and clearly affected voting blocs in the Court.

The Court's working environment may also be affected by external events. One need only recall how the power structure in the Court was dramatically modified by Franklin D. Roosevelt's attempt to "pack" the Court in 1937, or the changes in voting alignments associated with appointments to the Court at various times.[23] The idiosyncratic perspectives of individual justices or groups of justices may affect the success of the chief justice in marshaling his Court and avoiding the dissenting position. Changes in the idiosyncratic profile of the Court should be correlated with changes in the chief justice's dissent rate. It should make a difference whether a chief justice presides over a Court that is never called on to integrate a new member into the group and a Court frequently called to such a task. Similarly, it should matter whether all appointments to a given Court are made by the same president or several presidents. Appointments by several presidents open the possibility for enhancing idiosyncratic variation across appointees. Other things being equal, the more varied the number of chemists adding to a brew, the greater the uncertainty about the ultimate product—and the greater challenge to the brew master to maintain consistent quality standards. Consequently, we may expect some positive relationship between the number of presidents appointing justices to each Court and the dissent rates of the chief justices.

I suggested earlier that the ability of the chief justice to marshal his majorities in the face of turnover is influenced by the complexity of the cases in a given time period. It should be easier for the chief to integrate new members with differing ideological profiles into the Court when the cases are less rather than more complex. Thus the combination of complexity and turnover in the Court should predict the dissent rates of the chief justices over time.

To construct an indicator to complexity of cases, I first removed all cases in which chief justices dissented. I then calculated the conflict rate for the Court from the remaining cases. This measure was used to indicate case complexity. For turnover, I used an index that combines the average number of appointing presidents per term per Court and the average number of appointments to the Court per term per Court. The formula for the index is $\sqrt{I} \times J$ where I is appointing presidents and

Table 2.2. Predictors of Chief Justices' Dissent Rates

Chief Justice	Years of Service	Number of Appointments to Court	Number of Appointing Presidents	N of Cases	N of Non-unanimous Cases
Marshall	34	10	5	1,180	80
Taney	28	14	8	1,670	219
Chase	8	4	1	1,076	107
Waite	14	6	4	2,597	256
Fuller	22	11	5	4,753	639
White	10	7	2	2,502	274
Taft	8	4	2	1,692	164
Hughes	11	7	2	2,004	301
Stone	5	4	2	609	247
Vinson	7	2	1	633	452
Warren	16	8	3	1,557	1,005

J is appointments of justices. This index assigns the highest value when the contribution of each component is equal and the lowest value when the contributions are maximally disparate. Because there is no a priori reason to think one component more important than the other, this index is considered a reasonable means of measuring the combined effects of the two turnover components.

Table 2.2 contains the data necessary for constructing measures on the predictors. As the table shows, the number of appointments varied from two (the Vinson Court) to fourteen (the Taney Court). Similarly, the number of appointing presidents has fluctuated from one (the Vinson and Chase Courts) to eight (the Taney Court). The empirical equation to be tested is $DR = a + bX + cY + e$ where X is complexity of cases and Y is turnover. The regression coefficient for complexity is .202 and that for turnover is .147. The signs are as specified, adjusted R^2 is .938, both coefficients are significant at .01, and F is significant at .0001.

Although this result may appear impressive, it was derived via ordinary least squares (OLS) regression. A Durbin-Watson analysis for autocorrelation produced a coefficient of 2.807 indicating the presence of autocorrelation in the residuals.[24] Thus the OLS results could be contaminated by the interdependence of contiguous measures on the predictors. One possible consequence of such contamination is to overstate the ability of the predictor variables to account for variation in

Table 2.3. Dissent Percentages Predicted Compared to Percentages
Observed

Chief Justice	Observed	Predicted
Marshall	.58	.72
Taney	2.22	2.82
Chase	2.97	.92
Waite	1.70	1.57
Fuller	2.32	3.27
White	1.53	1.52
Taft	.93	1.86
Hughes	2.24	3.40
Stone	13.49	12.51
Vinson	12.44	11.92
Warren	12.13	12.86

dissent rate across chief justices. An analysis of a correlogram and the partial autocorrelation coefficients for the regression indicated that the residuals were characterized by an autoregressive process of order one.[25] Consequently, the coefficients for the model were reestimated specifying an autoregressive process and using the pseudogeneralized least squared (GLS) estimation technique of the Statistical Analysis System.[26]

The reestimated coefficients, .206 and .166 respectively, differ little from the original coefficients. The signs are in the predicted direction, complexity is significant at .0001 and turnover at .003, and adjusted R^2 is .97. The goodness of fit for the reestimated model may be seen in Table 2.3, in which the observed and predicted values from the model are arrayed. As can be seen from this table, the residuals are randomly distributed with an approximate mean of zero. This means that the series is free of serial dependency, trend, and drift.[27]

I infer that Model 4 shows sufficient promise to warrant further investigation. Further testing under various controlled conditions would be a logical next step in searching for the antecedents of variation in chief justices' dissent rates.

To this point, I have omitted Chief Justice Burger because he has yet to complete his tenure. Nevertheless, one may be curious to know how well Model 4 would predict Burger's dissent rate for the first twelve years of his service on the Court, the 1969–80 terms inclusive.[28]

In that time span, Burger dissented at a rate of 13.6 percent. The rate predicted by Model 4 is 9.43. Thus the model underpredicts Burger by about 31 percent. This is not to say that the model has no predictive capacity in Burger's case. Clearly it does, even though it was developed using chief justices other than Burger. But we might wonder why the model was less successful with Burger than with the earlier chief justices. It may be that Burger's first twelve terms were atypical and that upon completion of his years as chief, the model will do as well with him as with the other Court leaders. It may also indicate that complexity of cases and turnover are having a greater impact on Burger than on earlier chiefs. The correct explanation, however, can be found only after additional research.

Model 5. The results with Model 4 suggest that if one were to incorporate Chief Justice Burger in the predictive model, some adjustments would be necessary. Using the same eleven chief justices, I have tried one possible adjustment—replacing the term t with the lagged term $t - 1$. Dissent rate in this model $= a + bX_{t-1} + cY_{t-1} + e_t$. The argument here is that dissent rate is affected by the levels of complexity and turnover reached in the periods preceding the period of dissent, that is, that the disruption associated with such factors in one period carry over and cause a response in a later period. The regression equation for this model is $DR = -2.15 + .175X_{t-1} + .118Y_{t-1} + e_t$ or 10.04. This prediction is a little better than that provided by Model 4, but this model is significant neither for Burger nor for the other eleven chief justices. Clearly the dissent response to complexity and turnover is not a lagged response.

In this chapter, I have suggested that dissent by a chief justice of the Supreme Court is an important event. It brings conflict in the Court to the attention of various publics, some of whom may seek to punish the Court or exploit Court conflict for personal or political reasons.[29] From the standpoint of a chief justice, to dissent is to relinquish control over opinion assignments, thereby reducing his influence on the development of law and social policy at the national level. Since a chief justice would not likely relinquish such prerogatives lightly, one is encouraged to seek an explanation for such behavior.

This investigation has determined that dissent cases in the Supreme Court as a percentage of total cases with full opinions varied appreciably in the period 1801–1969. Until the Stone era, such cases constituted 7 to 17 percent of all opinion cases. In the Stone, Vinson, and Warren Courts, however, conflict occurred in 49 to 75 percent of total opinion cases. The Stone Court was found to be unique when change in conflict rate was examined. I have suggested that Supreme Court cases and interpersonal relations in the Court became more complex beginning with the Stone period.[30] Such an explanation cannot account totally for the great increase in dissent cases in the Stone era. Earlier inferences regarding Stone's leadership abilities may continue to have some validity. But to the extent that such inferences are based on dissent levels across all Courts, the leadership hypothesis is affected because by that criterion Stone was more effective than Vinson and Warren. Given these facts, I have suggested the hypothetical explanation that over the long term Court conflict measures case complexity. Although it is still possible to view conflict in the Court as an indicator of weak leadership skills possessed by a particular chief justice (as has traditionally been done with Stone), such an approach is not productive over the long term. It is perhaps more reasonable to view variation in conflict as an indicator of case complexity because it accords with the notion that the judicial system functions best when dissent in the Court is caused by "hard cases."

This examination of dissent by chief justices has determined that dissent rate across eleven Courts is a legitimate variable, with levels of dissent voting reaching only 1 percent for John Marshall but surpassing 13 percent for Chief Justice Stone. The largest jump in dissent rate also came in the Stone era. The mean rate for chief justices before Stone was 1.9 percent, but for Stone through Warren, the mean rate was 12.5 percent.

In seeking explanations for these variations across Courts, five different models have been explored. The first two incorporated attributes of the chief justices, and the third took into consideration the influence on the Court of part of its external environment. Models 4 and 5 focused on conflict and turnover in the Court and the problems associated with integrating new justices into ongoing groups.

Analysis of Models 1 through 3 produced no significant reasons for rejecting the null hypotheses. These models provided no ground for believing that chief justices' dissent rates are significantly influenced by age at time of appointment, number of years served, prior judicial or legislative service, or pressure on the Court via variation in stable and unstable configurations of political power. But in exploring the relationships between case complexity/turnover and dissent rates of chief justices, significant results were obtained. As promised earlier, I reached no theoretical conclusions in this chapter. Nevertheless, the investigative work suggests the general hypothesis that the career levels of dissent reached by chief justices of the U.S. Supreme Court are significantly influenced by the complexity of the cases decided by the Court, the frequency of appointments to the Court, and the presidents making these appointments.

An application of the prediction equation from Model 4 to the first twelve terms of the Burger Court did not substantially weaken support for the model. Using Model 4 to forecast Chief Justice Burger's dissent rate, however, gave a result 31 percent below the actual rate. Possible reasons for the error have been suggested, to wit: Burger's tenure is incomplete and may be atypical, and Burger may be affected more by case complexity and turnover than earlier justices.[31]

Finally, it should be repeated that the effort here is strictly exploratory. Other more sophisticated models may be developed. This study has not exhausted the many considerations that could, theoretically, affect a chief justice's dissent rate. For example, a model limited to the high-dissent justices, Stone through Burger, might incorporate different predictors than those used here or require the addition of variables not employed in this chapter. Breakdowns of the data on a basis other than completed terms of chief justices may also provide additional insights. The inclination of a chief justice to dissent might depend on the identity of the senior associate justice in a majority that does not include the chief,[32] for that justice would become the opinion assignor in the case. Or it might depend on the identity of the justice who seems likely to get the opinion assignment from the senior justice in the majority. It might also be affected by the subject matter of the case and the chief's emotional or other interest in the matter, by how the chief justice views his role, or by his attitude toward dissent or the importance of unanimity in the Court. But these matters are beyond the scope of the present chapter and must be left for elucidation to future research. For the present, given the unique factors that should discourage chief justices from dissenting, it is significant that the chiefs seem affected substantially in their dissent voting by some of the causes of dissent voting in the Court. Future attempts to improve our understanding of the processes operating to produce chief justices' dissents cannot afford to ignore such a consideration.[33]

The research on which this paper is based has been supported by the National Science Foundation, Grant GS2682. Although the responsibility for this chapter is entirely mine, I wish to acknowledge the helpful assistance provided by my colleague William Berry and the editors of this volume, Sheldon Goldman and Charles M. Lamb.

1. Philip B. Kurland, *Felix Frankfurter on the Supreme Court* (Cambridge, Mass.: Belknap Press, 1970), pp. 488-89.

2. J. Woodford Howard, Jr., "On the Fluidity of Judicial Choice," *American Political Science Review* 62 (1968): 43-56; Saul Brenner, "Fluidity on the United States Supreme Court: A Reexamination," *American Journal of Political Science* 24 (1980): 526-35; Saul Brenner, "Fluidity on the Supreme Court: 1956-1967," *American Journal of Political Science* 26 (1982): 388-90.

3. For example, Stuart S. Nagel hypothesized that "during periods in which there is a relatively high (i.e., above average) degree of disagreement between members of the Court (and thus high controversy), congressional attack is more likely to occur." In examining seven historical periods running from the 1800s through the 1950s, Nagel found some support for the hypothesis (*The Legal Process from a Behavioral Perspective* [Homewood, Ill.: Dorsey Press, 1969], p. 266).

4. Harlan B. Phillips, *Felix Frankfurter Reminisces* (New York: Reynal, 1960), p. 198.

5. Benjamin N. Cardozo, *Law and Literature* (New York: Harcourt Brace, 1931), p. 34.

6. *Northern Securities Co.* v. *U.S.*, 193 U.S. 197 (1904); *Bank of U.S.* v. *Dandridge*, 25 U.S. 64, 90 (1827).

7. Learned Hand, *The Bill of Rights* (Cambridge, Mass.: Harvard University Press, 1958); John P. Frank, *The Marble Palace* (New York: Knopf, 1968); David J. Danelski, "The Influence of the Chief Justice in the Decisional Process," in Walter F. Murphy and C. Herman Pritchett, eds., *Courts, Judges and Politics: An Introduction to the Judicial Process,* 3d ed. (New York: Random House, 1979), pp. 695-703.

8. David J. Danelski, "Causes and Consequences of Conflict and Its Resolution in the Supreme Court," Chapter 1 of this volume.

9. 297 U.S. 1, 79 (1936).

10. I.e., if "men make the difference," unanimity is not to be expected in a Court whose membership is collegial and ever-changing.

11. E.g., *Brown* v. *Board of Education*, 347 U.S. 483 (1954). See S. Sidney Ulmer, "Earl Warren and the *Brown* Decision," *Journal of Politics* 33 (1971): 689-702.

12. Dissent may also be a function of interpersonal relations, but those relations may be affected by the external environment or the introduction of disturbances from the external environment. Without such disturbances, interpersonal relations among the same justices may stabilize over time, thereby damping down any changing impact on dissent rates.

13. Stephen C. Halpern and Kenneth N. Vines, "Dissent, the Judges' Bill and the Role of the Supreme Court," paper delivered at the Annual Meeting of the American Political Science Association, August 30-September 2, 1974, Chicago, Illinois.

14. For other recent uses of the alternative model approach in judicial research, see Thomas Likens, *Discretionary Review by the Supreme Court, Part I: The Model*

(Newton, Mass.: Educational Development Corporation, Undergraduate Mathematics and Its Applications Project, Unit 306, 1979); Thomas Likens, *Discretionary Review by the Supreme Court, Part II; Analysis of the Model* (Newton, Mass.: Educational Development Corporation, Undergraduate Mathematics and Its Applications Project, Unit 307, 1979). See also Greg A. Caldeira, "The United States Supreme Court and Criminal Cases, 1935-1976," *British Journal of Political Science* 11 (1982): 449-70; Greg A. Caldeira and Andrew T. Cowart, "Budgets, Institutions, and Change in Criminal Justice Policy," *American Journal of Political Science* 24 (1980): 413-38. I have profited particularly from the work of Caldeira.

15. Only three chief justices (White, Hughes, and Stone) served as associate justices before becoming chief, so, considering all eleven chiefs, experience as chief justice is essentially equivalent to experience on the Court. I believe, however, that experience as chief is most likely to teach the justice what he needs to know and do to avoid the dissenting position.

16. There may be theoretical problems connected with the interpretation of a regression equation in which the N of cases is as small as here. In all cases, R^2 has been adjusted by the formula

$$\text{Adjusted } R^2 = R^2 - \left(\frac{k-1}{N-k}\right) (1 - R^2)$$

where k is the number of independent predictors, N is number of cases, and R^2 on the left side of the equation is the unadjusted variance explained. The adjusted R^2 adjusts for the relationship between the number of cases and the number of predictors. It is, therefore, a more conservative measure than R^2.

17. Although earlier research cannot be cited to support such a contention, the possibility has not previously been ruled out in the context in which it is examined here.

18. Richard Funston, "The Supreme Court and Critical Elections," *American Political Science Review* 69 (1975): 795-811; see also Bradley C. Canon and S. Sidney Ulmer, "The Supreme Court and Critical Elections: A Dissent," *American Political Science Review* 70 (1976): 1215-18.

19. Nagel, *Legal Process*, p. 266.

20. Walter F. Murphy, *Elements of Judicial Strategy* (Chicago: University of Chicago Press, 1964); Howard, "On the Fluidity of Judicial Choice"; J. Woodford Howard, Jr., *Mr. Justice Murphy: A Political Biography* (Princeton: Princeton University Press, 1968).

21. 320 U.S. 591 (1944).

22. 443 U.S. 193 (1979).

23. S. Sidney Ulmer, "Homeostatic Tendencies in the United States Supreme Court," in S. Sidney Ulmer, ed., *Introductory Readings in Political Behavior* (Chicago: Rand-McNally, 1961), pp. 167-88.

24. For a technical discussion of the significance of autocorrelation, see David McDowall, Richard McCleary, Errol E. Meidinger, and Richard A. Hay, Jr., *Interrupted Time Series* (Beverly Hills: Sage, 1980), pp. 15ff.; Arthur S. Goldberger, *Econometric Theory* (New York: Wiley, 1964).

25. See Douglas Hibbs, "Problems of Statistical Estimation and Causal Inference

in Dynamic Time Series Models," in Herbert Costner, ed., *Sociological Methodology* (San Francisco: Jossey-Bass, 1974), pp. 252-308.

26. SAS Institute, *SAS User's Guide* (Raleigh, N.C.: SAS Institute, 1979).

27. Trend is defined as motion in a specific up or down direction or, more technically, as "any systematic change in the level of a time series process" (McDowall et al., *Interrupted Time Series,* pp. 19-20). Drift implies the absence of trend and a process that drifts up or down. For an exposition of the analytical consequences of trend and drift, see John M. Gottman, *Time Series Analysis* (New York: Cambridge University Press, 1981).

28. There were four appointments in Burger's first twelve terms versus eight in the Warren era. Two presidents made appointments in the Burger period compared to three in the Warren era. The conflict rate for the Burger Court for twelve terms, calculated after removing the cases in which Burger dissented, is 53.87 percent.

29. Nagel, *Legal Process,* p. 266.

30. Although I have made no attempt to explain why the cases have become more complex, Halpern and Vines may be read to suggest that the "judges' bill" was one key factor ("Dissent, the Judges' Bill and the Role of the Supreme Court").

31. For a treatment of Burger's propensity for conflict in the D.C. Court of Appeals, see Charles M. Lamb, "A Microlevel Analysis of Appeals Court Conflict: Warren Burger and His Colleagues on the D.C. Circuit," Chapter 8 of this volume.

32. As suggested by Joel Grossman.

33. This is not to rule out the possibility that such factors as case complexity and turnover might help explain dissent voting by associate justices.

3

Changing Voting Patterns in the Warren and Burger Courts

EDWARD V. HECK

The United States Supreme Court is continually being asked to resolve some of the most significant and controversial political problems facing the nation. The issues raised in the cases accepted for review are— almost by definition—those not resolved elsewhere in the political system. At any given time the Court consists of individuals far more diverse in background and attitudes than the stereotype of the Court as a body of "nine old men" suggests. Only on rare occasions is the Court dominated by the appointees of a single president. Most justices have taken strong stands on the significant questions of the day, either before their appointment or in opinions written after accession to the highest court. It is therefore hardly surprising that political scientists studying the Court have tended to focus more on conflict than on consensus.[1]

The most visible form of conflict on the Supreme Court is, of course, dissent, the public expression of disagreement with the decision of the majority. Scholars who have traced overall dissent rates in the Court over time have found that the frequency of dissent has increased in the twentieth century. Stephen C. Halpern and Kenneth N. Vines documented a sharp rise in the percentage of cases evoking dissent after the passage of the 1925 Judges' Bill.[2] Similarly, S. Sidney Ulmer, in Chapter 2 of this book, reports illuminating data on the dissent rate during the tenure of each chief justice from Marshall to Burger. Never from Marshall to Hughes did the overall conflict rate, defined as the percentage of nonunanimous cases, exceed 17 percent. In the Stone Court, the conflict rate leaped to 48.6 percent, climbing to 75 percent in the Vinson years and 68.8 percent during the tenure of Chief Justice Earl Warren. The level of conflict has remained high in the Burger era.

In addition to tracing changing dissent rates over time, scholars have sought to identify the causes or correlates of dissent. In a thorough inventory of proffered explanations, Steven A. Peterson has categorized propositions about the causes of dissent under four headings: legal culture, the court as an organization, the sociopolitical system, and the individual judges. Many of the posited causes of dissent have been tested only indirectly at best. Yet some progress appears to have been made in identifying factors bearing on an individual judge's tendency to dissent. Although proposed explanations have run the gamut from role orientations to psychological needs, the evidence seems generally to support the conclusion that high dissent rates are a function of disagreement with the policy views dominant in the Court in a given period.[3]

If dissent is an indicator of ideological conflict between an individual justice and the Court collectively, voting with the majority indicates agreement with the shifting alliance of justices who constitute the Court's majority decision coalition. Consensus, rather than conflict, comes to the forefront if we shift our focus from individual dissent rates to the opposite side of the coin—majority participation rates. Perhaps more significant than the frequent dissenter is the justice most often in the majority, the Court's "center of gravity."[4] Although voting with the majority does not necessarily indicate task leadership within the Court, an extremely high majority participation rate does suggest an ideological position characteristic of the Court as a whole.[5] It is of particular interest that changes in individual justices' majority participation rates may point to significant shifts in the overall policy direction of the Court.[6]

In this chapter, therefore, I will examine data on the majority participation rates of individual justices for each natural court of the Warren and Burger eras through the retirement of Justice Potter Stewart in July 1981. The analysis proceeds at two levels. At the purely descriptive level, the data presented here extend earlier studies of overall patterns of dissent through the first dozen terms of the Burger Court and show in detail how majority participation rates have shifted as the membership of the Court has changed. This descriptive treatment also offers an opportunity to consider more generally the relationship between voting patterns and the appointment process. At the second level, the goal is to use the data on voting patterns in the modern Supreme Court to examine theoretical propositions about conflict and consensus, with emphasis on the impact of freshman justices, the place of the chief justice in the Court's voting alignments, and the effect of bloc structure on majority participation rates.

An investigation of the impact of freshman justices is appropriate because the appointment of new justices may be a force for change in the Court's voting patterns. The literature on "freshman effects" is extensive and somewhat controversial.[7] It is clear that many freshman justices—at least in the Warren and Burger Courts—joined identifiable voting blocs during their first natural court.[8] Such a newcomer might well be expected to have a significant impact on patterns of consensus and conflict. Thus it seems reasonable to hypothesize that *the center of gravity will normally be occupied by a sitting justice who is closely allied with the newest member of the Court* (H1). Moreover, *a justice whose rates of agreement with a series of new justices are high should maintain his position at the Court's center of gravity over several natural courts* (H2).

History offers little clear guidance about the place of the chief justice in the Court's voting patterns. A chief justice who aggressively and successfully pursued consensus in his Court and rarely dissented (Marshall or Taft, for example) might well emerge as the center of gravity of his Court.[9] On the other hand, a chief imbued with enthusiasm for debate and expression of individual views, such as Stone, would naturally be a frequent dissenter.[10] Ulmer's data in Chapter 2 of this volume show substantial variation in frequency of dissent among chief justices from Marshall to Warren. Ulmer's effort to explain this variation clearly suggests that the dissent rate of the chief justice is in large part a function of the dissent rate for the Court as a whole. Left unanswered is the question of whether the chief justice will dissent more or less frequently than associate justices with whom he serves. A modest hypothesis, consistent with the proposition that a chief justice would not wish to squander leadership opportunities by frequent dissent, is that *the chief justice will generally be close to the center of gravity of the Court he heads* (H3).

A final hypothesis concerns the bloc structure of the Court. Bloc analysis, a staple tool of students of judicial behavior for decades, remains a useful means of summarizing the interagreement rates of groups of justices. In this chapter bloc analysis is used as a secondary tool for examining the relationship between majority participation scores and the bloc structure of natural courts. The justice most frequently in the majority should normally be one who has formed close voting alliances with several other justices. On a Court with large, cohesive blocs, he would most likely be a member of the largest bloc. Thus I hypothesize that *the justice most frequently in the majority will normally be a member of the largest bloc on the Court* (H4).

The data on which this analysis rests include votes on all cases decided on the merits with full opinion (unanimous as well as non-unanimous), plus *per curiam* decisions evoking dissent on the merits.[11] When several cases were decided with a single opinion, each case has been counted separately. The period covered is the twenty-eight years between the appointment of Chief Justice Warren in 1953 and the retirement of Justice Stewart in 1981. The period is divided into eleven natural courts, each of which embraces the tenure of a unique group of nine justices initiated by the seating of at least one new member. The voting data are summarized in Tables 3.1, 3.2, and 3.3 in the form of percentages of the majority participation of each justice in each natural court. Interagreement rates for each pair of justices in each natural court have also been calculated and are reported in the text when they bear directly on the analysis. Summary data on the bloc structure of each natural court are also incorporated into each table.[12]

THE EARLY WARREN COURT

Table 3.1 reports majority participation rates for the early Warren Court years (1953–62). Each of the five natural courts of this period began with the appointment of a new justice by President Dwight Eisenhower. The table reveals that Justice Clark occupied the Court's center of gravity for most of this period, with Chief Justice Warren generally recording the second highest majority participation score. Among the remaining justices some intriguing shifts took place as the Court's membership changed, but no definitive pattern emerged.

The voting patterns of the 1953–55 Court were shaped by the close alliance between Justice Tom Clark and the newly appointed chief justice. A moderate on both civil liberties and economic liberalism issues in this period, Clark agreed with Warren in just over 95 percent of the cases in which both justices participated, the highest interagreement rate for any pair of justices in this Court.[13] Warren, Clark, and Burton formed a three-member bloc with an average interagreement score of just under 90 percent. Occupying the center of gravity were Clark with only ten dissents and the chief justice with twelve. Frank-

Table 3.1. Majority Participation Rates, 1953-1962 (Early Warren Court)

Justice	1953-55 Percent (Ranking)	1955-56 Percent (Ranking)	1956-57 Percent (Ranking)	1957-58 Percent (Ranking)	1958-62 Percent (Ranking)
Clark	94.8(1)	94.4(1)	91.7(1)	77.3(3)	86.8(1)
Warren	93.7(2)	92.3(2)	86.0(2)	78.9(2)	79.3(4)
Frankfurter	92.1(3)	80.3(8)	64.0(9)	73.9(5)	73.9(7)
Minton	87.2(4.5)	87.9(4)	--	--	--
Jackson	87.2(4.5)	--	--	--	--
Burton	86.2(6)	81.4(6)	80.0(4)	70.5(8)	--
Reed	84.5(7)	80.8(7)	78.6(5)	--	--
Black	79.2(8)	88.7(3)	72.3(7)	73.2(7)	72.2(8)
Douglas	72.1(9)	82.4(5)	66.0(8)	69.9(9)	63.1(9)
Harlan	--	77.8(9)	75.5(6)	73.5(6)	76.2(5)
Brennan	--	--	84.1(3)	89.1(1)	84.7(3)
Whittaker	--	--	--	76.8(4)	74.7(6)
Stewart	--	--	--	--	85.3(2)
Court cohesion	78.8	77.6	66.2	64.5	66.9
Sprague criterion	89.4	88.8	83.6	82.2	83.4
Size of largest bloc	3	3	2	3	3
(Members)	(Warren, Clark, Burton)	(Black, Warren, Clark)	(Reed, Clark)[a]	(Warren, Black, Douglas)	(Brennan, Warren, Black)

[a]Most cohesive pair.

furter and Warren's interagreement rate was 86.9 percent, and Frankfurter's majority participation score of 92.1 percent ranked third. Black
and Douglas, the only justices whose dissent rates were in excess of 20
percent, remained isolated from their more conservative brethren,
including the new chief justice.

The appointment of Justice John Marshall Harlan in March 1955
initiated the second natural court of the Warren era. Voting most often
with Frankfurter and Burton, Harlan immediately became the Court's
most frequent dissenter. Far more significant than Harlan's appointment in shaping patterns of consensus and conflict in 1955–56 was the
shifting posture of Chief Justice Warren. Earlier quantitative studies
have amply demonstrated Warren's gradual movement toward the liberal wing of the Court during his first three terms.[14] More recent studies
based on the private papers of the justices have revealed that the close
cooperation between Warren and Justice Frankfurter that had marked
their joint pursuit of unanimity in the *Brown* decision soon gave way to
mutual distrust and hostility.[15] As the estrangement of Warren and
Frankfurter deepened, their interagreement rate dipped to 74.9 percent.
Meanwhile, the Warren-Black interagreement score surged to 94.4
percent. Although Warren began to move away from Clark's position on
civil liberties issues in this period, overall he agreed with the Texan on
more than 90 percent of the Court's votes. The trio of Clark, Warren,
and Black formed a cohesive bloc, and these three were the justices
most frequently in the majority.[16] Frankfurter's forty-seven dissents
testify to his increasing dissatisfaction with Warren and the Court's
overall direction.

Voting patterns in the brief period between the recess appointment
of Justice William J. Brennan, Jr., in October 1956 and the seating of
Justice Charles E. Whittaker the following March remained broadly
similar to those of 1955–56, though care must be taken not to make too
much of these figures because only fifty-two cases were decided during
these months. Clark and Warren again recorded the highest majority
participation scores, with newcomer Brennan voting with the majority
in 84 percent of the cases. The overall Court cohesion score dropped to
66 percent, but no three-member blocs formed in this Court. The three
most cohesive pairs—Reed and Clark, Warren and Black, and Warren
and Brennan—did, however, include the justices most frequently in the
majority.

The fourth natural court of the Warren years, covering the year and a half between Whittaker's appointment and the retirement of Justice Burton in October 1958, was marked by the emergence of a cohesive bloc consisting of Warren, Black, and Douglas. On the fringes of this bloc was Brennan, who was somewhat less likely than his senior colleagues to take civil libertarian or prounion positions.[17] As the moderate liberal who sometimes voted on the conservative side, Brennan was with the majority more often than any other justice (89.1 percent of the cases). A distant second was the chief justice, followed by Clark and Whittaker.

The appointment of Justice Stewart in 1958 initiated a period of membership stability that continued until the retirement of Justice Whittaker in April 1962. Despite some landmark decisions this Court was by no means dominated by the liberals. Rather, the 1958–62 Court was splintered into warring factions, with no group able consistently to attract the decisive votes of the centrist judges. In this situation, Justice Clark regained his old position at the Court's center of gravity, despite fifty-six dissenting votes and a majority participation score of only 86.8 percent on a Court more noted for conflict than consensus. Ranked second was the newly appointed Justice Stewart, a "swing voter," whose tilt toward the conservative justices produced many 5–4 votes against civil liberties claims. Even though Brennan, Warren, and Black formed a cohesive bloc, frequent dissents in civil liberties cases account for these justices' lower majority participation rates.

Taken as a whole, the data for the early Warren Court years seem to offer at least modest support for my hypotheses about the place of the chief justice in the Court's voting patterns (H3) and the relationship between bloc structure and majority participation scores (H4). Clearly, the chief justice was never far out of the mainstream in this period, yet Warren's generally high majority participation scores reflect as much his own search for a coherent judicial philosophy as any quality inherent in the office of chief justice. Justice Clark was a member of the largest bloc (or most cohesive pair) in the three of the four natural courts in which he occupied the center of gravity. Moreover, Chief Justice Warren's high majority participation scores appear to be in part a function of close alliances with other justices. Still, it cannot be denied that the relationship between bloc membership and voting with the majority is tenuous and subject to a wide variety of conditions unique to each natural court. In the 1958–62 Court, for example, Clark was the justice most frequently in the majority even though he was a member of no cohesive bloc. Rather, he was a swing voter, frequently joining Warren, Black, and Douglas in support of the economic underdog but voting with such colleagues as Harlan and Frankfurter in opposition to civil liberties claims. Because the data in Table 3.1 are based on all cases, it is possible for a justice to emerge as the Court's center of gravity simply because he lacked a consistent ideology encompassing both civil liberties and economic regulation issues.[18]

Finally, expectations about the impact of newly appointed justices (H1 and H2) do not seem to be borne out by the experience of the early Warren years. Only the alliance between Clark and the newly appointed Chief Justice Warren in 1953–55 is a clear example of the effect of a new appointment on patterns of conflict and consensus. Nor did Clark or any other justice maintain a dominant position over several Courts by allying with a series of newly appointed justices.

To understand patterns of conflict and consensus in the early Warren Court, it is necessary to consider the nature of appointments to the Court during the Eisenhower years. The Eisenhower Court lacks a clear identity (in contrast to the Roosevelt Court) because Eisenhower did not seek consistently to shape the Court by filling vacancies with individuals reflecting a common position on the salient issues of the day. Instead, he appointed five justices with diverse views who did not vote as a bloc. The center of gravity, therefore, went almost by default to a holdover justice with moderate views. Whereas Eisenhower's five appointments had little impact, President John F. Kennedy's two appointments in a single year brought about a remarkable change in the Court's voting patterns.

THE LATE WARREN COURT

The contrast between the voting patterns of the early Warren Court and those of the late Warren Court is striking. With the appointments of Justices Arthur Goldberg, Abe Fortas, and Thurgood Marshall by Presidents John Kennedy and Lyndon Johnson, a cohesive liberal bloc came to dominate Supreme Court decision making. The Court's center of gravity shifted markedly—from Clark to Brennan. Forming close alliances with the chief justice and each of the new appointees of this period, Justice Brennan remained the justice most frequently in the majority until 1969, when the liberal bloc was shattered by the retirement of Warren and the resignation under fire of Justice Fortas. The

Table 3.2. Majority Participation Rates, 1962-1969 (Late Warren Court)

Justice	1962-65 Percent (Ranking)	1965-67 Percent (Ranking)	1967-69 Percent (Ranking)
Brennan	97.1(1)	92.2(1)	98.4(1)
Warren	94.1(2)	88.7(2)	94.1(3)
Goldberg	89.0(3)	– –	– –
White	86.0(4)	84.7(3)	80.3(6)
Douglas	83.5(5)	76.4(7)	75.4(7)
Black	81.1(6)	81.0(6)	68.4(8)
Clark	76.9(7)	83.6(4)	– –
Stewart	76.0(8)	70.0(8)	82.5(5)
Harlan	56.3(9)	58.8(9)	67.8(9)
Fortas	– –	81.7(5)	92.4(4)
Marshall	– –	– –	96.4(2)
Court cohesion	72.0	69.5	73.0
Sprague criterion	86.0	84.7	86.5
Size of largest bloc	3	3	4
(Members)	(Warren, Brennan Goldberg)	(Brennan, Warren, Fortas)	(Marshall, Brennan, Warren, Fortas)

1962 to 1969 period was truly the "heyday of Warren Court liberalism."[19]

The opportunity to reorient the Court fell to President Kennedy as a result of the disability retirement of Justice Whittaker in April 1962, followed in short order by the stroke that forced Justice Frankfurter off the bench for the final months of the 1961–62 term and led to his retirement the following August. To replace these conservative stalwarts, Kennedy selected two members of his executive branch team, Deputy Attorney General Byron White and Secretary of Labor Arthur Goldberg.[20] The impact of these appointments may be brought into sharp focus by comparing majority participation scores for 1958–62 (Table 3.1) with those of 1962–65 (Table 3.2). Brennan, who had filed 66 dissents in the earlier period, cast only 15 dissenting votes in 1962–65, voting with the majority in just over 97 percent of the cases. Close behind was Warren, followed by newcomers Goldberg and White. Douglas attained his highest majority participation score of the Warren-Burger eras (83.5 percent). No longer the center of gravity on a reconstituted Court, Clark dissented more frequently than any justice except Stewart and Harlan. Completely isolated from the new majority in both civil liberties and economic regulation cases, Harlan expressed disagreement with the result in more than 40 percent of the cases of this period, casting 222 dissenting votes.

Data on interagreement rates for each pair of justices in the 1962–65 Court indicate that Brennan's place as the justice most frequently in the majority was secured by a combination of his alliances with the two freshman justices and his position within the largest bloc. No sitting justice had a higher rate of agreement with the newcomers than Brennan, who voted with Goldberg in 89 percent of the Court's cases and with White 84.2 percent of the time. Moreover, Brennan was part of a cohesive bloc with Warren and Goldberg, and both Douglas and Black were on the fringes of this bloc. The dominance of these justices is clearly reflected in the many landmark civil liberties decisions of these years.

This natural court ended when Goldberg acceded to President Johnson's urgent request that he resign from the Court to accept the post of U.N. ambassador. To fill Goldberg's place, Johnson selected Abe Fortas. Although Fortas was somewhat more inclined to dissent than his predecessor, patterns of consensus and conflict in the 1965–67 Court were generally similar to those of 1962–65. Brennan and Warren retained the top two spots on the majority participation chart, but their positions did not prevail as frequently as during Goldberg's brief tenure. With twenty-three dissents, Brennan's majority participation score fell to 92.2 percent, and Warren dissented thirty-three times in two terms.

As in the previous natural court, Brennan and Warren allied with a freshman justice to form a three-member bloc to which Douglas was marginally attached. By 1965–67, however, Black stood outside the bloc structure, voting with his erstwhile allies on such issues as First and Fifth Amendment claims but siding with the conservatives in cases involving appeals by civil rights demonstrators or Fourth Amendment claims. With Black's support, the liberals prevailed in such pathbreaking decisions as *Miranda* v. *Arizona*.[21] Still, Black's increasingly frequent defections occasionally left the foursome of Douglas, Warren, Brennan, and Fortas one vote shy of a majority, notably in cases arising from civil rights demonstrations.

In the fall of 1967, however, the liberals' position was strengthened by Clark's retirement and President Johnson's selection of Thurgood

Marshall as his replacement. Voting with Fortas, Warren, and Brennan in more than 90 percent of the Court's cases, Justice Marshall became the fourth member of the most cohesive bloc of the Warren Court years. With Marshall as his staunchest ally (95.2 percent interagreement rate), Brennan was on the winning side in all but six cases decided by the 1967–69 Court, recording an almost incredible majority participation rate of 98.4 percent. Close on his heels was Marshall, followed by bloc partners Warren and Fortas. Although Justice Douglas was a reliable ally of the Brennan-Marshall-Warren-Fortas bloc in decisions favoring civil liberties claims, he dissented in approximately one-fourth of the Court's cases, including a number of civil liberties cases in which the majority was unwilling to go as far as he preferred. By 1967–69 Black had moved far enough away from his former allies to file 119 dissents, only 2 fewer than Harlan.

Overall, the data reported in Table 3.2 clearly portray patterns of consensus and conflict in the last seven and a half years of the Warren Court and provide even stronger support for each of my hypotheses than do the early Warren Court data. What stands out is the extent to which voting patterns in this period reflect the dominance of a subgroup of justices centered around Brennan and Warren. Particularly striking is the record of Justice Brennan, who filed only forty-four dissents between 1962 and 1969, for an overall majority participation score of 96.8 percent. Among the factors that account for his position must be counted his close ties with the chief justice and with a series of freshman colleagues—Goldberg, Fortas, and Marshall. In each Court the subgroup including Brennan and Warren generally needed only one or two additional votes to prevail. Even when the bloc split, Brennan was usually with the majority.[22]

As hypothesized, the center of gravity in each natural court was occupied by a justice closely allied with a new member of the Court (H1), who maintained his position through alliances with a series of freshman justices (H2). Moreover, the chief justice was never far out of the mainstream (H3), and the justice at the center of gravity and his allies were invariably members of the largest bloc (H4).

As with the early Warren Court years, explanations for these patterns of conflict and consensus are associated with the appointment process. With vacancies to fill on a fractionalized Court, Kennedy was able to tip the balance by appointing White and Goldberg to fill the seats of Whittaker and Frankfurter. President Johnson assured continuation of the trend with his selection of Fortas and solidified the dominance of the liberal bloc with the appointment of Marshall.

By 1968, of course, the Warren Court's posture had become a campaign issue for Republican presidential nominee Richard Nixon, who pledged to appoint justices who would support the "peace forces" rather than the "criminal forces."[23] Within a few months of Nixon's election, the retirement of Warren and the resignation of Fortas, both key members of the liberal bloc, provided the new president with a golden opportunity to fulfill his campaign pledge.

THE BURGER COURT

In seeking to appoint Supreme Court justices who shared his views, Nixon behaved like most earlier presidents, though he was perhaps more explicit than any president since Roosevelt about the policy goals he sought to promote through his Supreme Court appointments. In sharp contrast to Roosevelt, Nixon's opportunities came early in his presidency. Within three years of his inauguration Nixon had appointed four justices including the chief. Although the opposition of the Senate and later the American Bar Association prevented Nixon from filling three of the vacancies with the appointees he had originally preferred, Warren E. Burger, Harry A. Blackmun, Lewis F. Powell, Jr., and William H. Rehnquist were all on record as generally sympathetic to the president's law and order approach.[24]

Table 3.3 reports data on majority participation rates for the first dozen years of the Burger Court. The 1969–72 period includes all cases argued or decided by the Burger Court between Chief Justice Burger's appointment in the summer of 1969 and the seating of Justices Powell and Rehnquist in January 1972. Through most of the 1969–70 term Burger headed a Court of eight justices while the Senate debated and rejected in turn Nixon's nominations of Clement Haynsworth and G. Harrold Carswell. The Court returned to full strength for the 1970–71 term following Senate approval of Harry A. Blackmun to fill Fortas's seat but was reduced to seven members when Justices Harlan and Black retired as the 1971–72 term was about to begin. The cases decided by the remaining justices in this term are included in the 1969–72 data. The 1972–75 period includes all cases argued and decided between the seating of Powell and Rehnquist as freshman justices and the retirement of Justice Douglas in October 1975. The 1975–81 Court, with Stevens

Table 3.3. Majority Participation Rates, 1969-1981 (Burger Court)

Justice	1969-72 Percent (Ranking)	1972-75 Percent (Ranking)	1975-81 Percent (Ranking)
White	87.0(1)	86.7(3)	86.5(2)
Stewart	86.8(2)	82.6(5)	83.8(5)
Marshall	85.1(3)	69.3(7)	67.4(8)
Blackmun	83.1(4)	88.8(2)	85.5(4)
Brennan	81.5(5)	67.2(8)	67.1(9)
Harlan	80.9(6)	– –	– –
Burger	77.6(7)	84.8(4)	86.2(3)
Black	71.3(8)	– –	– –
Douglas	65.6(9)	55.2(9)	– –
Powell	– –	89.7(1)	89.9(1)
Rehnquist	– –	79.7(6)	77.8(6)
Stevens	– –	– –	77.1(7)
Court cohesion	69.6	67.7	68.4
Sprague criterion	84.8	83.9	84.2
Size of largest bloc	2	3	3
(Members)	(Burger, Blackmun)[a]	(Powell, Burger, Blackmun)	(Powell, Burger, Rehnquist)

[a]Most cohesive pair.

as the freshman justice, covers nearly six full terms through the retirement of Justice Stewart.

Majority participation scores for 1969–72 indicate that with his first two appointments Nixon was able to alter substantially the voting patterns that had prevailed in the late Warren Court. Brennan's majority participation rate dropped from 98.4 to 81.5 percent, fifth highest of the justices. In his place as the Court's center of gravity was Justice White, followed closely by Stewart. Although Marshall clung to third place, his majority participation percentage dropped substantially. Yet the Nixon appointees were not a dominant force within the Court. Through the first two and a half years of the Burger Court, the new chief justice was among the Court's three most frequent dissenters with a majority participation score of 77.6 percent. This transitional Court can be more accurately characterized as the Stewart-White Court than as a Nixon Court.[25]

The relationship between bloc structure and majority participation rates is substantially less apparent in this period than in the late Warren

Court. Only the two pairs of Brennan-Marshall (87.8 percent inter-agreement rate) and Burger-Blackmun (94.6 percent) qualify as blocs. Stewart and White occupied the center of gravity in this Court because one or both of them often held the balance of power between the liberal Warren Court holdovers (Douglas, Brennan, and Marshall) and the Nixon appointees. Both White and Stewart frequently voted with the two newcomers. White was on the fringe of the Burger-Blackmun bloc, allying with the new associate justice in 83.9 percent of the cases in which both participated, and Stewart was Burger's closest ally other than Blackmun. Thus the 1969–72 data provide some support for the "freshman justice" hypothesis, though the link between majority participation rate and a voting alliance with new members of the Court is much weaker than in the late Warren Court.

With the appointments of Justices Powell and Rehnquist, the balance of power shifted more clearly toward the Nixon appointees. Nixon appointees Powell and Blackmun achieved the highest rates of majority participation during 1972–75. Justice White dropped to third, and Chief Justice Burger moved up from seventh to fourth. The liberal holdovers became the Court's three most frequent dissenters. Justice Brennan, who had dissented only 44 times between 1962 and 1969, cast 206 dissenting votes in the 1972–75 period, and his majority participation score dropped to 67.2 percent. Completely outside the mainstream in his last years on the Court, Douglas dissented in nearly 45 percent of the cases in which he participated.

Interagreement data for this period unambiguously support the hypothesis that the justices at or close to the Court's center of gravity should be members of the largest bloc. Three Nixon appointees (Powell, Burger, and Blackmun) formed a cohesive bloc, with both White and Rehnquist on the bloc's fringes. In fact, each Nixon appointee voted with each other Nixon appointee in at least 80 percent of the cases during this period.[26] Although this bloc was not as cohesive as the Brennan-Warren-Marshall-Fortas bloc in the last two years of the Warren Court, the tendency of the Nixon justices to vote together made the newcomers a powerful force within the Court.

With some minor variations, the patterns established in 1972–75 prevailed throughout the six years of stable membership initiated by the appointment of Justice John Paul Stevens in 1975. Powell remained at the Court's center of gravity, voting with the majority in just under 90 percent of the cases decided in the 1975–81 period. Clustered behind

Powell were White, Burger, and Blackmun. Showing no hesitancy to dissent in his early years on the Court, Justice Stevens quickly staked out an idiosyncratic position, dissenting in approximately 23 percent of the cases in which he participated. With the departure of Douglas, Marshall fell to eighth place, and Brennan had the lowest rate of participation in the majority, dissenting in almost one-third of the cases decided in this six-year period.

Although the bloc structure of the 1975–81 Court bore some resemblance to that of 1972–75, the ties holding the Nixon appointees together loosened noticeably. The onetime "Minnesota Twins" disagreed in more than one-fifth of the cases in this period, an agreement rate substantially below their 88.3 percent figure for 1972–75. As Blackmun and Rehnquist began moving in opposite directions, their agreement rate dropped to 71.4 percent. Still, Powell, Rehnquist, and Burger formed a cohesive bloc, and both White and Stewart frequently aligned with Burger and Powell. Brennan and Marshall voted together in 91.3 percent of the cases and still remained largely isolated from the rest of the Court.

The changes observed in the Burger Court years, as in the late Warren Court period, suggest once again the importance of the appointment process as a factor influencing patterns of conflict and consensus. With his first two appointments, Nixon was able to shift the balance of power away from Brennan and Marshall. After four appointments the Court's complexion had changed sufficiently to convert Brennan and Marshall into dissenters more likely to express opposition to the Court's decisions than such earlier dissenting pairs as Holmes and Brandeis or even Black and Douglas. At the same time, the Nixon experience may suggest the limits of presidential influence on the Court. Although the Nixon appointees voted together frequently enough to reorient the Court, they disagreed among themselves often enough to ensure that they could not dominate the Court as thoroughly as had Brennan and his allies in the late Warren Court. The independence of the Nixon appointees when the future of the Nixon presidency was at stake is, of course, well known.[27] Moreover, the gradual emergence of divergent views among the Nixon four suggests that even justices who generally share the views of a president when appointed may in time move in different directions as the Court confronts new issues.

The data for the Burger years supply further support for my

hypotheses about the place of the chief justice in patterns of conflict and consensus (H3) and about the relationship between bloc structure and majority voting (H4), though the evidence is not without its ambiguities. After a brief period of frequent dissent, Burger has moved back into the Court's mainstream. Powell, the justice most frequently in the majority since his appointment in 1972, has invariably been a member of the largest bloc on the Court. The data offer only the most limited support, however, for my freshman justice hypothesis.

What conclusions can be drawn from this survey of Supreme Court voting patterns over a twenty-eight-year period? At the descriptive level, the most significant point is that the major outlines of conflict and consensus did change significantly during these years. Changes in majority participation rates over time clearly tracked changes in the Court's direction. Following Justice Brennan's majority participation scores over a quarter of a century highlights the Court's shifts from moderate conservatism through liberalism to a new conservatism that left Brennan isolated from the Court's mainstream. In general, these changes may be traced to the appointment process, lending support to the proposition that the Court, in time, reflects in a general way the policy preferences of the same dominant national coalition that prevails at the presidential level.[28]

Moreover, the data analyzed in this chapter tend to support the hypotheses about general patterns of conflict and consensus set out above, though not without ambiguity. A preponderance of the evidence clearly supports the hypothesis that the justice at the center of gravity should normally be a member of the largest bloc on the Court (H4). Justice Clark through much of the early Warren Court, Justice Brennan in the late Warren Court, and Justice Powell since his appointment in 1972 were able to maintain their dominant positions because they had close allies within the Court. It seems safe to conclude that when there is a large, cohesive bloc within the Court, the justice most frequently in the majority will be a member of the largest bloc. Of course, the caveat that there is not always a large, cohesive bloc within the Court must be entered, a condition that sometimes allows a "swing voter" associated with no bloc on a divided Court (Clark in 1958–62 or White in 1969–72) to occupy the Court's center of gravity. The experience of the Warren and Burger years also supports the expectation that the chief justice is not likely to be far outside the Court's mainstream (H3), though Burger did dissent frequently before other Nixon appointees joined him on the bench.

As for the place of the freshman justice in patterns of conflict and consensus, it seems safe to say only that it depends on the circumstances. On occasion, a freshman justice may emerge as the Court's center of gravity. If several new justices form a voting bloc (as did the Nixon appointees) or use their votes to strengthen an existing bloc (as in the cases of Goldberg, Fortas, and Marshall), the impact of the new justices may be substantial. In other circumstances, however, the influence of a freshman on patterns of consensus and conflict may be negligible. Overall, the hypothesis that the justice most frequently in the majority will generally be an ally of a freshman justice (H1) must be rejected. Evidence that a justice can maintain his position at the center of gravity by allying with a series of new colleagues (H2) appears to be limited to the unique circumstances of the late Warren Court.

This chapter's close focus on the Supreme Court over a twenty-eight-year period provides students of the judicial process with a detailed description of patterns of conflict and consensus that highlights the importance of the appointment process as a factor affecting majority participation and dissent. It is clear that the validity of the generalizations emerging from this investigation must ultimately rest on further confirmation in research on earlier periods and on future Courts.

1. Steven A. Peterson, "Dissent in American Courts," *Journal of Politics* 43 (1981): 433.

2. Stephen C. Halpern and Kenneth N. Vines, "Institutional Disunity, the Judges' Bill and the Role of the U.S. Supreme Court," *Western Political Quarterly* 30 (1977): 471-83.

3. Peterson, "Dissent in American Courts," pp. 413-25; Joel B. Grossman and Richard S. Wells, *Constitutional Law and Judicial Policy Making*, 2d ed. (New York: Wiley, 1980), pp. 232-34.

4. Glendon Schubert, *Quantitative Analysis of Judicial Behavior* (Glencoe, Ill.: Free Press, 1959), p. 102.

5. A plausible alternative explanation is that the justice with the highest majority participation score could be the one most likely to swallow dissent for institutional reasons. It seems unlikely, however, that this will be the case in an era noted for the intense individualism of the justices and marked by frequent concurring as well as dissenting opinions. See Grossman and Wells, *Constitutional Law,* pp. 231-32.

6. Edward V. Heck, "Changing Voting Patterns in the Burger Court: The Impact of Personnel Change," *San Diego Law Review* 17 (1980): 1041-45.

7. See, e.g., J. Woodford Howard, Jr., *Mr. Justice Murphy: A Political Biography* (Princeton: Princeton University Press, 1968), pp. 231-64; Elliot E. Slotnick, "Judicial Career Patterns and Majority Opinion Assignment on the Supreme Court," *Journal of Politics* 41 (1979): 640-48.

8. Edward V. Heck and Melinda Gann Hall, "Bloc Voting and the Freshman Justice Revisited," *Journal of Politics* 43 (1981): 857-60.

9. See S. Sidney Ulmer, "Exploring the Dissent Patterns of the Chief Justices: John Marshall to Warren Burger," Chapter 2 of this volume; Alpheus T. Mason, *The Supreme Court from Taft to Burger* (Baton Rouge: Louisiana State University Press, 1979), pp. 61-66.

10. David J. Danelski, "The Influence of the Chief Justice in the Decisional Process of the Supreme Court," in Sheldon Goldman and Austin Sarat, eds., *American Court Systems: Readings in Judicial Process and Behavior* (San Francisco: W. H. Freeman, 1978), pp. 511-13.

11. The rationale for this selection of cases is that it includes the cases that have received individual attention from the Court as a whole or at least the dissenting justice(s) (in the case of nonunanimous *per curiam* decisions). For the 1953-69 period, I have used Glendon Schubert's Supreme Court voting data, made available through the Interuniversity Consortium for Political and Social Research. I coded the data for 1969-81.

12. Procedures for matrix construction, bloc identification, and calculation of the "Sprague criterion" for each natural court follow the rules set out in John D. Sprague, *Voting Patterns of the United States Supreme Court: Cases in Federalism, 1889-1959* (Indianapolis: Bobbs-Merrill, 1968), pp. 7-8, 31-46, 53-60.

13. The data reported here tell us nothing about the ideological positions of the justices. To characterize individual justices or blocs as liberal, moderate, or conservative, it is necessary to rely on data that tap the ideological dimension. Unless otherwise noted, all such characterizations in this chapter are based on Glendon Schubert, *The Judicial Mind: The Attitudes and Ideologies of Supreme Court Justices, 1946-1963* (Evanston: Northwestern University Press, 1965), pp. 97-146, and David W. Rohde and Harold J. Spaeth, *Supreme Court Decision Making* (San Francisco: W. H. Freeman, 1976), pp. 137-45.

14. Schubert, *Judicial Mind*, pp. 118-19.

15. Bernard Schwartz, "Felix Frankfurter and Earl Warren: A Study of a Deteriorating Relationship," in *Supreme Court Review 1980* (Chicago: University of Chicago Press, 1981), pp. 115-42; G. Edward White, *Earl Warren: A Public Life* (New York: Oxford University Press, 1982), pp. 173-90.

16. The statistics reported in the tables encompass all issues decided by the Court. An analysis limited to a particular issue category, such as civil liberties, might well yield different results.

17. Edward V. Heck, "The Socialization of a Freshman Justice: The Early Years of Justice Brennan," *Pacific Law Journal* 10 (1979): 716-17.

18. For evidence of the unique nature of Clark's voting patterns, see Harold J. Spaeth, "Unidimensionality and Item Invariance in Judicial Scaling," *Behavioral Science* 10 (1965): 299. In this article Clark was classified as "authoritarian" because of his opposition to civil liberties claims and his support of the claims of economic underdogs. In a later study, Clark was the only justice classified as a "New Dealer" (Rohde and Spaeth, *Supreme Court Decision Making*, pp. 143-45).

19. For a detailed discussion of this period, analyzing leading opinions as well as votes, see Edward V. Heck, "Justice Brennan and the Heyday of Warren Court Liberalism," *Santa Clara Law Review* 20 (1980): 841-87.

20. White took his seat on April 16, 1962. Although Frankfurter officially remained a member of the Court until his retirement in August, his illness prevented him from voting in any of the cases decided after White's appointment. Thus a new natural court of eight members was created by White's appointment and brought to full strength when Goldberg joined the Court in October 1962.

21. 384 U.S. 436 (1966).

22. For example, in *Schmerber* v. *California*, 384 U.S. 757 (1966), Brennan joined with the Court's four conservatives to reject a variety of constitutional claims raised by a defendant seeking reversal of a conviction for driving while intoxicated.

23. James F. Simon, *In His Own Image: The Supreme Court in Richard Nixon's America* (New York: David McKay, 1973), pp. 4-9.

24. Ibid., pp. 83-86, 143-46, 233-35, 245.

25. Philip B. Kurland, "1971 Term: The Year of the Stewart-White Court," in *Supreme Court Review 1972* (Chicago: University of Chicago Press, 1973), pp. 181-329. Kurland applied the label to the 1971–72 term during which Powell and Rehnquist joined the Court. The data presented here suggest that this characterization fits the 1969–72 period as a whole.

26. Interagreement percentages for each pair of Nixon appointees were as follows: Powell-Burger, 86.1; Powell-Blackmun, 82.6; Powell-Rehnquist, 81.9; Burger-Blackmun, 88.3; Burger-Rehnquist, 88.1; and Blackmun-Rehnquist, 82.1.

27. *U.S.* v. *Nixon*, 418 U.S. 683 (1974).

28. Robert A. Dahl, "Decision-Making in a Democracy: The Supreme Court as a National Policy-Maker," *Journal of Public Law* 6 (1957): 279-95, esp. p. 293.

4

Felix Frankfurter, Judicial Activism, and Voting Conflict on the Warren Court

HAROLD J. SPAETH and
MICHAEL F. ALTFELD

Given Felix Frankfurter's reputation for judicial restraint, this chapter analyzes decisions amenable to resolution on the basis of restraint. In so doing it sheds considerable light on the conflict between Frankfurter's supposed role conception and reality gleaned from an examination of his opinion behavior and also from patterns of voting conflict and consensus among Warren Court justices generally. Specifically, we examine Frankfurter's voting behavior and opinions on state action and federal agency cases regulatory of business and labor decided during his tenure on the Warren Court, 1953–61.[1] Cases are grouped into four subsets: state regulation of labor, state regulation of business, cases involving the National Labor Relations Board (NLRB), and federal administrative agencies regulatory of business. Because earlier research demonstrated that Frankfurter's restraint was thoroughly subordinated to his substantive attitudes toward business and labor,[2] we are especially interested in how Frankfurter accommodated his reputation for restraint via his opinions when he assumed an activist posture. Although no assumption is made that attitudes toward business and labor motivated the justices' behavior in the cases analyzed, it is prudent, given previous studies,[3] to allow for the possibility that these attitudes may at least partially explain patterns of conflict and consensus during these Warren Court years.

STATE REGULATION OF LABOR

Twelve formally decided nonunanimous cases concerned state regulation of labor unions. Except for Douglas, Black, and Warren, the

Table 4.1. State Labor Cases: Percentages of Interagreement in Split Decisions

	Dou	Blk	War	Brn	Clk	Har	Bur	Min	Ree	Stw	Frk	Wht
Douglas												
Black	80											
Warren	82	78										
Brennan	14	40	17									
Clark	33	20	27	86								
Harlan	29	20	0	83	100							
Burton	22	14	33	100	100	100						
Minton	40	20	60		100	100[b]	100					
Reed	40	20	60		100	100[b]	100	100				
Stewart	50[a]	0[a]	0[a]	50[a]	100[a]	100[b]						
Frankfurter	18	0	18	83	91	100	89	80	80	100[a]		
Whittaker	17	0	0	67	83	80	100			100	100	
Average	39	27	34	60	76	74	76	75	75	63[a]	69	61
Percentage of time in majority	33	20	27	86	100	100	100	100	100	100	91	83

Indices of interagreement
Dou-Blk-War = .80
Rest of justices = .92
[a] = 2 cases
[b] = 1 case

justices were rarely in voting conflict with one another. The result was a sharply bifurcated Court, as Table 4.1 shows. Whereas Glendon Schubert considers an index of interagreement of .70 to be high,[4] here Douglas-Black-Warren are at .80 and the other nine participating justices are at .92. Six justices voted with the majority without fail: Clark, Burton, Harlan, Minton, Reed, and Stewart. Three split from the majority only once: Frankfurter, Brennan, and Whittaker. By contrast, Douglas, Warren, and Black agreed with the majority on only four, three, and two occasions, respectively. In other words, of twenty-seven dissents, twenty-four were cast by Douglas, Black, and Warren (eight apiece). Frankfurter was obviously in greatest voting conflict with these three justices. The likely reason for the unusually sharp division on the Court is that eleven of the twelve state labor cases involved federal preemption of state court jurisdiction to resolve unfair labor practices. These cases form an unusually good cumulative scale ($R = .987$). Only Douglas, Black, and Warren proved to be prounion.

A second feature of the cases involving state regulation of labor is

Table 4.2. Votes on State Regulation of Labor Unions

Justice	Prostate	Antistate	Percentage of Support
Whittaker	6	0	100
Stewart	2	0	100
Frankfurter	10	1	91
Harlan	6	1	86
Burton	7	2	78
Clark	9	3	75
Brennan	5	2	71
Reed	3	2	60
Minton	3	2	60
Black	1	9	10
Warren	1	10	9
Douglas	1	11	8
Jackson	0	0	–

that in every case a prostate vote was concomitantly antiunion and vice versa. Accordingly, one may argue, equally persuasively, that attitudes toward state regulation, rather than those toward labor unions, motivated the justices' voting in this set of cases. As shall be seen, this argument collapses when we analyze the other three sets of cases. But when the justices' votes are arrayed in a pro- and antistate fashion in Table 4.2, the pattern supports considerations of federalism except for Douglas, Black, and Warren.

In these cases, Frankfurter's votes accorded with his reputation for restraint, and only Whittaker and Stewart exceeded his proportion of prostate votes. Inasmuch as Frankfurter did not write in the case in which he voted antistate—*Capital Service* v. *NLRB* (1954)—his five opinions in this set of cases all support considerations of federalism.[5] It is noteworthy that Frankfurter assigned the Court opinion in six of these twelve cases. At no time during his Warren Court tenure was Frankfurter more than third in seniority regarding opinion assignment. Warren, Black, and Reed outranked him. Frankfurter disproportionately assigned three of these six cases to himself. By comparison, neither Warren nor Black self-assigned. Reed retained one of his two, assigning the other to Frankfurter.

STATE REGULATION OF BUSINESS

Unlike the state labor cases, those involving state regulation of business make up a more structurally complex set exhibiting less conflict

Table 4.3. State Business Cases: Percentages of Interagreement in Split Decisions

	Dou	Blk	War	Clk	Brn	Min	Ree	Bur	Wht	Stw	Jac	Frk	Har
Douglas													
Black	61												
Warren	59	78											
Clark	58	73	88										
Brennan	67	71	90	100									
Minton	25	75	64	67									
Reed	18	55	50	55		82							
Burton	30	30	47	55	25	75	82						
Whittaker	42	26	42	47	47			88					
Stewart	36	36	64	73	73				89				
Jackson	33	17	20	33		67	50	67					
Frankfurter	36	45	50	55	57	67	55	55	53	73	100		
Harlan	32	50	59	59	62	0[a]	100[a]	67	37	55		73	
Average	41	51	59	64	66	58	61	56	52	62	48	60	53
Percentage of time in majority	48	70	84	91	100	92	82	60	47	73	67	64	59

Indices of interagreement
Dou-Blk-War-Clk-Brn = .75
Min-Ree-Bur = .80
Bur-Wht-Stw-Jac-Frk-Har = .69
[a] = 1 case

on the Warren Court. Although seventeen of the thirty-three cases concerned state taxation, the remainder involved a congeries of nontax state activities. Five of the cases also concerned the federal regulatory commissions. Nor was a prostate vote invariably antibusiness. In five cases, a prostate vote supported business. Table 4.3 indicates that the Court was not as bifurcated as it was in the labor cases, and the interagreement ratios are not as high and low as earlier. The Court upheld the states in nineteen of the thirty-three decisions and eighteen times when the state's regulation was antibusiness. The Court's pro-/anti-business proclivity overrode a pro-/anti-state orientation. Two-thirds of the thirty-three cases produced an antibusiness result: the eighteen antibusiness regulation decisions that the Court upheld, plus the four probusiness decisions reversed. The likelihood that this pattern occurred by chance is one in ten.[6]

As Table 4.3 shows, the justices divided themselves into three distinguishable blocs. The liberal grouping of Douglas, Black, and Warren expands to five with the addition of Brennan and Clark. Opposite them was a six-member bloc that, on the basis of findings in the sources cited in note 3, we will label conservative, while Minton, Reed, and Burton formed a centrist group. Although the interagreement indices are lower than in the labor cases, only the six-member conservative group falls below Schubert's specification of "high," and then only by a single percentage point. There was markedly less voting conflict in the state business cases than in the labor cases. The lack of exceptionally high interagreement ratios also evidences a lack of polarization. Whereas fifty-one of the fifty-nine cells in Table 4.1 reveal an interagreement ratio $\langle$.33 or $\rangle$.75, in Table 4.3 only twenty of sixty-seven do so. The undoubted reason is that the state business cases addressed a vastly broader range of issues than did the labor cases.

Unlike the labor cases, in which six of the twelve participating justices always voted in the majority, only Brennan did so here, followed by Minton and Clark at 92 and 91 percent respectively. At the other extreme, Douglas again was with the majority less than half the time (48 percent), along with Whittaker (47 percent). Frankfurter fell from 91 percent in labor cases to 64 percent here. Warren and Black, who, along with Douglas, were part of the majority in less than half the labor cases, stand at 84 and 70 percent here. Douglas dissented most often, seventeen times, and voted in dissent with every justice except Brennan, who was always in the majority. Frankfurter dissented twelve times, most often with Harlan (six) and Whittaker (five). Black and Whittaker rank next in frequency of dissent (ten each), followed by Harlan (nine) and Burton (eight). Whereas the justices averaged 2.25 dissents per labor case (twenty-seven in twelve cases, of which Douglas, Black, and Warren cast twenty-four dissenting votes), the proportion in the state business cases is 2.5 (eighty-two dissents in thirty-three decisions). As in Table 4.1, Frankfurter again conflicted most often with Douglas, Black, and Warren, and his rate of agreement with Brennan, Burton, Clark, Stewart, and Whittaker also declined considerably.

Evidence of what we surmised as explaining the interagreement in Table 4.1 is substantiated by the pattern of pro- and antistate votes shown in Table 4.4. If, for example, one compares the percentage of prostate votes that a justice cast in the labor cases (Table 4.2) with that in the business cases, an interesting grouping emerges. Of the five most prostate justices in the labor cases, only Harlan was prostate in business cases. Deference clearly is a sometime thing. Even more graphic is the switch manifested by Douglas, Warren, and Black. Douglas, who supported state regulation of labor at a rate of only 8 percent, increased his support to 61 percent in cases involving state regulation of business. Warren went from 9 to 69 percent and Black from 10 to 70 percent prostate. Indeed, only three justices deferred to the states with more than half their votes in both the labor and business cases: Harlan, Brennan, and Clark. Brennan's proportion of support, 71 percent, is identical between the two sets, while Clark's support deviates by only eight points. Harlan, by contrast, falls from 86 percent prostate in labor cases to 59 percent in business cases. The remaining nine justices show an average variance of fifty-four points in their support of state action.

Obviously, something is at work here. If it were considerations of federalism, a markedly less drastic shift in the justices' ratios of pro- and antistate votes would appear in Tables 4.2 and 4.4. Because in all but five cases a prostate vote was concomitantly antibusiness, the likely explanation is that the justices—with the possible exceptions of Harlan, Brennan, and Clark—subordinated any states' rights sentiments to their substantive attitudes toward business. If the votes are scored as pro- and antibusiness, rather than pro- and antistate, the following antibusiness percentages result: Brennan, 81; Black, 79; Clark, 73; Warren, 69; and Douglas, 64. By comparison, Whittaker voted probusiness 74 percent of the time, followed by Frankfurter with 64, Stewart, 55, and Harlan, 50 percent. Compatibly with the findings in the sources referred to in note 3, the former group is identified as liberal toward economic regulation generally, while the latter is conservative. Accordingly, the justices were divided in cases involving state regulation of business not so much by their attitudes toward federalism as toward business per se.

Frankfurter wrote fifteen opinions in the thirty-three state business regulation cases. Among the other justices, only Douglas wrote as frequently. Frankfurter, interestingly, had no reticence about authoring an opinion when it accompanied an antistate vote. Although he wrote opinions for only 43 percent of his antistate votes, as opposed to half of his prostate votes, he wrote nine antistate opinions as opposed to six prostate. A marked difference also exists between Frankfurter's pro- and antistate opinions. Of his six prostate opinions, two were opinions of the Court, three were special concurrences, and only one was a

Table 4.4. Votes on State Regulation of Business

Justice	Prostate	Antistate	Percentage of Support
Brennan	15	6	71
Black	23	10	70
Warren	22	10	69
Clark	22	11	67
Douglas	20	13	61
Harlan	13	9	59
Stewart	5	6	45
Frankfurter	13	20	39
Reed	3	8	27
Minton	3	9	25
Burton	5	15	25
Jackson	1	5	17
Whittaker	3	16	16

dissent. But when Frankfurter coupled an antistate vote with an opinion, only one was that of the Court, one a regular concurrence, and seven dissents.[7]

One may assume that when a justice has a reputation for judicial restraint, he will take pains to explain his posture when he votes antistate because such a vote represents a departure from his supposed philosophical position. Frankfurter's efforts to explain his antistate dissents would seem consistent with this view. But Frankfurter's behavior is also exactly what we would expect from an individual who was, in reality, restraintist only insofar as it favored his policy preferences yet valued his legal reputation as an advocate of restraint. Therefore, Frankfurter would take great pains not to explain the conflict between his role conception and his antistate votes but rather would try to explain them away. An examination of Frankfurter's antistate opinions should indicate which of the foregoing assumptions is correct.

Frankfurter's opinion for the Court in *Kake* v. *Egan* (1962), holding that Alaska could regulate commercial fishing of nonreservation Indians, appears to be pro- rather than antistate. But a stay of execution of the state court's decision was extended until the end of the salmon fishing season. The majority's posture was antistate only because Douglas dissented from the stay of execution. Accordingly, to indict Frankfurter for an antistate opinion here would be caviling. We hold the same view with regard to his concurrence in *Phillips Petroleum* v.

Wisconsin (1954) and his dissents in *Marin County* v. *U.S.* (1958) and *Utah PSC* v. *U.S.* (1958). All three involved action by federal regulatory commissions as well as by the states. As is typical of such cases, a restraintist justice cannot pay obeisance to both, and Frankfurter chose to defer to the agencies rather than the states. One may read Frankfurter's concurrence in *Phillips Petroleum* as deferring less to the expertise of the Federal Power Commission than to the nationalistic language of the interstate commerce clause, but again we will not cavil. These four opinions, although more or less antistate, arguably do not besmirch Frankfurter's reputation for restraint.

We cannot say the same for Frankfurter's other five antistate dissents. In *Braniff Airways* v. *Nebraska Board* (1954), he complained that interstate commerce was burdened by state taxation and that the nexus between the taxed object (airplanes) and the taxing state was so tenuous as to constitute "an obvious inroad" on the commerce clause.[8] In his second antistate dissent, *International Harvester* v. *Goodrich* (1956), at issue was the constitutionality of a New York statute that granted highway tax liens priority over the security interests of conditional vendors of trucks operated by motor carriers. Frankfurter held that the due process clause barred New York from according priority to liens arising prior to the conditional sale of the trucks to the carrier.

Frankfurter's remaining antistate dissents all occurred in cases that received front-page coverage. *Detroit* v. *Murray Corp.* (1958) was one of three companion cases that concerned state taxation of federal property. The majority held that federal property used or leased by private persons loses its immunity from state taxation. Frankfurter, wrapping himself in the mantle of *McCulloch* v. *Maryland* (1819), insisted that in *Murray* the state "professedly and directly" levied "an ad valorem property tax on what is indubitably government property."[9] Although Frankfurter joined with Burton and Harlan in Whittaker's dissent, none joined him.

Northwestern States Portland Cement v. *Minnesota* (1959) upheld net income taxes on that portion of an out-of-state corporation's business earned from and fairly apportioned to business activities in the taxing state even though the taxed activities resulted from interstate operations. In this case, the cement company shipped 48 percent of its product from Iowa to Minnesota and sold it there. The company maintained only a small sales office in the latter state. Frankfurter, in dissent, vigorously argued that the tax violated the commerce clause.

The nationalistic tenor of his opinion was coupled with a measure of restraintist rhetoric, however. The states' apportionment formulas, he observed, will "present far-reaching problems of accommodating federal-state fiscal policy. But a determination of who is to get how much out of the common fund can hardly be made wisely and smoothly through the adjudicatory process. In fact, relying on the courts to solve these problems only aggravates the difficulties and retards proper legislative solution."[10] Again, neither of the other dissenters, Whittaker and Stewart, joined Frankfurter's opinion, although Frankfurter joined the former's.

Frankfurter sounded an unabashedly nationalistic refrain in *Youngstown Sheet & Tube* v. *Bowers* (1959), the last of his antistate dissents. The Court ruled that the import-export clause did not bar a state from taxing imported raw materials stored within the state for immediate use. Frankfurter, joined by Harlan, cited chapter and verse in support of the thesis that "guided by the experience of the evils generated by the *parochialism* of the new States, the wise men at the Philadelphia Convention took measures to make of the expansive United States a free trade area and to withdraw from the States the *selfish* exercise of power over foreign trade, both import and export."[11] Unlike *Northwestern States*, Frankfurter made no effort to couple his antistate sentiments with assertions of judicial incompetence.

Given Frankfurter's legacy of votes and opinions in state business regulation cases, how is it possible to characterize him as an advocate of judicial restraint? Was his behavior here deviant from his overall posture? Perhaps. Analysis of his record in the sets of cases still to be analyzed should answer this question. Alternatively, is it possible that Frankfurter's apologists have disregarded his dissenting opinions? Others have not. Anthony Lewis, for example, in an analysis of *Northwestern States* and *Youngstown*, contrasted Frankfurter's dissents in these cases, which Lewis described as "fervent," with Paul Freund's characterization of the majority as having "shown a marked degree of self-restraint."[12] Although Frankfurter displayed deference to the states in the labor cases, this deference was equally antilabor. In the state business regulation cases, Frankfurter's deference disappeared, but his economic conservatism remained. This probusiness bias, as noted, was manifest in his votes. Yet perhaps of even greater significance is that when Frankfurter wrote an antistate opinion in these cases, eight of the nine produced a probusiness result. The sole exception was his regular concurrence in *Phillips Petroleum*.[13] All seven of his antistate dissent-ing opinions accompanied a probusiness vote. Clearly, then, the only label that accurately fits Frankfurter's voting and opinion behavior in the state cases regulatory of business and labor is that of economic conservative.

We turn now to the other aspect of judicial restraint to be consid-ered: decisions of the federal regulatory commissions. As in the state cases, we divide them between those regulating labor and those reg-ulating business.

FEDERAL AGENCY LABOR REGULATION

During Frankfurter's tenure on the Warren Court, it nonunanimously decided twenty-three cases involving the NLRB: nine in which the NLRB was prounion and fourteen in which it was antiunion. The Court upheld the NLRB thirteen times, although its prounion orientation overrode its support of the NLRB. Of the twenty-three cases, seventeen produced a prounion result. Eight of nine prounion NLRB decisions were upheld, and nine of fourteen antiunion decisions were reversed. This distribution, when arranged in a 2 x 2 table, is statistically significant.[14]

Patterns of conflict and consensus previously displayed in the state action cases (Tables 4.1 and 4.3) remain recognizable in Table 4.5. Douglas, Black, and Warren continued to form the core of the liberal bloc, with Brennan often joining them. In the NLRB cases, however, Stewart replaced Clark as the fifth member of the liberal bloc. Totally unlike the state business cases, an eight-member liberal-moderate bloc appeared here. Not only was this bloc markedly larger than the others indicated in Table 4.5, its interagreement index is ten points higher than the other three blocs. The conservative bloc shrank to three justices— Harlan, Frankfurter, and Whittaker—from the six in the state business cases.

There was somewhat more judicial conflict than in the state busi-ness cases because of the behavior of Douglas and Black, on the one hand, and that of Harlan, Frankfurter, and Whittaker, on the other. Yet there was less polarization than in the state labor cases. Whereas 86 percent of the cells in Table 4.1 show an interagreement ratio $\langle.33$ or $\rangle.75$, here only 42 percent do so. This ratio, however, exceeds 30 percent in the state business set. The proportion of the time each justice

Table 4.5. NLRB Cases: Percentages of Interagreement in Split Decisions

	Dou	Blk	War	Brn	Stw	Clk	Ree	Min	Jac	Bur	Har	Frk	Wht
Douglas													
Black	83												
Warren	70	78											
Brennan	56	69	81										
Stewart	64	82	91	91									
Clark	39	48	70	69	64								
Reed	57	57	100			86							
Minton	33	33	83			67	83						
Jackson	0	33	100			100	100	100					
Burton	42	42	75	100		75	100	83	100				
Harlan	32	42	53	81	73	58	0	50		50			
Frankfurter	11	21	37	58	57	58	43	67	67	58	87		
Whittaker	7	20	33	40	40	73				60	53	91	
Average	41	51	73	72	69	67	70	67	75[a]	71	52	54	43
Percentage of time in majority	61	70	91	94	91	78	100	83	100	92	63	47	47

Indices of interagreement
Dou-Blk-War = .77
Dou-Blk-War-Brn-Stw = .77
War-Brn-Stw-Clk-Ree-Min-Jac-Bur = .87
Har-Frk-Wht = .77
[a] = 3 cases.

voted with the majority provides further evidence of polarization. The six who voted in the majority more than 91 percent of the time provided 45 percent of all votes for the majority position in NLRB cases. Only three justices supported the majority at this high a level in the state business set, and they cast only 30 percent of all votes for the majority.

At the other extreme, Whittaker and Frankfurter voted with the majority less than half the time (47 percent). Whittaker's 47 percent is the same as in state business cases. Frankfurter, by contrast, fell from 64 percent and again was in greatest voting conflict with Douglas, Black, and Warren. Douglas, although proportionately third least supportive of the majority, nonetheless rose to 61 percent.

Whereas Douglas dissented most frequently in the state action sets (although Black and Warren tied him in the labor cases), Frankfurter achieved that distinction in the NLRB cases with ten. Douglas followed

Table 4.6. Votes on the Pro-/ and Antiunion Decisions of the NLRB

Justice	NLRB Prounion	Percentage of Support	Justice	NLRB Antiunion	Percentage of Support
Warren	9-0	100	Burton	5-0	100
Reed	5-0	100	Reed	2-0	100
Stewart	2-0	100	Minton	2-0	100
Jackson	1-0	100	Jackson	2-0	100
Black	8-1	89	Whittaker	10-2	83
Burton	6-1	86	Frankfurter	8-2	80
Douglas	7-2	78	Clark	8-6	57
Brennan	3-1	75	Harlan	5-7	42
Minton	3-1	75	Brennan	4-8	33
Clark	6-3	67	Warren	4-10	29
Frankfurter	3-6	33	Stewart	2-7	22
Whittaker	1-2	33	Douglas	1-13	7
Harlan	1-6	14	Black	0-14	0

with nine, Whittaker eight, and Harlan and Black seven. Each justice except Warren dissented at least once with Frankfurter. Harlan did so most frequently, and each of his seven dissenting votes occurred in a case in which Frankfurter also dissented. Douglas, by comparison, had the company of only Black (six times) and Warren (twice), in addition to one Frankfurter vote, when he dissented in the NLRB cases. Overall, however, the number of dissents declined from the 2.5 per case in the state business set to 2.26 here (fifty-two in twenty-three decisions), only 1 percent above that of the state labor cases.

Table 4.6 strongly supports the implication that justices vote on the basis of their pro- and antiunion attitudes rather than their degree of deference to the NLRB. Of the thirteen justices, only Jackson, Reed, Burton, Minton, and Clark supported the NLRB more than half the time regardless of whether the NLRB was pro- or antiunion. All but Clark gave unstinting support. Collectively, twenty-six of their twenty-eight votes upheld the agency (93 percent). Clark, by comparison, upheld the NLRB 67 percent of the time when it was prounion and 57 percent when it was antiunion. Among these five justices, only Clark deferred to the states with more than half his votes in the state action sets (see Tables 4.2 and 4.4). Jackson did not participate in any of the state labor cases. Burton, Minton, and Reed supported state regulation of business at respective proportions of only 25, 25, and 27 percent. If a judicial activist is defined as one who fails to support state or federal regulatory agencies with at least half his votes even when the decisions are controlled for by liberal and conservative outcome, Harlan took an activist position toward the NLRB in the cases decided during Frankfurter's tenure on the Court. No other justice displayed such behavior in the state action cases.

The remaining seven justices displayed the pattern of voting that dominated behavior in the state action cases (see Tables 4.2 and 4.4): deference to the states when they regulated business but not when they regulated labor, or vice versa. These seven show an average variance of 64 points between the pro- and antiunion portions of Table 4.6. Black is most extreme at 89 points. Stewart follows at 78; then Douglas and Warren at 71, Whittaker, 50, Frankfurter, 47, and Brennan, 42. In the state action sets, Brennan, Clark, and Harlan upheld the states in their regulation of both labor and business.

Evidence that the justices' substantive attitudes toward labor, rather than deference to the NLRB, motivated their voting behavior may be had by rescoring the votes in Table 4.6 on a pro- and antiunion basis and comparing them with the bloc alignments given in Table 4.5. The Douglas-Black-Warren bloc voted prounion 61 of 69 times (88 percent); with the addition of Brennan and Stewart, the ratio becomes 81 of 97 (84 percent). The eight-member liberal-moderate bloc voted prounion 66 of 101 times (65 percent), while the Whittaker-Frankfurter-Harlan bloc did so in only 16 of their 53 votes (30 percent). Furthermore, the twenty-three NLRB cases form a marginally acceptable cumulative scale ($R = .949$; $MMR = .707$). The scale is considered only marginally acceptable because Clark cast 5 of the 8 computable nonscale votes.[15] Accordingly, we conclude that the justices voted as they did primarily because of their substantive economic attitudes toward labor unions. This explanation, based on the individual justices' degree of economic liberalism or conservatism, comports with the findings presented in both of the state action sets.

Frankfurter wrote more frequently than any of his colleagues in the NLRB decisions: thirteen opinions in nineteen participations (68 percent), which is markedly greater than his 45 percent in each of the state action sets. Eight of Frankfurter's opinions were dissents, one a regular concurrence, and four opinions of the Court, the latter of which Frankfurter self-assigned. Apart from these four cases, Warren assigned the Court's opinion in eighteen; the remaining case was decided *per curiam*. Frankfurter's greed in retaining the Court's opinion for himself at every opportunity is perhaps explained by Warren's failure to assign any of the NLRB cases to him. Frankfurter, however, was part of the majority opinion coalition in only five cases in which Warren made the assignment. If unanimous decisions are added, Frankfurter received more than his fair share: three of eighteen.

Similar to his behavior in the state business cases, Frankfurter had no hesitance to author anti-NLRB opinions. Indeed, he accompanied each of his eight anti-NLRB votes with an opinion. When he voted to uphold the NLRB, he wrote an opinion in only five of his eleven votes. Moreover, six of his eight anti-NLRB opinions were dissents, and the NLRB was prounion in most of these cases. Frankfurter's other two anti-NLRB opinions were those of the Court. Frankfurter's opinions supportive of the NLRB included two opinions of the Court, two dissents, and one regular concurrence. In each of Frankfurter's support-ive opinions, the NLRB was antiunion. The observation made regard-ing the character of Frankfurter's opinions in the state business regula-tion set applies no less to the NLRB cases: if a justice warrants his reputation for restraint, he will write as often as possible when his vote opposes agency action. When he votes for the agency, written opinion is unnecessary. As in state regulation of business, Frankfurter flaunted these considerations. Not only were his eight dissents double the number written by any other justice, but six of them opposed the NLRB's action.

Frankfurter was able to conceal his lack of deference in the first of his two anti-NLRB opinions of the Court. *NLRB* v. *Avondale Mills* was decided together with *NLRB* v. *Steelworkers* (1958). We count them separately only because Warren concurred in the latter but dissented in the former. The cases concerned the validity of employer-imposed no-solicitation rules. In *Steelworkers*, the Court upheld the NLRB's dis-missal of alleged unfair labor practices against the employer, but in *Avondale Mills* it denied enforcement of an NLRB order. Hence the partial cloaking effect in Frankfurter's majority opinion, even though Black, Douglas, and Warren thought that the NLRB had sufficiently supported both its decisions. Frankfurter's second anti-NLRB majority opinion involved a cease-and-desist order barring a union from engag-ing in a secondary boycott. Frankfurter held that the NLRB improperly applied the pertinent provisions of the National Labor Relations Act. Although Frankfurter did not explicitly say so, the result rejects defer-ence, notwithstanding his acknowledgement that the distinction between legitimate primary activity and prohibited secondary activity "does not present a glaringly bright line" and that the board "has more or less felt its way during the fourteen years it has had to apply" the provision at issue.[16]

We now turn to Frankfurter's six anti-NLRB dissenting opinions. In *Mastro Plastics* v. *NLRB* (1956), Frankfurter, joined by Harlan and Minton, held that the NLRB's construction of a provision of the Taft-Hartley Act conflicted with its plain meaning. Although Taft-Hartley "must be considered as an organic whole," no "controlling considerations preclude giving the ordinary meaning to what Congress has written" here. Accordingly, "we need not agree with a legislative judgment in order to obey a legislative command. It is enough for us that Congress did not legislate idly, but did intend the . . . provision to have an effect."[17] With these words, Frankfurter cloaked his lack of deference to the board with the higher duty of deference to Congress. Similarly, in *NLRB* v. *Borg-Warner* (1958), although Frankfurter's dissent did not explicate the basis for his lack of deference to the NLRB, the unstated rationale appears to be the same: he chose to defer to Congress rather than the board when they behave incompatibly.

In *NLRB* v. *Truitt Manufacturing* (1956), Frankfurter was joined by Harlan and Clark in faulting the NLRB on different grounds: for "mak[ing] a rule of law out of one item—even if a weighty item—of the evidence." Instead, the board should have considered "the totality of the conduct." Its failure to do so left the NLRB's "judgment without reasonable foundation."[18] There was no mincing of words here. The board was simply wrong.

No justice joined Frankfurter's dissent in *NLRB* v. *Lion Oil* (1957). Whereas the majority reversed the court of appeals, thereby affirming the NLRB's decision, Frankfurter skillfully juxtaposed the disagreement between the appellate court and the board to conceal his opposition to the latter. He noted that the NLRB did not raise the respondent employer's alternative defense in its arguments before the Supreme Court; neither was it "clear from the record that respondent urged this objection before the Board." If the latter was the situation, the alternative defense may not be "open for judicial consideration." Nevertheless, "it is not for this Court in the first instance to construe this contract." Rather, "it is for the Court of Appeals to judge whether the record as a whole supports the Board's findings of unfair labor practices."[19] Harlan joined Frankfurter's dissent in *NLRB* v. *Walton Man-*

ufacturing (1962), the last of his dissents opposing a prounion ruling of the NLRB. The refrain accords with that of *Lion Oil*: "I do not think the Court of Appeals applied an erroneous standard of review or grossly misapplied the correct standard, and . . . it is not for this Court to 'pass on the Board's conclusions in the first instance or to make an independent review of the review by the Court of Appeals.[20]

The Pontius Pilate posture adopted by Frankfurter in *Lion Oil* and *Walton Manufacturing* also manifested itself in his only dissenting opinion that objected to an antiunion decision of the NLRB: *NLRB* v. *Electrical Workers* (1953). Frankfurter argued that courts of appeals have primary responsibility for enforcing NLRB orders. The appellate court "found that the Board employed an improper standard as the basis for its decision" and "does not travel beyond its proper bounds in asking the Board for greater explicitness in light of the correct legal standards for judgment."[21] This and other of Frankfurter's anti-NLRB opinions indicate a deviousness not present in his antistate business regulation opinions. There his lack of restraint appeared starkly naked. Here he was able to use deference to Congress and the courts of appeals to offset his lack of deference to the NLRB. The substantive reason for Frankfurter's anti-NLRB votes, however, was the same as for his opposition to state business regulation: economic conservatism.

FEDERAL AGENCY BUSINESS REGULATION

The remaining set of data involves agency cases regulatory of business. We again divide these decisions into those in which the regulatory commission was antibusiness (twenty-eight) and those in which the agency was probusiness (nineteen). These agencies were upheld in thirty-one of forty-seven of the Court's nonunanimous decisions (66 percent), but the Court's antibusiness orientation slightly overrode its support for the agencies: thirty-two of the decisions produced an antibusiness result (68 percent). When the agencies were antibusiness, the Court sustained their rulings in twenty-two of twenty-eight cases (79 percent); when they were probusiness, the Court upheld only nine of nineteen (47 percent). This distribution, when arrayed in a 2 x 2 table, slightly exceeds a probability of .05 ($x^2 = 3.62$ with 1 degree of freedom).

Patterns of conflict and consensus displayed in the state labor, state business, and NLRB cases (Tables 4.1, 4.3, and 4.5) remain recogniz-

Table 4.7. Federal Agency Business Cases: Percentages of
Interagreement in Split Decisions

	Dou	Blk	War	Clk	Brn	Min	Ree	Bur	Stw	Har	Frk	Wht
Douglas												
Black	73											
Warren	66	91										
Clark	64	80	89									
Brennan	66	76	86	86								
Minton	53	85	73	71								
Reed	60	77	80	79		79						
Burton	30	48	52	69	44	73	60					
Stewart	29	47	47	44	65							
Harlan	13	26	35	46	45	38	22	75	65			
Frankfurter	15	33	45	51	48	47	47	70	71	88		
Whittaker	14	32	36	44	46			89	59	82	71	
Average	44	61	64	66	62	65	63	61	53	48	53	50
Percentage of time in majority	57	78	87	91	97	73	87	63	65	50	57	50

Indices of interagreement
Dou-Blk-War-Clk-Brn = .78
Dou-Blk-War-Clk-Brn-Min-Ree = .75
Blk-War-Clk-Brn-Min-Ree = .81
Blk-War-Clk-Brn = .85
Blk-War-Clk = .87
Min-Ree-Bur = .71
Bur-Stw-Har-Frk-Wht = .74
Har-Frk-Wht = .80
Har-Frk-Wht-Bur = .79

able in Table 4.7. A solid five-member liberal bloc existed, four of
whose members served throughout Frankfurter's tenure on the Warren
Court. When Minton and Reed are added, each of whom participated in
only fifteen of the forty-seven decisions, the liberal bloc's interagreement index drops only from .78 to .75. Greater cohesion occurred
when Douglas is excluded (.81) and still more when Minton and Reed
are partitioned out (.85). Nonetheless, unlike the dominant bloc in the
NLRB decisions, which excluded the Court's two most economically
liberal members, Douglas and Black, here the liberals dominated. The
only cost to them was the rightward movement of Burton and Stewart to
the Whittaker-Frankfurter-Harlan bloc.

Even though the seven most liberal justices whose positions are shown in Table 4.7 confronted the five most conservative, polarization was less than in the other sets, with the possible exception of state business regulation. Only twenty-two of fifty-nine cells (37 percent) contain ratios ⟨.33 or ⟩.75. The comparable proportion for state labor and NLRB was 86 and 42 percent, respectively. State business produced a 30 percent proportion. But unlike state business, only two justices participated with the majority more than 90 percent of the time (Brennan and Clark). This pair cast 24 percent of the majority votes (69 of 286), while the three justices who voted with the majority in the state business cases more than 90 percent of the time (Brennan and Clark again, joined by Minton) cast 30 percent of the majority votes there. Moreover, no justice failed to participate in the majority with less than half of his votes, whereas in the other three data sets at least two justices fell below 50 percent.

Dissenting most frequently, thereby reflecting conflict, were Douglas, Frankfurter, and Harlan, each with 20 dissents. Indeed, this trio accounted for over half the dissents cast in the agency business cases (60 of 117). Markedly more than in other sets, except for the highly skewed state labor cases, bloc members largely dissented only with their fellow bloc members. Thus Frankfurter never dissented when Douglas, Black, Warren, Brennan, or Reed did so. Dissents, overall, averaged 2.5 per case, equal to that in the state business cases and above the 2.25 contained in the two labor sets.

The pattern of votes continues to indicate that the justices' economic policy preferences rather than tenets of activism or restraint explain their behavior. Excluding Jackson with his single participation, only five of the twelve justices whose votes are shown in Table 4.8 supported the agencies regardless of whether they were pro- or antibusiness. Four of the five are the same ones who supported the NLRB with more than half their votes when the NLRB was prounion as well as antiunion: Burton, Reed, Minton, and Clark. Brennan joined them in the agency business cases. Yet unlike the NLRB cases, in which this group's support for the agency was high regardless of whether the NLRB was pro- or antiunion, here it was much more equivocal. Thus Clark, Minton, Burton, and Brennan varied at least 23 points in support when the agencies were probusiness from their percentage of support when the agencies were antibusiness. The seven remaining justices occupy the poles of the interagreement matrix (Table 4.7) and show an average variance of 58 points between the pro- and antibusiness portions of Table 4.8.

Table 4.8. Votes on Pro- and Antibusiness Decisions of the Federal
Agencies Regulatory of Business

Justice	Agency Probusiness	Percentage of Support	Justice	Agency Antibusiness	Percentage of Support
Frankfurter	17-2	89	Black	24-2	92
Harlan	15-2	88	Minton	9-1	90
Burton	10-2	83	Warren	25-3	89
Stewart	5-1	83	Brennan	14-2	88
Whittaker	9-3	75	Clark	23-4	85
Minton	3-2	60	Douglas	21-7	75
Brennan	7-6	54	Reed	6-3	67
Reed	3-3	50	Burton	9-6	60
Clark	9-9	50	Stewart	4-7	36
Warren	6-13	32	Frankfurter	10-18	36
Black	4-15	21	Harlan	8-15	35
Douglas	2-17	11	Whittaker	2-14	13
Jackson	0-0	—	Jackson	0-1	0

When the votes in Table 4.8 are scored for the justices' pro- and antibusiness leanings, further evidence emerges that these men marched to the beat of their attitudes toward business, rather than those pertaining to agency expertise. Douglas, Black, and Warren collectively cast 83 percent of their votes in an antibusiness direction (115 of 139). If the votes of Brennan and Clark are added, the proportion is 78 percent (167 of 213). At the conservative extreme, Frankfurter, Whittaker, and Harlan collectively voted probusiness with 88 of their 115 votes (77 percent). The addition of Burton and Stewart raises the total to 116 of 159 votes (73 percent). Efforts to construct a cumulative scale produced a coefficient of reproducibility of only .924. Apparently the variety of situational contexts in which the federal commissions regulate business precluded formation of a more acceptable scale. Nonetheless, Black, Douglas, Warren, Brennan, and Clark ranked most antibusiness, and Whittaker, Harlan, Frankfurter, Burton, and Stewart demonstrated the most probusiness attitudes.

A count of opinions shows that Douglas, Frankfurter, and Harlan wrote most frequently in these agency business cases. As in all but the federal labor cases, Frankfurter disproportionately wrote in dissent. Whereas 53 percent of his state business opinions were dissents, as were 63 percent of his NLRB opinions, here 76 percent were dissents (thirteen of seventeen). He wrote two opinions of the Court, one of which he self-assigned.[22] Unlike the other sets, in which he typically self-assigned, Frankfurter assigned four of five to others.

Compatibly with his behavior in the state business and NLRB decisions, Frankfurter had no qualms about writing when he voted in derogation of judicial restraint. In the twenty cases in which he voted against the agency, he wrote in ten. Conversely, he wrote in only seven of the twenty-seven cases in which he supported the agency's action. The pattern of Frankfurter's opinions clearly reveals the dominance of his economic conservatism. Eight of his ten antiagency opinions occurred when the agency's actions were antibusiness; when he wrote upholding the agency, the agency's decisions were invariably probusiness. Moreover, seven of his antiagency opinions appeared as dissents. One antiagency decision appeared as an opinion of the Court and two appeared as regular concurrences, in both of which the agency had been probusiness.

In Frankfurter's antiagency opinion of the Court, *St. Joe Paper Co.* v. *Atlantic Coast Line Railroad Co.* (1954), the authority of the Interstate Commerce Commission (ICC) to initiate a merger, rather than the affected carriers, was at issue. Frankfurter stated that the pertinent provision of the Bankruptcy Act incorporated by reference the Interstate Commerce Act, which meant that the reorganization must be initiated by the merging railroads themselves: "One carrier cannot be railroaded [pun intended?] by the Commission into an undesired merger with another carrier."[23] The dissenters argued that the case did not involve a forced ("cram down") merger at all, inasmuch as none could occur without a vote of the debtor railroad's shareholders.

Frankfurter displaced his rush-to-judgment activism of *St. Joe Paper* with an effort to eat his restraintist cake and have it too in his antibusiness antiagency concurrence in *Secretary of Agriculture* v. *U.S.* (1956). The majority opinion, which Frankfurter joined, held that the ICC's order relieving railroads of liability for stated percentages of damages suffered by eggs during shipment lacked substantial evidence to support it. Frankfurter's concurrence, which none of the majority joined, stated that "this Court must stay its hands" when the commission documents the bases for its orders and that such bases require only "such substantiality of proof as is appropriate to the subject matter."[24]

Frankfurter's other concurrence, *Phillips Petroleum* v. *Wisconsin* (1954), which was also antibusiness, was discussed earlier in connection with his opinion behavior in the state business regulation cases.

Because a vote in this case could not simultaneously defer to both the state and the federal regulatory commission, an advocate of restraint must of necessity overrule one or the other. But Frankfurter managed to come as close as possible to deferring to neither the state nor the FPC. He emphasized that the type of natural gas sales involved was not constitutionally subject to state regulation and overruled the FPC, which had held that it had no jurisdiction over the rates in question. Frankfurter's rationale conflicted with the plain-meaning rule he used to justify his position in *Mastro Plastics* v. *NLRB*. Instead, the section of the Natural Gas Act which was at issue "is not to be construed on its face. It comes to us with an authoritative gloss. We must construe it as though Congress had, in words, added to the present text some such language as . . . 'the basic purpose of the legislation is to occupy the field in which the States may not act.'"[25]

Frankfurter's other antiagency opinions all appeared as pro-business dissents. In *SEC* v. *Drexel & Co.* (1955), Burton joined Frankfurter in holding that the Securities and Exchange Commission (SEC) lacked jurisdiction to set fees payable by a parent company in a reorganization plan proposed by a subsidiary. The subsidiary's plan required the parent to initiate certain proceedings, which were consolidated with the subsidiary's reorganization plan. "But," noted Frankfurter, "Congress particularized. It did not vest this fee-fixing authority of the Commission in a comprehensive provision. It dealt with the problem distributively. It was explicit in relating the power to fix fees to the particular proceeding." Even though Congress was "duly mindful of the abuses of excessive fees in the conduct of inter-company affairs" and *"effectively* equipped the Commission with power to regulate fees in the various proceedings which required approval by the Commission," the act "is a reticulated statute, not a hodgepodge."[26]

In *General Stores Corp.* v. *Shlensky* (1956), Burton again joined Frankfurter's dissent. The SEC and a shareholder had opposed a petition for arrangement of debts under the Bankruptcy Act. The three federal courts that heard the matter all upheld the SEC's motion, but Frankfurter asserted that the district court, in exercising discretion, "was guided by inappropriate standards," which left its discretion "without a supporting basis." Why? Because the "usually careful district judge" used "a loose generality" rather than "the ratio decidendi" of the controlling case.[27]

As in the two preceding cases, only one justice other than Frankfurter dissented in *U.S.* v. *Storer Broadcasting* (1956). Here, however, that justice—Harlan—wrote his own opinion. At issue were Federal Communications Commission (FCC) rules limiting the number of television stations a broadcaster could own. Because Storer had reached but not exceeded the limit, Frankfurter held that the broadcaster was not an aggrieved party and thus the FCC rules did not apply. Although Frankfurter admitted that the case "raises issues on which judges not unnaturally divide," nonetheless "procedural and jurisdictional limitations on judicial action by the federal courts are not playthings of lawyers nor obstructions on the road of justice." Rather, "they are means designed to keep the courts within appropriate limits."[28] Here, then, Frankfurter concealed his lack of deference to the agency by referring to the limited decision-making competency of the courts, and in contrast to his other antiagency opinions, he arguably did exercise restraint.

As in the preceding case, only Frankfurter and Harlan dissented in *Denver & Rio Grande Western* v. *Union Pacific* (1956), and again each wrote separately. The ICC had established through routes for specified commodities. Frankfurter viewed the ICC's action as lacking sufficient support because the justifications it provided "collide with congressional policy." The ICC's failure to justify its order "by findings that support it and by evidence that supports the findings" warrants remand to the agency "for clarification and reconsideration" since it is "not our duty to find reasons to support the Commission's order."[29] Although Frankfurter's willingness to remand to the ICC is more restraint-oriented than is outright reversal, it does not equate with unequivocal affirmance—which is what the majority ordered.

Any belief, even the most Pollyannaish, that Frankfurter regularly exercised restraint should not have survived his opinion in *FHA* v. *The Darlington* (1958). If Frankfurter believed in restraint, he would have recognized that silence in this case might have left the gold much less tarnished. He did, after all, join Harlan's dissent, as did Whittaker. But he could not keep his pen in its inkwell. The result was a ringing declaration of unconstitutionality, notwithstanding the "very weighty presumption of constitutionality that I deem it essential to attribute to any Act of Congress." The reason: "the unavoidable application of the . . . Act to the Darlington mortgage did substantially impair the 'vested rights' of respondent."[30] The majority exercised restraint not only toward congressional legislation but also toward the dissenters.

Douglas's majority opinion could have twisted the knife. Instead he merely concluded that "invocation of the Due Process Clause to protect the rights asserted here would make the ghost of *Lochner* v. *New York* walk again."[31]

Frankfurter's remaining pair of antiagency dissents were one-paragraph words of emphasis to his concurrence in Harlan's dissents in *Sunray Mid-Continent Oil* v. *FPC* (1960) and *Sun Oil* v. *FPC* (1960). Frankfurter's objection was the one he most frequently used: the agency's failure to support its decision with reasons therefor.

Our analysis of patterns of conflict and consensus in non-unanimous state action and agency cases regulatory of business and labor decided during the eight years Felix Frankfurter served on the Warren Court shows that the individual justices' substantive economic attitudes dominated their behavior[32] and that those of like mind acted together in conflict with their ideological opponents. As an economic conservative, Frankfurter associated most frequently with his fellow conservatives in opposition to the liberals and had no reluctance to write when his vote opposed agency and state action. Although he wrote relatively as often when he voted to uphold the states and agencies as when he opposed them (twenty-four versus twenty-six times), his twenty-four restraintist opinions applied to only 40 percent of his sixty restraintist votes. His twenty-six activist opinions, by comparison, applied to 52 percent of his fifty activist votes. Moreover, the bulk of his antistate and antiagency opinions appeared as dissents: twenty of twenty-six (77 percent). Only ten of his twenty-four prostate and proagency opinions appeared as such (42 percent).

As noted, such behavior is exactly what would be expected from a genuine spokesman for restraint who believes it necessary to explain his activist votes. It is also, however, exactly what would be expected from a justice who values his reputation as an advocate of restraint yet, in fact, practices restraint only when the state or agency action in question favors his personal policy preferences. The analysis of Frankfurter's votes, along with those of the other justices, clearly shows that the latter interpretation of Frankfurter's opinion behavior is by far the more correct one—that activism and restraint are means to substantive ends rather than palliatives that mute discord and enhance accord. Indeed, Frankfurter's voting behavior was far less restraintist than that of Minton, Reed, and Clark, all of whom supported NLRB and agency

decisions regulatory of business at least half the time regardless of
whether such decisions were pro- or antiunion or business. Furthermore, that most of Frankfurter's activist votes were in dissent indicates
that the majority of the justices, in each case, was willing to take a
position of restraint, whether verbalized or not, which Frankfurter, the
putative restraintist, was not.

All this, of course, leaves the question why Frankfurter has retained
a reputation as an advocate of restraint. Several hypotheses, amenable
to future research, suggest themselves in answer. First, Frankfurter's
attachment to restraint antedated his service on the Court, which
suggests that though Frankfurter verbalized restraint during the 1920s
and 1930s, he changed his tune after his appointment to the Court in
1939. Second, Frankfurter grew conservative and more activist with
age. This hypothesis flies in the face of empirical analyses of his
service on the Stone and Vinson Courts.[33] Third, the cases selected for
analysis do not span the waterfront of decisions in which restraint is
properly operative. Technically, this is true. Previous research has
identified fifty-two cases that were formally decided during the first
eight terms of the Warren Court.[34] The bulk of these cases involved the
Federal Rules of Civil Procedure, the doctrine of comity, venue, and
diversity of citizenship. Frankfurter did indeed exercise restraint in
these areas, but these cases bear little relationship to any underlying
consideration other than the propriety of the Supreme Court's resolution of the controversy. Furthermore, among these sets only the comity
cases connect as closely with the heart of restraint as cases involving
economic state action and administrative agency activity. That Frankfurter voted in a restrained fashion in the judicial power universe does
not gainsay his activism in the cases we have analyzed.

A fourth hypothesis would involve Frankfurter's reputation for
restraint based on his opinions for the Court. Our analysis provides
some support for this allegation. Including his judgment of the Court,
Frankfurter wrote ten majority opinions upholding the states and federal regulatory commissions, as opposed to three that did not. Yet if an
exclusive focus on majority opinions explains Frankfurter's reputation,
what does this say about the scholarship of those who have so sharply
limited their focus? No matter how strongly one advocates restraint,
that a reputable scholar would identify a justice with his own personal
policy preferences based solely on majority opinions passes credulity.[35]
Another hypothesis would be that after his appointment to the Court,

Frankfurter could no more claim to be an advocate of restraint than any of his colleagues. As Arthur S. Miller has pointed out: "All judges are 'result-oriented'; so, too, are all commentators upon the work of the judiciary."[36] That some analysts dress Frankfurter in the mantle of judicial restraint is their problem, not Frankfurter's. His propensity to write in dissent against the states and federal regulatory commissions supports this hypothesis, especially when his opinion-writing is coupled with his staunchly probusiness and antilabor voting record. Frankfurter deferred no more blindly than any of his colleagues. When a result of which a justice approves can be rationalized by invocation of restraint, the justice will do so—a Douglas, Black, or Warren no less than a Frankfurter, Harlan, or Whittaker. But when restraint does not fit the desired result, the cloak remains in the closet in preference to those that better conceal the nakedness of the justice's policy preferences.[37]

A final hypothesis suggests that Frankfurter's reputation for restraint results from his pre-Court reputation, which he maintained during his justiceship by peppering his opinions with references thereto at every opportunity. In short, Frankfurter was typecast when he took his seat on the Court; accordingly, observers in general, and votaries in particular, recognized only the pepper of Frankfurter's restraint while remaining senseless to the salt of his activism. Our analysis of the contents of Frankfurter's activist opinions indicates the use of restraint rhetoric to cloak his activism; however, by no means did he do so with any regularity. Whether, in fact, Frankfurter relied on canons of restraint to justify his votes with greater frequency than did his colleagues requires content analysis of the justices' opinions—an enterprise far beyond the scope of this work. Two points may be noted in this regard, however. First, during Frankfurter's tenure on the Court most state and federal agency business regulation reviewed by the Court was economically liberal, even though the comparable labor regulation appears not to have been. But because business regulation occurred more often than that involving labor unions, it is plausible that restraint could be used more readily by liberal justices than by those who were economic conservatives, such as Frankfurter. Second, as detailed, Frankfurter had no compunction about voting in an activist fashion and coupling these votes with dissenting opinions.

Whatever the explanation, our analysis of Frankfurter's record reveals him to be nothing more nor less than a stalwart economic conservative who used judicial restraint and activism with equal facility. When restraint supported his and his conservative colleagues' policy preferences, he used it; when it did not, activism suited him just as well. These conclusions, in short, clearly emerge both from our examination of conflictual and consensual voting patterns and from our survey of Frankfurter's opinion behavior.

As for future research, Felix Frankfurter's failure to abide by the canons of restraint necessarily did violence to the role his votaries ascribed to him. But whether this discrepancy between his alleged role and his actual behavior acerbated conflict with his colleagues remains an unanswered question. So also does consideration of whether activism or restraint needs necessarily provoke conflict. An examination of their use by justices on other Courts or an analysis of activism and restraint by justices such as Clark, Reed, and Minton, whose voting behavior manifested greater restraint than that of their colleagues, may provide an answer.

We wish to thank Arthur S. Miller, Professor Emeritus of Law, George Washington University, and Stuart H. Teger, Esq., of Detroit, for their suggestions and assistance.

1. Although Frankfurter did not retire from the Court until August 28, 1962, he participated in no cases decided after April 9, 1962. Because of our concern with conflict, we limit our analysis to orally argued nonunanimous decisions. Multiple cases decided by a single opinion are counted once. The only exception is *NLRB* v. *Steelworkers* and *NLRB* v. *Avondale Mills*, 357 U.S. 357 (1958); the former was decided by a 7-2 vote, the latter by 6-3. Counting this case as two decisions produces an N of 109. Six of the 109 cases, however, pertain to both state action and federal agency activity. If these are counted twice, the N increases to 115. A categorized listing of the 115 cases that displays the votes and opinions of each justice may be had by writing the authors.

2. Harold J. Spaeth, "The Judicial Restraint of Mr. Justice Frankfurter—Myth or Reality," *Midwest Journal of Political Science* 8 (1964): 22-38. This study covered the state action and federal agency cases of only the first seven terms of the Warren Court and paid no attention to conflict and consensus among the justices.

3. Harold J. Spaeth, "An Analysis of Judicial Attitudes in the Labor Relations Decisions of the Warren Court," *Journal of Politics* 25 (1963): 290-311; Harold J. Spaeth, "Warren Court Attitudes toward Business: The 'B' Scale," in Glendon Schubert, ed., *Judicial Decision-Making* (New York: Free Press, 1963), pp. 79-108; Glendon Schubert, *The Judicial Mind: The Attitudes and Ideologies of Supreme Court Justices, 1946-1963* (Evanston: Northwestern University Press, 1965), pp. 127-46; David W. Rohde and Harold J. Spaeth, *Supreme Court Decision Making* (San Francisco: W. H. Freeman, 1976), pp. 137-45.

4. Glendon Schubert, *Quantitative Analysis of Judicial Behavior* (Glencoe, Ill.: Free Press, 1959), p. 91.

5. Although Frankfurter's *Capital Service* vote was antistate, it did uphold the NLRB. Thus he supported the other prong of restraint—deference to agency expertise.

6. Fisher's exact test produces $p = .08$.

7. Frankfurter received equitable treatment on the seventeen occasions when he was available for receipt of the opinion of the Court—an average of once every eight cases. Warren kept no cases for himself; neither did Reed or Black. Frankfurter, however, self-assigned at his only opportunity, and Warren assigned him two cases.

8. 347 U.S. 590, at 608.

9. 355 U.S. 489, at 502.

10. 358 U.S. 450, at 475-76.

11. 358 U.S. 534, at 551 (emphasis added).

12. Anthony Lewis, "A Gain for States' Rights," *New York Times,* March 1, 1959, p. 56.

13. By comparison, when Frankfurter wrote in support of the state's regulation, five of his six opinions were antibusiness. This pattern should occasion no surprise inasmuch as in twenty-eight of the thirty-three business regulation cases a prostate vote was concomitantly antibusiness.

14. Fisher's exact test produces $p = .0157$.

15. Ideally, nonscale votes should be randomly distributed. See Harold J. Spaeth and David J. Peterson, "The Analysis and Interpretation of Dimensionality: The Case of Civil Liberties Decision Making," *Midwest Journal of Political Science* 15 (1971): 413-41. We also distrust the "goodness" of the NLRB scales because, unlike the state labor cases, these twenty-three concern a wide variety of labor union activities. The mere fact that the cases, when scored as pro- and antiunion, R⟩ .90 does not mean that the situational context in which an attitude "object" (here labor unions) reaches the Court should be disregarded.

16. *Electrical Workers* v. *NLRB*, 366 U.S. 667, at 673, 674.

17. 350 U.S. 270, at 293, 296.

18. 351 U.S. 149, at 155.

19. 352 U.S. 282, at 294, 295.

20. 369 U.S. 404, at 421.

21. 346 U.S. 464, at 478-79, 480.

22. Inasmuch as Frankfurter was part of the majority opinion coalition in twenty-seven of the agency business cases, his two opinions of the Court were less than his fair share.

23. 347 U.S. 298, at 310.

24. 350 U.S. 162, at 175, 176.

25. 347 U.S. 672, at 685-86.

26. 348 U.S. 341, at 349-50 (emphasis added).

27. 350 U.S. 462, at 469, 470.

28. 351 U.S. 192, at 214, 213.

29. 351 U.S. 321, at 337, 340, 344.

30. 358 U.S. 84, at 93.

31. Ibid. at 91-92 (citation omitted).

32. To obtain some additional evidence for this conclusion, we used Pearson's R to correlate the percentage of support for the states, the NLRB, and the federal agencies by the justices when those entities were regulating business and labor (in the case of the states) or were pro- or antilabor or business in the case of the NLRB and the federal regulatory agencies, respectively. Regarding state regulation, the correlation was $-.52$ (significant at $\langle.05\rangle$) indicating that if a justice was activist toward state regulation of labor, he was likely to be restraintist toward state regulation of business, and vice-versa. In the area of federal regulation of business, the correlation was $-.73$ (significant at $\langle.01\rangle$) indicating that if a justice was restraintist when such decisions were probusiness, he was likely to be activist when they were antibusiness, and vice-versa. In the case of the NLRB, the correlation was only $-.08$. Although this result is in the right direction, it is not statistically significant, and we are at a loss to explain its weakness. Nevertheless, the three coefficients, taken as a whole, do indicate a strong relationship between restraint and activism on the one hand and the justices' policy preferences on the other.

33. C. Herman Pritchett, *The Roosevelt Court: A Study of Judicial Politics and Values, 1937-1947* (New York: Macmillan, 1948), pp. 239-63; Schubert, *Judicial Mind*, pp. 127-41; Peter G. Renstrom, "The Dimensionality of Decision Making of the 1941-1945 Stone Court" (Ph.D. dissertation, Michigan State University, 1972), pp. 80-142.

34. Harold J. Spaeth, "Judicial Power as a Variable Motivating Supreme Court Behavior," *Midwest Journal of Political Science* 6 (1962): 54-82.

35. See Arthur S. Miller, "In Defense of Judicial Activism," in Stephen C. Halpern and Charles M. Lamb, eds., *Supreme Court Activism and Restraint* (Lexington, Mass: Lexington Books, 1982), pp. 175-76.

36. Ibid., p. 173.

37. See Harold J. Spaeth and Stuart H. Teger, "Activism and Restraint: A Cloak for the Justices' Policy Preferences," in Halpern and Lamb, eds., *Supreme Court Activism and Restraint*, pp. 277-301.

II
The United States
Courts of Appeals

5

Factors Affecting Variation in Rates of Dissent in the U.S. Courts of Appeals

DONALD R. SONGER

Nonunanimous decisions of collegial courts have been a frequent focus of research in political science for more than three decades. The public expression of dissent has been taken as an objective indicator that legitimate decisional alternatives were open to the judges. Decisions with dissent have therefore been viewed as appropriate data with which to test the influence of judicial attitudes, values, and role orientations on case outcomes. The level of dissent has also frequently been used as an objective indicator of the extent of conflict and consensus in a court. Although unanimous decisions are not necessarily devoid of internal conflict nor lacking in legitimate decisional alternatives, most behavioral research on the courts has confined its analysis to decisions containing dissent.[1]

This chapter explores conflict and consensus in the United States courts of appeals. A first step will be to describe the variations in the level of dissent among circuits, changes in the rate of dissent over time, and differences in the rate of dissent between two major issue areas. After describing the extent of variation, several hypotheses concerning factors that often are believed to affect the level of dissent will be examined. No attempt is made to explore factors related to the tendency of individual judges to dissent.

The data consist of 6,618 cases with full opinions (including *per curiams*) published in the *Federal Reporter* for the years 1953 through 1975. A random sample consisting of 150 criminal cases and 150 labor relations cases per year was selected.[2] For years in which fewer than 150 labor cases were published with full opinions, all labor cases were included. The cases used in analysis are part of a larger data set

Table 5.1. Changes in Dissent Rate in Two Issue Areas,
1953-1975

	Percentage of Nonunanimous Decisions	
Year	Criminal	Labor Relations
1953	8.7	6.7
1954	7.5	7.2
1955	3.8	4.9
1956	9.3	10.7
1957	7.3	6.4
1958	8.0	11.1
1959	8.0	9.1
1960	4.7	10.5
1961	7.3	6.9
1962	6.7	6.3
1963	6.1	7.8
1964	6.0	8.8
1965	8.7	10.0
1966	4.7	8.0
1967	4.7	12.0
1968	8.7	5.0
1969	5.5	7.4
1970	9.5	11.5
1971	6.7	13.7
1972	3.3	8.5
1973	4.0	7.0
1974	8.7	7.3
1975	13.4	2.7
Mean	7.0	8.3
Standard deviation	2.28	2.45

collected for a study on judicial impact which is still in progress.
Although the particular twenty-three-year period selected was determined by the needs of the impact analysis, the existence of data
covering such an extended period made it possible in the present study
to explore changes over time in dissent in the courts of appeals.

VARIATION IN RATES OF DISSENT

To begin the description of dissent in the United States courts of
appeals, the rate of dissent has been computed separately for each issue
area in each of the twenty-three years of the period subjected to analysis.
The data are presented in Table 5.1. Throughout the period from 1953

Table 5.2. Dissent Rates by Circuit in Two Issue Areas

	Percentage of Nonunanimous Decisions	
Circuit	Criminal	Labor Relations
1	6.1	2.4
2	6.8	11.6
3	7.0	7.8
4	6.9	12.1
5	5.6	6.9
6	7.7	8.8
7	6.8	10.4
8	3.1	3.9
9	5.7	5.4
10	2.7	5.4
DC	21.1	16.9
Mean	7.2	8.3
Standard deviation	4.6	4.0

to 1975 the dissent rate has remained low compared to that of the Supreme Court for the same period. Moreover, differences between the two issue areas are modest. The mean dissent rate for criminal cases was found to be 7.0 percent and that for labor relations cases was 8.3 percent. Within each issue area, however, there was substantial fluctuation over time. The dissent rate for criminal cases reached a high of 13.4 percent in 1975 and a low of 3.3 percent in 1972. The dissent rate for labor relations cases varied from 13.7 percent in 1971 to 2.7 percent in 1975.

There has, however, been no consistent linear trend over time. This absence of a secular trend is in striking contrast to the findings of a considerable growth in the level of dissent for state supreme courts reported in Chapter 9 of this volume by Henry R. Glick and George W. Pruet, Jr.

Substantial variation in the rate of dissent also exists among the eleven circuits of the courts of appeals, as shown in Table 5.2. The pattern of variation among the circuits over the twenty-three-year period is noticeably different for the two issue areas. For criminal appeals, the District of Columbia Circuit stands in marked contrast to all the other circuits. Its 21.1 percent rate of dissent was nearly three times that of the Sixth Circuit, which had the second highest level of dissent (7.7 percent).

In contrast, there was considerably more variation throughout all the circuits for labor relations cases. Although the District of Columbia still exhibited the highest rate of dissent (16.9 percent), three other circuits (the second, fourth, and seventh) had dissent rates above 10 percent. The difference between the patterns in the two issue areas is highlighted by observation of the effect of the District of Columbia Circuit on the standard deviation for each. When all eleven circuits are included in the analysis, variation as measured by the standard deviation is higher for criminal cases than for labor cases (4.6 as compared to 4.0). When only the ten numbered circuits are compared, however, the standard deviation for criminal cases drops dramatically to 1.6 and the standard deviation for labor cases declines only modestly to 3.1.

FACTORS AFFECTING DISSENT

Over the years an extensive literature on American appellate courts has provided many explanations of the causes of dissent and factors related to its incidence. In his recent summary of this literature, Steven A. Peterson has identified twenty separate propositions relating to the causes of dissent, but he suggests that very few have been convincingly confirmed.[3] Because a disproportionate share of the tests of these propositions is limited to the Supreme Court, explorations of the causes of dissent in other bodies is needed.

In an attempt to meet this need identified by Peterson, ten general hypotheses were tested with the data from the courts of appeals. Organization of the discussion of these hypotheses follows three categories suggested by Peterson: the influence on dissent of the legal culture, organizational and institutional factors, and the sociopolitical system. When possible, each hypothesis was stated in a manner congruent with Peterson's propositional inventory, although he does not always state his hypotheses in a manner that is easily tested. Each of the hypotheses was tested separately for the sample of criminal cases and labor cases. For several of the general hypotheses, two or more methods of operationalization were employed so that a total of thirty-four separate tests of the causes of dissent are presented.

LEGAL CULTURE AS AN INFLUENCE OF DISSENT

Although the traditionalists' assumption that judicial outcomes could be explained almost entirely by a proper understanding of precedent and other legal influences has long since been discredited by the research of legal realists and behavioralists, few would go so far as to say that legal considerations are irrelevant to judicial decisions. Richard J. Richardson and Kenneth N. Vines argue that the behavior of lower federal courts can best be conceptualized as the result of pressures emanating from two sources, which they identify as the "legal subculture" and the "democratic subculture." The legal subculture includes rules and norms governing the judicial process and the behavior of judicial actors. Important examples would be the expectation that judges remain insulated from political pressures and interests and that great weight be accorded legal precedent in judicial decision making.[4] Peterson reports that a number of researchers have concluded that legal factors relating to the nature of the cases and decisions are related to the occurrence of dissent.[5]

Hypothesis 1: Difficult questions of law produce more dissent. Since the courts of appeals lack the control of their dockets possessed by many supreme courts, they handle a large volume of routine litigation. J. Woodford Howard views the magnitude of the routine litigation in the courts of appeals as a major factor in depressing dissent.[6] Similarly, Joel B. Grossman and Richard S. Wells argue and Stephen C. Halpern and Kenneth Vines present findings that the Judiciary Act of 1925, which enlarged the Supreme Court's discretionary jurisdiction, was an important reason for the increasing dissent in the Court. Peterson reports that although there has been no definitive test of this proposition, some indirect support for it may be found in statements by the justices.[7]

An empirical test of this hypothesis is complicated by the absence of any way to determine unambiguously which cases "objectively" contain more "difficult questions of law." In light of this problem, several categories of cases were examined which might reasonably be suspected of containing a greater proportion of cases with complex legal questions than other cases. If "tough questions of law" do produce more dissent, one could expect the rate of dissent in these categories to be significantly higher than in cases not in the category.

Attention first centered on the effects of the Criminal Justice Act of 1964. A significant reform embodied in this legislation was the provision for the first time of free counsel to indigent defendants on their first appeal from the conviction of any felony. Such a reform might reasonably be expected to increase the number of frivolous criminal appeals to the courts of appeals because indigent defendants would often have nothing to lose from appeal. Hypothesis 1 would then lead to the prediction that the rate of dissent on criminal appeals would be higher before than after 1964.

The data employed in this first test provide no support for the hypothesis. No significant differences were found between the rate of dissent for criminal appeals in the periods before and after 1964. In fact, there is a very slight difference in the opposite direction (7.19 percent for the later period compared to 7.02 percent for the pre-1964 cases). The results are essentially unaffected if only the period immediately before and after 1964 (using either a two- or four-year interval) is examined. One may therefore safely conclude that the 1964 Criminal Justice Act had no effect on the dissent rate for criminal appeals.

The history of a case subsequent to decision by the courts of appeals may provide additional indicators of the difficulty of the legal questions involved. Although several factors probably enter into any calculation over the decision of whether to seek appellate review, it is reasonable to assume that one important consideration is the evaluation by the potential appellant's attorneys of the merits of their legal argument. If they believe the appeals court decision turned on a close or difficult question of law, they are more likely to be encouraged to seek Supreme Court review than if they believe their position lacks substantial legal merit. If the first hypothesis is valid, it would therefore be expected that the rate of dissent would be substantially higher in cases in which the losing party sought Supreme Court review than in cases in which no review was sought.

A similar logic would suggest a further test. Within the subset of cases in which review was sought, it might be reasoned that the Supreme Court would be more likely to accept for review those cases presenting difficult questions of law. Therefore, a higher rate of dissent would be expected in cases accepted for review than in those in which review was denied. The data to test these propositions are presented in Table 5.3.

When each of these two methods is applied separately to labor relations and criminal appeals, four tests of Hypothesis 1 are obtained. In all four of the tests, the results are in the predicted direction. Rates of dissent are higher for cases in which Supreme Court review was sought than for those in which no review was sought, and decisions actually reviewed by the Supreme Court had more dissent in the courts of

Table 5.3. Dissent Rates for Cases Classified according to History
after Court of Appeals Decision

	Criminal			Labor		
Supreme Court Review Sought	Appeals Court Vote		Dissent Rate	Appeals Court Vote		Dissent Rate
	Unanimous	Divided		Unanimous	Divided	
No	1,906	126	6.2%	2,337	174	6.9%
Yes	1,299	115	8.1%	574	91	13.7%
	$x^2 = 4.71, p < .05$			$x^2 = 32.42, p < .001$		
	gamma = .14			gamma = .36		
Supreme Court Review						
Denied	1,240	92	6.9%	533	80	13.1%
Granted	59	23	28.0%	41	11	21.2%
	$x^2 = 32.44, p < .001$			$x^2 = 2.86$, ns		
	gamma = .68					

appeals than those denied review. In three of the four tests the differences reach generally accepted levels of statistical significance.
There is considerable variation among the four tests in the magnitude of
the effects with the difference between criminal cases granted and
denied review exhibiting the strongest relationship (gamma = .68).

Although these results provide moderately strong support for the
hypothesis that dissent is more likely in cases containing difficult legal
questions, one caveat is in order. Previous studies have shown that the
Supreme Court is more likely to review cases whose decisions involved
dissent below.[8] Moreover, it is possible that the decision to seek review
is encouraged by the presence of dissent regardless of the nature of the
legal issues involved. Caution should be used in interpreting the tests of
Hypothesis 1 because of the possibility that the indicators of difficult
questions employed may not be truly independent.

*Hypothesis 2: Overturning precedent is associated with increased
dissent.* This second hypothesis is closely related to the first. A case
involving the straightforward application of clear precedent is likely to
be considered an "easy" question of law, which will result in a consensual decision. In contrast, to overturn established precedent, given
the weight the legal culture places on the importance of *stare decisis,*

would seem to create a difficult problem for judges.[9] To date, this hypothesis has not been tested for judges on the courts of appeals, though there is some support in studies of Supreme Court voting. For example, Howard Ball concludes from a study of cases in which the Supreme Court overturned precedent that supporters of the earlier decisions were most likely to dissent. Similarly, John R. Schmidhauser concludes that the typical dissenter "has been a tenacious advocate of traditional legal doctrines which were being abandoned during his tenure."[10]

It would appear to be impossible to test the application of this hypothesis to the courts of appeals with the method scholars have applied to the Supreme Court. Judges of the courts of appeals will rarely admit to overturning Supreme Court precedent directly. Application of many precedents to specific fact situations that are not identical to the facts of the precedent-setting case, however, often contains some ambiguity. Judges who wish to reach a result contrary to that implied by the precedent may do so by distinguishing the case at hand from the apparent precedent.

Given the difficulty of classifying decisions according to whether they were consistent in a legal sense with Supreme Court precedent, decisions were instead classified according to whether they were consistent with the current decisional trends of the Supreme Court. To determine these trends, all criminal cases with full opinions in the twenty-three-year period studied were classified according to whether they were pro- or antidefendant. The percentage of prodefendant decisions for each year was then calculated. An appeals court decision was classified as consistent with the decisional trend of the Supreme Court if the direction of the decision was the same as the majority of decisions of the Supreme Court. In a similar manner, all labor relations cases were classified as being pro- or antimanagement.[11]

The operationalized hypothesis tested was that the rate of dissent would be higher for decisions in which the outcome was contrary to the decisional trends of the Supreme Court. The findings, however, provided no support for the hypothesis. In each period, the dissent rate in labor relations cases was higher when the court of appeals made a promanagement decision regardless of the decisional trend of the Supreme Court. For criminal cases, the dissent rate was consistently higher for prodefendant decisions regardless of the decisional trends of the Supreme Court.

These results may have been affected by the high proportion of consensual decisions involving clear-cut precedent. I have shown elsewhere that unanimous affirmances by the courts of appeals are likely to be such cases and that a significant proportion of reversals contain a choice situation that permits judicial preferences to determine the outcome.[12] The analysis was therefore repeated with only those decisions in which the courts of appeals reversed the district court or the NLRB. The results were the same: no support was found for the hypothesis.

ORGANIZATIONAL AND INSTITUTIONAL FACTORS

Peterson argues that in the courts, as in other bodies, decision making is constrained by the organization's structure and norms.[13] It is therefore probable that organizational factors affect dissent.

Hypothesis 3: The greater the workload, the less the dissent. Howard reports that the judges he interviewed from three circuits of the courts of appeals regarded heavy caseloads as the chief depressant of dissent. Writing dissenting opinions is a time-consuming process that is likely to interfere with other tasks for a judge struggling to keep up with a heavy caseload. Consequently, Kenneth C. Haas argues that heavy caseloads produce pressure to reach accommodations that will preserve unanimity.[14]

To test this hypothesis the number of cases filed per judge was computed for each circuit for each of the twenty-three years in the period analyzed.[15] The hypothesis was then tested by examining the relationship between the dissent rate for each year and the mean caseload per judge for the same year. The Pearson product-moment correlation between the dissent rate and the mean caseload per year was computed separately for each issue area. For criminal cases the correlation was $r = .23$. For labor relations cases the correlation was $r = .20$. Neither of these values for r approaches traditional standards of statistical significance. Therefore it may be concluded that increases in the caseload of appeals court judges over time do not appear to have had a significant impact on the dissent rate.[16]

The increase in the caseload per judge over the period studied has been dramatic. During the 1950s the mean caseload fluctuated between 50 and 57, but starting in 1962 it increased every year in an almost linear manner until it reached 172 filings per judge in 1975. But during this time, the dissent rate experienced only minor, apparently random, fluctuations.

Workload was equally ineffective in explaining variation in dissent rate between the circuits. In each of the four time periods used in the analysis, the average caseload per judge for the circuit had no statistically significant relationship to variation in dissent rate per circuit. It therefore appears safe to reject the notion advanced by the appeals court judges themselves that heavy workloads are a major depressant of dissent.

Hypothesis 4: The greater the diversity of background characteristics among judges on a court, the higher will be the dissent rate. A number of studies have investigated the thesis suggested by John W. Patterson and Gregory J. Rathjen that a court consisting of members with similar backgrounds may be expected to produce less internal conflict than one composed of members from different backgrounds.[17] No consensus exists, however, on which characteristics are most important in this regard. The analysis below tests this hypothesis by examining the effects of heterogeneity of party affiliation, ideology, and the presence or absence of a district court judge on the panel. Separate tests were conducted for each of the two issue areas.

Two studies of state supreme courts have concluded that courts with diverse party memberships have higher rates of dissent than those composed solely of members of the same party. Dean Jaros and Bradley C. Canon found a correlation of $r = .20$ between party heterogeneity and frequency of dissent. In contrast, Patterson and Rathjen, using a slightly different methodology, found party heterogeneity, with a correlation of $r = .46$, to be more strongly related to dissent rate than any of the other nine variables tested.[18]

Examining ideological heterogeneity, Burton M. Atkins found that every member of the District of Columbia Circuit was more likely to dissent when placed on a panel with members of a different voting bloc than when all three panel members were of the same bloc.[19] Although Atkins did not directly examine the dissent rate of panels, his findings for individual behavior are consistent with the hypothesis being explored.

There is little support in the literature, however, for the proposition that increasing the heterogeneity of an appeals court panel by including a district judge sitting by designation produces more dissent. Justin J.

Table 5.4. Diversity in Panel Composition and Rate of Dissent

	Labor Cases			Criminal Cases		
	Appeals Court Vote		Dissent	Appeals Court Vote		Dissent
Panel Composition	Unanimous	Divided	Rate	Unanimous	Divided	Rate
Political Party						
Same	353	52	14.2%	321	39	10.1%
Diverse	713	111	13.5%	602	99	12.9%
		$x^2 = 0.09$, ns			$x^2 = 0.99$, ns	
Ideology						
Same	294	23	7.3%	255	18	6.6%
Diverse	767	140	15.4%	655	107	14.0%
		$x^2 = 12.37, p \langle .001$ gamma = .40			$x^2 = 10.54, p \langle .01$ gamma = .40	
Presence of District Court Judge						
Circuit judge only	2,563	221	7.9%	2,267	206	6.9%
Circuit and district judges	348	44	11.2%	432	36	7.7%
		$x^2 = 4.57, p \langle .05$ gamma = .19			$x^2 = 0.34$, ns	

Green and Burton Atkins found that when district judges sit by designation on appeals court panels, they file only one-fourth of the expected number of dissents based upon the frequency with which they sit on panels. Ninth Circuit judges interviewed by Stephen L. Wasby also seem to reject the hypothesis by maintaining that district court judges did not contribute to inconsistency in the circuit more than did circuit judges.[20]

Six tests of Hypothesis 4 are presented in Table 5.4. In each of the two issue areas the effects of heterogeneity on dissent are separately tested for each of the three characteristics discussed above. Only those decisions in which the characteristics of all three panel members could be determined were included in the analysis.[21]

The strongest support for the hypothesis comes from the analysis of diversity in regard to policy views.[22] For both criminal and labor relations cases, panels whose membership reflected diverse policy positions had a dissent rate more than twice as high as the rate for more homogeneous panels. Both of the relationships meet the conventional standards of statistical significance. Similar results were obtained when the analysis was repeated for different portions of the twenty-three-year time period studied.

The most surprising result was the finding that there was no significant relationship between diversity in party membership and the rate of dissent. In fact, for labor cases a slightly higher rate of dissent was recorded for panels composed entirely of members of the same party (particularly if all three were Democrats). One possible explanation for this absence of effect may be provided by the Patterson and Rathjen study of state supreme courts.[23] They found that heterogeneity in regard to political factors had the greatest effect on dissent rates when the state supreme court was elective rather than appointive and when it was a third-level rather than a second-level court. Moreover, political factors explained less variance for single dissents than for multiple dissents. Because courts of appeals are second-level courts with appointive panels and only single dissents, all three criteria would lead to the prediction that diversity of party membership would have a reduced impact on dissent rates.

The test involving the presence of a district court judge produced mixed results. For labor relations cases there was a modest, statistically significant relationship in the predicted direction. The magnitude of the effect (gamma = .19), however, was only half that produced by diversity in policy views (gamma = .40). For criminal cases, although there was a very slight relationship in the predicted direction, it was statistically insignificant.

Hypothesis 5: Intercourt relations affect the manifestations of dissent. Courts of appeals are inescapably bound within a judicial system in which they interact in significant ways with courts both above and below. The possibility exists that the nature of their relations with other courts will have a significant impact on conflict within their own panels.

Two distinct tests were employed. Richardson and Vines argue that "dissent on the circuit court is primarily a function of the reversal of lower court decisions."[24] Most dissenting judges expressed support for

Table 5.5. Dissent Rates in Appeals Court Decisions Affirming and Reversing Decisions Below

Appeals Court Decision	Criminal			Labor		
	Unanimous	Divided	Dissent Rate	Unanimous	Divided	Dissent Rate
Affirm	2,545	138	5.1%	1,775	123	6.4%
Reverse	569	91	13.8%	841	115	12.0%
	$x^2 = 62.81, p \langle .001$			$x^2 = 25.16, p \langle .001$		
	gamma $= .49$			gamma $= .33$		

a district judge being reversed, thus reducing the loneliness of dissent. On the three circuits studied by Richardson and Vines, the dissent rate for reversals was as much as six times the rate found in decisions affirming the district court. The data in the present study permitted a test of the Richardson and Vines thesis for all eleven circuits. The data are displayed in Table 5.5.

The analysis of both criminal and labor cases provides strong support for the hypothesis.[25] Although the magnitude of the differences in dissent rates between reversals and affirmances does not reach the levels discovered by Richardson and Vines for civil liberties cases, the differences are both substantial and statistically significant. The larger differences are found in criminal appeals, with a 13.8 percent dissent rate in reversals compared to a 5.1 percent rate for affirmances. The higher rate of dissent for reversals was manifested in every circuit except the seventh.

The nature of the relationship between the courts of appeals and the Supreme Court may also have significance for conflict in the circuits. It was hypothesized that sharp changes in policy by the Supreme Court would tend to upset established relationships on the courts of appeals. The proportion of prodefendant and promanagement decisions of the Supreme Court changed significantly in 1970. The proportion of promanagement decisions jumped from zero in 1969 to 40 percent in 1970. The proportion of prodefendant decisions declined from 79 percent in 1968 to 63 percent in 1969 and then fell to 50 percent in 1970. As indicated above, these new decisional trends remained relatively stable for the remaining five years included in the present data set. Such a change was hypothesized to lead to an increase in the rate of dissent in the courts of appeals. When all cases in the twenty-three-year period studied are included in analysis, there are no significant differences in the dissent rates before and after the Supreme Court policy change, although it might be argued that any increase in the dissent rate would be only temporary during a period of adjustment. The data provide some support for this interpretation. For labor cases, the dissent rate in the two years before the Supreme Court policy shift was only 6.51 percent. In the two years following the shift it soared to 12.5 percent (significant at the .05 level). For criminal cases the change in the dissent rate is in the predicted direction but is not statistically significant. If only reversals (in which, as noted above, appeals court judges appear to have greater discretion) are included in the analysis, the changes are more dramatic. For reversals of labor decisions the dissent rate increased from 8.6 percent to 20.8 percent in the two years after the policy shift by the Supreme Court. For criminal appeals the dissent rate increased from 9.1 percent to 16.9 percent.

Overall it may be concluded that there is substantial support for Hypothesis 5. Both reversals of district court decisions and policy changes by the Supreme Court increased the rates of dissent in the courts of appeals.

Hypothesis 6: There will be fewer dissents in threat situations. Studies of the effect of external threat on coalition formation have been limited to the Supreme Court. Peterson concludes from an analysis of the literature that the evidence on the impact of threat situations on dissent is mixed.[26] Part of the dispute in the literature revolves around the proper definition of a threat situation. Consequently, no consensus exists on the designation of the periods of time in which the courts faced serious external threats.

Because of this lack of consensus, three separate tests of the hypothesis were performed. Each test examined the dissent rate in time periods characterized by a prominent scholar as involving a threat situation for the Supreme Court and compared them to the dissent rate in nonthreat periods. Stuart Nagel's study of "court-curbing" periods includes one such period (1955-59) in the time frame covered by the present study. David W. Rohde and Harold J. Spaeth identify the two periods involving the greatest threat to the Supreme Court's power as 1958 and 1968. Wasby argues that in general the period of the Burger Court was marked by a relative absence of threat compared to the Warren Court years.[27]

For the first test, the years 1955–59 (threat) were compared first to all other years studied and then to 1953–54 plus 1960–62 (the five nonthreat years closest to the five threat years). In the second test, the years 1958 and 1968 (threat) were compared to all other years and to the two years on either side of the threat years. For the third test, the years 1954–68 (threat) were compared to 1969–75.

For all three tests, performed separately for each issue, the results were the same. No significant differences were found between the dissent rates in threat and nonthreat periods. Although no support was found for the hypothesis, it is probably not fair to say that the data convincingly refute the hypothesis. Although there is some reason to suspect that external threats to the Supreme Court may imply threats to the lower federal courts, there is no firm evidence to date that establishes this connection.

SOCIO-POLITICAL SYSTEM
AS AN INFLUENCE ON DISSENT

The effects of a wide variety of social, economic, and political characteristics of decision making at all levels in the federal system have been conclusively demonstrated in numerous studies. It is therefore reasonable to expect that the social and political context within which judges find themselves will have an influence on significant aspects of their decision making.

Hypothesis 7: Urbanization is associated with increased dissent levels. Urbanization is one of a number of environmental factors associated with increased social and political complexity. Consequently, urbanization can be expected to produce the conditions that lead to increased demands and conflict in the larger political system, which in turn might be expected to lead to increased legal conflict. It is not surprising therefore that a number of studies have discovered an association between urbanism and dissent rates on state supreme courts.[28]

To test the applicability of this hypothesis to variations in the rate of dissent among circuits, an index of urbanism for each circuit had to be constructed. First, census data on the proportion of each state's population living in urban areas was obtained for each state in a given circuit. This percentage was multiplied by the number of nonsenior circuit judges from that state, and the sum of these scores from each state was divided by the number of nonsenior judges in the circuit.

Separate indices were computed from 1960 and 1970 census data and were compared to circuit dissent rates for the six-year period, which included the census year. Each issue area was thus subjected to two tests of the hypothesis. Pearson product-moment correlations were then computed between each circuit's index of urbanism and its rate of dissent for the six-year period.

The results provide strong support for the hypothesis. For each of the two issues in each of the two time periods there was a strong relationship between high levels of urbanization and high rates of dissent. For labor cases the correlations were $r = .89$ with 1960 census data and $r = .87$ with 1970 data. For criminal appeals the results were $r = .88$ for 1960 data and $r = .87$ for 1970 data. In each of the four tests, more than three-fourths of the variation in dissent rates among circuits is explained by differences in urbanization. Thus on the courts of appeals as in state supreme courts, urbanization appears to be associated with conditions that result in increased judicial conflict.

Hypothesis 8: Changing societal values are associated with increased levels of dissent. It has often been argued that conflict on courts mirrors conflicts that divide society at large. Consequently, Nagel has suggested that high dissent rates on the Supreme Court coincide with times of considerable societal conflict. Grossman and Wells concur. They suggest that public expression of dissent seems "more appropriate in a period of great political and social change."[29] Although these conclusions are based on observation of Supreme Court behavior, their logic should be applicable to the courts of appeals as well.

Perhaps the clearest public manifestation of changing societal values (at least in the two issue areas included in the present study) during the period examined was the 1968 presidential election. Nixon campaigned forcefully on the need to reverse the criminal procedure decisions of the Warren Court, and his theme apparently struck a responsive chord in a large portion of the public. The hypothesis would therefore lead to the prediction that the rate of dissent on criminal appeals would be high either in the period immediately before and/or after the 1968 election. The data, however, provide no support for the hypothesis. In the two years preceding the election the dissent rate was 6.7 percent and in the two years following the election it was 7.5 percent. Neither rate is significantly different from the 7.0 rate for the entire twenty-three-year period. Similar results are obtained using three- and four-year periods.

The 1950s are popularly viewed as a period of relative calm preceding widespread social upheaval in the 1960s. The hypothesis thus leads to the prediction that rates of dissent would have been lower in the 1950s. The data again provide no support for the hypothesis. For criminal appeals the dissent rate was marginally higher in the 1950s than in the 1960s (7.5 percent versus 6.3 percent). For labor cases the results are in the predicted direction, but the difference is trivial (8.1 percent versus 8.2 percent). Hypothesis 8 is therefore not supported.

Hypothesis 9: Cases raising constitutional issues are more likely to produce dissent than those decided on nonconstitutional grounds. This hypothesis is related to the preceding one because constitutional issues are more likely to be important and to attract widespread public notice and generate societal conflict. Moreover, judges may be more likely to express publicly their disagreements with the majority position on such important issues than on issues of relatively minor significance. Howard reports that no judge is expected to compromise on important principles, but when the disputed point will make little real difference, many judges are inclined to go along with the majority.[30]

It proved impossible to test this hypothesis with data from labor relations cases. By the 1950s too few labor cases reaching the courts of appeals raised constitutional questions to make analysis meaningful. In 44 percent of the criminal cases examined, however, one or more constitutional issues were discussed in the opinion of the court.

The data in Table 5.6 provide some support for the hypothesis. Although the relationship is relatively weak (gamma = .16), it is in the predicted direction and does reach generally accepted standards of statistical significance.

Hypothesis 10: The policy direction of a court's decision is related to the incidence of dissent. The leading work to examine this question is the Richardson and Vines study of three courts of appeals during the 1960s. They found that on two of the three circuits, dissent in civil liberties cases was usually an expression of nonlibertarianism.[31] In contrast, dissent in labor cases was found to be more often in a prolabor direction. A test of these conclusions with data from all eleven circuits is provided in Table 5.7.

The data in Table 5.7 provide strong confirmation of the Richardson and Vines thesis. Dissents in criminal cases are much more likely to occur when a court makes what is usually labeled a "liberal"

Table 5.6. Dissent Rates for Criminal Appeals Decisions in Appeals
Courts Raising Constitutional and Nonconstitutional Issues

Constitutional Issue Present	Unanimous	Divided	Dissent Rate
No	1,824	118	6.1%
Yes	1,373	123	8.2%
	$x^2 = 5.88, p \langle .05$		
	gamma $= .16$		

Table 5.7. Dissent Rates for Different Policy Positions Supported by
Appeals Court Decisions

	Criminal				Labor		
Decision	Unani-mous	Divided	Dissent Rate	Decision	Unani-mous	Divided	Dissent Rate
Prodefendant	569	89	13.5%	Promanagement	1,059	120	10.2%
Antidefendant	2,543	140	5.2%	Antimanagement	1,563	112	6.7%
	$x^2 = 57.48, p \langle .001$				$x^2 = 11.14, p \langle .001$		
	gamma $= -.48$				gamma $= -.48$		

(i.e., prodefendant) decision whereas in labor cases dissents occur
more frequently from a "conservative" (i.e., promanagement) decision.
The difference in dissent rates in criminal appeals (13.5 percent versus
5.2 percent) is particularly striking and represents one of the strongest
relationships discovered in the present study. But it is not immediately
apparent why liberals and conservatives should have different rates of
dissent in different issue areas. Additional research would be helpful to
clarify this point and to compare these results to analysis based on other
issue areas and other courts.

This chapter has examined variation in the rates of dissent in all
eleven United States courts of appeals.[32] Most previous studies of
dissent have concentrated on the supreme courts of either the states or
the nation. Among the findings were that some of the factors that have
been shown to be related to the incidence of dissent in supreme courts
are not helpful in explaining dissent in the courts of appeals. The most

important of such negative findings was that appeals court panels whose membership includes both Democrats and Republicans are no less likely to issue unanimous opinions than are panels that are exclusively Democratic or Republican.

The present study also provided one of the few opportunities to test hypotheses on changes in patterns of dissent over time. Although considerable variation was discovered, none of the hypotheses relating to change over time was supported. The impact of the variables with the greatest explanatory effects on dissent rates (ideological diversity, urbanization, and reversals of decisions below) did not appear to change significantly over the twenty-three-year period studied. The changes in dissent rates over time which were discovered therefore remain unexplained, appearing as merely random variation. The presence of this unexplained variation is yet another reason for students of courts to devote more effort to the relatively neglected task of studying change over time in the courts.

Factors discovered to be most strongly related to high rates of dissent were the presence of difficult legal issues in cases, ideological diversity in the panels, urbanism, reversals of decisions below, and the policy direction of the decision. The finding of significant effects for the index of urbanism in the circuit suggests the need for more research on the consequences of social, economic, and political characteristics for outcomes on the courts of appeals. This area has been neglected in the past, presumably because circuits were not conceived of as units having any political meaning in the larger political system. The findings noted above suggest, however, that the nature of political conflict in the states making up each circuit may aggregate to produce significant differences between circuits.

A number of studies of the policy-making process in legislatures have suggested that significant differences often exist between different issue areas. We need to investigate more systematically the effects of differences in issue or policy areas on the judicial process and the behavior of judges. In the present study, the effects of difficult legal questions, reversals, and the policy direction of the appeals court decision were substantially different for criminal and labor cases. On the other hand, no differences of note were found for the effects of workload, party or ideological diversity on the panels, or urbanization.

Finally, one of the most surprising findings was the absence of effect of changes over time or differences between circuits in workload on the rate of dissent. This finding is in sharp contrast to the opinion of some judges that heavy workloads were one of the chief inhibitors of dissent. Perhaps the lesson to be learned is that although valuable insight may be obtained from interviews with judges, conclusions based on interviews need to be subjected to critical examination of the data.

I am appreciative of the funding received from *Project '87* which made possible the collection of a large portion of the data used in this study.

1. See, for example, Robert J. Sickels, "The Illusion of Judicial Consensus: Zoning Decisions in the Maryland Court of Appeals," *American Political Science Review* 59 (1965): 100-104; Burton M. Atkins and Justin J. Green, "Consensus on the United States Courts of Appeals: Illusion or Reality?" *American Journal of Political Science* 20 (1976): 735-48; Donald R. Songer, "Consensual and Nonconsensual Decisions in Unanimous Opinions of the United States Courts of Appeals," *American Journal of Political Science* 26 (1982): 225-39.

2. The sample of labor cases includes both those appealed from the U.S. district courts and from the National Labor Relations Board. The sample of criminal cases includes *habeas corpus* cases as well as those appealed from decisions on the merits. Both samples include cases decided *en banc* and by three-judge panels.

3. Steven A. Peterson, "Dissent in American Courts," *Journal of Politics* 43 (1981): 412-34.

4. Richard J. Richardson and Kenneth N. Vines, *The Politics of Federal Courts: Lower Courts in the United States* (Boston: Little, Brown, 1970), pp. 7-10.

5. Peterson, "Dissent in American Courts," p. 413.

6. J. Woodford Howard, Jr., *Courts of Appeals in the Federal Judicial System: A Study of the Second, Fifth, and District of Columbia Circuits* (Princeton: Princeton University Press, 1981), p. 193.

7. Joel B. Grossman and Richard S. Wells, *Constitutional Law and Judicial Policy Making*, 2d ed. (New York: John Wiley, 1980), p. 232; Stephen C. Halpern and Kenneth N. Vines, "Institutional Disunity, the Judges' Bill and the Role of the U.S. Supreme Court," *Western Political Quarterly* 30 (1977): 471-83; Peterson, "Dissent in American Courts," pp. 413-14.

8. Joseph Tanenhaus, Marvin Schick, Matthew Muraskin, and Daniel Rosen, "The Supreme Court's Certiorari Jurisdiction: Cue Theory," in Glendon Schubert, ed., *Judicial Decision-Making* (New York: Free Press, 1963), pp. 127-30.

9. Howard, *Courts of Appeals*, p. 164.

10. Howard Ball, "Careless Justice: The United States Surpeme Court's Shopping Center Opinions," *Polity* 11 (1978): 200-228; John R. Schmidhauser, "*Stare Decisis*, Dissent, and the Backgrounds of the Justices of the Supreme Court of the United States," *University of Toronto Law Journal* 14 (1962): 209.

11. For the years 1960-69, the decisional trend of the Surpeme Court was classified as prodefendant in criminal cases (mean = 76 percent). In other years it was antidefendant (mean = 49 percent prodefendant). For the years 1970-75, the Supreme Court was classified as promanagement in labor relations cases (mean = 56 percent). In other years it was classified as antimanagement (mean = 26 percent promanagement).

12. Songer, "Consensual and Nonconsensual Decisions."

13. Peterson, "Dissent in American Courts," p. 414.

14. Howard, *Courts of Appeals*, p. 205; Kenneth C. Haas, "The Reactions of the U.S. Courts of Appeals to Supreme Court Prisoners' Rights Decisions," paper delivered at the Annual Meeting of the American Political Science Association, August 31-September 3, 1979, Washington, D.C.

15. Data on caseloads were obtained from the annual reports of the director of the Administrative Office of the United States Courts.

16. These findings are consistent with those reported by Sheldon Goldman in "Voting Behavior in the United States Courts of Appeals Revisited," *American Political Science Review* 69 (1975): 493, n. 9.

17. John W. Patterson and Gregory J. Rathjen, "Background Diversity and State Supreme Court Dissent Behavior," *Polity* 8 (1976): 611.

18. Dean Jaros and Bradley C. Canon, "Dissent on State Supreme Courts: The Differential Significance of Characteristics of Judges," *Midwest Journal of Political Science* 15 (1971): 322-46; Patterson and Rathjen, "Background Diversity."

19. Burton M. Atkins, "Judicial Behavior and Tendencies towards Conformity in a Three Member Small Group: A Case Study of Dissent Behavior in the U.S. Court of Appeals," *Social Science Quarterly* 54 (1973): 41ff.

20. Justin J. Green and Burton M. Atkins, "Designated Judges: How Well Do They Perform?" *Judicature* 61 (1978): 369; Stephen L. Wasby, " 'Extra' Judges in a Federal Appeals Court; The Ninth Circuit," *Law and Society Review* 15 (1980-81): 374; see also Stephen L. Wasby, "Of Judges, Hobgoblins, and Small Minds: Dimensions of Disagreement in the Ninth Circuit," Chapter 7 of this volume.

21. Data on the party affiliation of judges were taken from the *Biographical Directory of Federal Judges.*

22. All of the analyses reported for the hypothesis, unlike those for the other hypotheses, were restricted to three-judge panels. If *en banc* decisions were included, the relationship between the measures of diversity and dissent rate would be stronger for ideological and party diversity. District judges, of course, cannot participate in *en banc* sittings of the courts of appeals.

23. Patterson and Rathjen, "Background Diversity," p. 621.

24. Richardson and Vines, *Politics of Federal Courts*, p. 136.

25. Additional support for this hypothesis comes from Charles M. Lamb, "A Microlevel Analysis of Appeals Court Conflict: Warren Burger and His Colleagues on the D.C. Circuit," Chapter 8 of this volume.

26. Peterson, "Dissent in American Courts," p. 419.

27. Stuart S. Nagel, "Court-Curbing Periods in American History," in Theodore

L. Becker and Malcolm M. Feeley, eds., *The Impact of Supreme Court Decisions: Empirical Studies*, 2d ed. (New York: Oxford University Press, 1973), pp. 9–21; David W. Rohde and Harold J. Spaeth, *Supreme Court Decision Making* (San Francisco: W. H. Freeman, 1976), p. 196; Stephen L. Wasby, *The Supreme Court in the Federal Judicial System* (New York: Holt, Rinehart and Winston, 1978), p. 166.

28. See, for example, Henry Robert Glick and Kenneth N. Vines, *State Court Systems* (Englewood Cliffs, N.J.: Prentice-Hall, 1973), pp. 80-82; Jaros and Canon, "Dissent on State Supreme Courts."

29. Nagel, "Court-Curbing Periods," p. 42; Grossman and Wells, *Constitutional Law*, p. 232.

30. Howard, *Courts of Appeals,* p. 209.

31. Richardson and Vines, *Politics of Federal Courts*, pp. 136-37.

32. Subsequent to the end of the period studied in this chapter, a new court of appeals was created by splitting the old Fifth Circuit into a new Eleventh Circuit and a reduced Fifth Circuit.

6
Parameters of Dissensus on Shifting Small Groups

JUSTIN J. GREEN

The research reported herein focuses on three aspects of the U.S. courts of appeals. First, the chapter surveys the theory underlying the study of dissensus in unanimous decisions by collegial courts. Second, it reports several recent changes in the structure and operation of the courts and how they have affected judicial decision making. Third, it updates a 1976 study of voting behavior on the courts of appeals. The prime objectives of both the 1976 research and this project are to determine whether the relatively low dissent rate on the courts of appeals masks disagreement among the judges and to provide the basis for future work in the broad area of judicial consensus. The findings have significant repercussions for research on the courts of appeals and suggest some precautions as well as strategies that might be adopted in the study of judicial behavior.

THEORY

The empirical study of dissensus on apparently consensual courts began with Robert J. Sickels's examination of zoning cases decided by the Maryland Court of Appeals.[1] He discovered that although all such cases were decided unanimously, the decisions were not always harmonious, and he suspected that an unidentified external factor was at work. His research revealed that the court assigned each zoning case to a justice, in rotation, and that he prepared the draft opinion. All other members then supported that opinion regardless of their views on the merits of the case. Sickels uncovered a dramatic instance of court norms effectively suppressing dissent; were it not for his research, the Maryland Court of Appeals would surely have been labeled consensual in its disposition of zoning cases.

In a sense, Sickels only confirmed the conclusion of many others who have read and studied the memoirs left by justices of the U.S. Supreme Court: judges do not always dissent even when they believe the majority to be in error. He advanced the study of judicial behavior by demonstrating this phenomenon through the analysis of a large number of cases rather than by using the files and recollections of individual justices in individual cases. Research and efforts to construct a theory of judicial behavior have been forced to come to grips with the behavior that Sickels identified, leading to much study of the conditions that elicit a dissent. An important element in the development of such a theory has been the construction of definitions of consensus and dissensus that permit the possibility of significant suppressed dissent and that, therefore, demand inquiry beyond the mere counting of votes. J. Woodford Howard has provided a widely adopted definition of dissensus that has proved most useful in stimulating research on how judges disagree: dissensus is discordant outcomes without dissent.[2] Discovery of dissensus so defined on a court requires aggregating cases in a search for underlying, masked disagreement.

In 1976 Atkins and Green published an article that follows in the Sickels tradition, though it antedates Howard's major contributions to theory in this area.[3] The principal conclusion drawn at the end of that study involving nineteen thousand cases decided between 1966 and 1970 was that although the dissent rate on the U.S. courts of appeals was extraordinarily low, considerable disagreement occurred among members of each circuit bench when deciding criminal appeals.

Donald R. Songer followed up these findings by attempting to determine whether panels of the courts of appeals are presented with a true choice, a prerequisite for disagreement, in the cases they decide.[4] By classifying judges as liberal or conservative based upon their votes in nonunanimous cases, which clearly present a choice of decisions, and then examining their votes in unanimous cases, Songer concluded that between 20 and 35 percent of the appeals decided unanimously presented true choice situations in which there was hidden disagreement.

Songer's research relied upon the trichotomous classification of judges based upon one set of decisions and the application of these labels to another set of votes. Both the Atkins and Green 1976 research and the follow-up research described here omit this intermediate, data-suppressing step. The classification scheme displays the weaknesses associated with labeling individuals as liberal or conservative, including arbitrarily setting lines dividing one group of judges from another, and does not appear essential to the overall research objective. For the reasons explained below, the coefficient of variation based upon a large number of unanimous panel decisions is a superior measure for investigating the extent of dissensus as defined by Howard.

STRUCTURAL AND OPERATIONAL CHANGES

Over the last two decades, courts and legislatures in all jurisdictions have struggled to cope with the pressures of rapidly rising caseloads. The adjustments have, in many cases, resulted in substantial structural change, such as the creation of new courts or the extensive reorganization of existing judicial bodies. Another common strategy has been to increase personnel. If the number of cases is too great for the judges to decide within a reasonable time, one fairly obvious solution is to expand the bench. This is not always a simple, noncontroversial change as the arguments over the size of the U.S. Supreme Court and the benches of the Fifth and Ninth circuits of the U.S. courts of appeals demonstrate.[5] A third approach, often initiated by the judges, has been to make changes in court rules and internal procedures to expedite the processing of cases and to lighten the judges', as opposed to the court's, workload. All three changes may well be accompanied by revamping the support system, making adjustments in staff, computerizing operations, and similar modifications designed to speed the disposition of a constantly lengthening docket.

Although the media have tended to focus on trial courts when discussing caseloads, the U.S. courts of appeals have long worked in the shadow of a rapidly lengthening docket. Between 1962 and 1982, for example, the number of filings in the courts of appeals increased 580 percent, from 4,823 to 27,984 cases.[6] The problem pervades the entire system; each circuit bench has been forced to address a continuous increase in the number of filings. Solutions to the difficulties posed by expanding caseloads have been both national and local in character. Federal agencies generated some of the changes, but each circuit was also free to address the problem in its own way. Four strategies were in common use throughout the period, and the results now form part of the judges' decision-making environment.

First, Congress in 1978 expanded the size of all but one circuit bench.[7] The total number of courts of appeals judges was increased by 36 percent, from 97 to 132. In some cases the expansion was substantial: the Fifth Circuit bench grew from 15 to 26 judges, the Ninth Circuit from 13 to 23. The Omnibus Judgeship Act of 1978 authorized the largest single expansion of the judiciary in the nation's history and reduced at least temporarily the per judge caseload of the courts of appeals. Relief, however, was minimal and short-lived. In 1970, 11,662 appeals were filed for 97 judges to hear, an average of 120 cases per year. In spite of the major expansion of the bench in 1978, the per judge caseload in 1982 reached an even higher level. In that year, 27,984 appeals were filed, or 212 for each of the 132 judicial positions, an increase of nearly 77 percent in twelve years. Clearly, during this time the workload of the courts of appeals far outstripped the expansion of personnel approved by Congress.

Second, all circuits have expanded the number of available judges by extensive use of senior judges, visiting appeals court judges, and district judges sitting "by designation." After the passage of the Omnibus Judgeship Act, use of these special judges was generally reduced although by 1980 some circuits, notably the Ninth, had returned to the former practice. To illustrate, between 1966 and 1970 a special judge sat on 52 percent of all panels of the courts of appeals. By 1980, this proportion had declined to 44 percent. The Ninth Circuit, however, rarely forms a panel composed entirely of active judges appointed to that circuit's bench.[8] If the Ninth Circuit is omitted from the 1980 data, special judges sat in 28 percent of the cases decided, a substantial decline from previous levels. The extensive use of special judges was a very controversial move, the effects of which are still under review.[9] Without doubt, use of the special judges permitted the courts of appeals to hear and decide thousands of cases that would otherwise have been delayed for months for want of available judges. The issue yet to be resolved conclusively is whether the quality of judicial decisions has been adversely affected by the dramatically increased use of special judges, especially district judges sitting by designation and, conversely, whether in recent years, when panels were more likely to consist solely of appointed judges, the quality of judicial decision making improved. The debate over the use of special judges continues in the literature. Unless and until overwhelming objective evidence can be assembled to demonstrate that a panel of two appointed judges and one special judge is less competent than one of three appointed judges, the use of special judges will increase as the workload of the courts of appeals continues to grow. That is, of course, an impossible research task. As long as Congress fails to provide sufficient judicial positions, the courts of appeals will, in effect, provide their own through the increased use of special judges.

Third, the circuits implemented internal rule changes to lighten the workload or to facilitate the prompt disposition of cases. Obviously, these changes varied from one circuit to the next, but of general note is the adoption of a "not for publication" rule. In 1971, the Judicial Conference of the United States asked each circuit to develop a plan under which only the most important decisions, those that established precedent or otherwise significantly contributed to the growth of the law, would be published.[10] Although all circuits adopted a not for publication rule, the extent to which it has reduced the amount of time spent writing opinions seems to vary widely by circuit, as several studies have demonstrated.[11] The intent of the conference's request was to allow judges more time to hear and decide cases by eliminating the burden of producing an opinion of publishable quality in each case. The unintended consequences of the rule are only now beginning to emerge.

Finally, two related structural changes are worth noting because of their potential value as precedent. In 1978, Congress authorized the geographically mammoth Fifth Circuit to form administrative subdivisions so as to improve efficiency of operation.[12] Since the bench was simultaneously increased to twenty-six judges, some organizational change was essential lest circuit management become impossible. Just two years later, Congress created the Eleventh Circuit by subdividing the Fifth Circuit.[13] This legislation is much too recent for its effects to be evaluated. Such research ought to be undertaken at the first opportunity, however, because discussion of according similar treatment to the Ninth Circuit continues in Congress and in legal circles.[14] That circuit is also geographically enormous, and significant further expansion from the present bench size of twenty-three could severely complicate the task of administering the circuit.

These structural changes are clearly important because of their effect on the administration of justice in the United States. They are also significant because they change the nature of the work group and may have a substantial effect on the internal operations of the courts of appeals. Even an apparently simple change, such as adding a seat to the bench, has a potentially significant effect on the highly complex interpersonal relationships on the court.[15] The number of possible panels increases geometrically as the bench is expanded. If panels are randomly constituted, judges will sit with each other less often and, presumably, know less about each other. If the expansion of the bench is successful in reducing the per judge workload to more manageable proportions, special judges will appear less often and this factor in the development of a bench's decisional patterns will shrink in significance.

AN UPDATE

The changes in the U.S. courts of appeals over the past twenty years amount to a laboratory, providing an opportunity to assess the effects of structural change on small group decision making. In the following pages, the Atkins and Green study of dissensus is updated to determine whether the broad outlines of judicial voting behavior noted at the time of its publication are still present. Whether or not change in behavior has occurred, the fact remains that the decision-making environment was transformed over the ensuing years. What does the literature claim the effects of these changes to be? Are there deviations from expectations, and if so, how are these to be fitted into the puzzle? To update the data for 1966–70, data were collected on all published criminal cases decided by three-judge panels of the courts of appeals in 1980.

To follow up the 1966–70 study, the best point of departure is dissent rates: have they changed markedly from a decade earlier and how do any changes fit with the structural modifications that have taken place in the interim? It must be conceded at the outset that the effect of the not for publication rules is generally unknown, although at least some helpful research is available. These rules were not in effect between 1966 and 1970 but, as Daniel H. Hoffman and others have demonstrated, they are clearly a factor today. Hoffman shows that the filing of a dissent significantly increases the probability of publication.[16] Numerous unanimous cases were not published in 1980, presumably because they were not of value as precedent, though similar decisions were published in 1966–70. Because no circuit is currently publishing all of its decisions, Hoffman's research suggests that the dissent rate will be higher in 1980, a function of the reduction in the base, that is, the number of decisions published.[17] Table 6.1 displays the dissent rates for the 1966–70 period and the analogous data for 1980.[18]

Table 6.1. Dissent Rate by Circuit

Circuit	1966–70[a]	1980
1	2.6	0.0
2	6.4	9.8
3	6.5	10.0
4	5.4	11.5
5	3.0	2.2
6	4.2	7.0
7	12.7	7.0
8	2.6	3.4
9	5.6	2.7
10	0.8	7.4

[a]*Source:* Burton M. Atkins and Justin J. Green, "Consensus on the United States Courts of Appeals: Illusion or Reality?" *American Journal of Political Science* 20 (1976): 743.

The results are somewhat mixed but do not support the expectation of a generally higher dissent rate in 1980. Overall, the dissent rate on the courts of appeals remained virtually unchanged, 5.8 percent in 1966–70 compared to 5.1 percent in 1980. The dissent rate should have been higher in 1980 than in 1966–70, but it was higher in only six of the ten circuits. Hoffman reports that the circuits publishing the lowest proportion of opinions after the adoption of the not for publication rules were the Fourth, Ninth, and Tenth. In these three circuits, the data might well be expected to approach the extreme—publication only of cases decided by split panels. The Fourth Circuit does indeed display a very high dissent rate, 11.5 percent, double the level of 1966–70. The dissent rate in the Tenth Circuit increased ninefold, but in the Ninth Circuit it was halved. Examining circuit caseloads to determine number of filings per judicial position reveals that the Fourth Circuit had the highest caseload, which is consistent with a decision to publish proportionally fewer cases and with an increase in the dissent rate. Workload in the Ninth and Tenth circuits ranks near the bottom of the order. A likely complicating factor is geography; the Ninth and Tenth circuits are both rather sprawling, and travel time must be a consideration. In sum, then, the effects of the not for publication rule are visible in some situations, such as the Fourth Circuit, but both in the overall dissent rate and those in the individual circuits, the expectation of a higher level of dissent in 1980 is not supported by the data.

Pursuing a tangent for a moment, consider the effect of the Omnibus Judgeship Act of 1978 on workload. Although it might be possible to determine the number of judicial positions needed to achieve a specified level of efficiency on the basis of caseload, geography, and other factors, clearly the number of new positions created in each circuit was a function, at least in part, of political considerations. Comparing the per judge caseloads of 1966–70 and 1980 suggests that the expansion of the circuit benches overcompensated for workload in the Fifth and Ninth circuits and did not compensate adequately in the First Circuit. All other factors being equal and, concededly, they are not, the dissent rate in the First Circuit should increase as a result of the proper application of the not for publication rule. It did not. In fact, no dissents were filed in the First Circuit in criminal cases in 1980, perhaps an extreme manifestation of the point often made in the literature that a heavy workload suppresses dissent.

Some additional correlates of the dissent rate are also worth examining with the more recent data. The literature strongly suggests that a principal suppressor of dissent is workload: judges simply do not have the time to write and file dissenting opinions when there are mountains of appeals to be heard and decided.[19] The 1966–70 data showed, as expected, a strong inverse correlation (rho of $-.564$) between workload, measured as filings per judge, and dissent rate. This situation was much changed in 1980. The workloads of the circuits were more uniformly distributed in 1980 than in 1966–70; particular circuits can no longer be singled out as having a substantially higher or lower than average workload as in the earlier period. More interestingly, the rank-order correlation between workload and the dissent rate is .423. Although not as strong a correlation as was present in 1966–70, it is in the opposite direction than would be hypothesized. The usually anticipated negative relationship between workload and dissent rates simply does not exist in the 1980 data.

These findings seem confusing and perhaps contradictory. That is to be expected because there are two powerful factors at work and neither is completely understood. On the one hand is the readily comprehended claim that a higher workload, such as in 1980, should suppress dissent. On the other hand, the not for publication rule should allow more time to write dissenting opinions and result in a higher dissent rate by suppressing the publication of numerous unanimous cases. Without substantial amounts of data on the not for publication decisions in each circuit for 1980, it is difficult to draw detailed conclusions. On balance, however, it is fair to say that consideration of dissent as a measure of disagreement leads to the conclusion that the courts of appeals were relatively more harmonious in 1980 than a decade earlier.

It must be conceded that the not for publication rule has a putatively substantial effect on research strategy as well as on the administration of justice. All research based upon published decisions of the courts of appeals must recognize the possibility of bias stemming from the application of the rule. The need to supply basic data and to resolve questions associated with the use of the rule is obvious. One way of continuing research on disagreement in the court while awaiting this research is to reduce the impact of the not for publication rule by adopting the research strategy first applied in 1976. At that time, the rationale for developing a new research approach was the concentration by scholars on nonunanimous decisions to the exclusion of 94 percent of the courts' production. The mathematically simple computation of the coefficient of variation based upon votes cast in unanimous cases was a way to bring all of the courts' decisions into the research design. Since then, the not for publication rule has provided a second persuasive reason for using the coefficient of variation. Adopting this approach would mitigate the effect of the rule in estimating the level of disagreement on the courts of appeals.

There are now three classes of cases decided by panels of the courts of appeals: split decisions (nearly all of which are published), published unanimous decisions, and unpublished unanimous decisions. Measuring disagreement by the dissent rate concentrates on the first group to the exclusion of the second and third. From the study of nonunanimous decisions, no conclusions can be drawn about disagreement in other kinds of cases. Using the coefficient of variation and unanimous published cases reveals more about the operations of the courts of appeals and provides the basis for research on unpublished decisions, but it still does not address directly questions of behavior in deciding unpublished cases. It is, therefore, a better but not optimal research strategy. The research, then, is directed only to the public image of the courts of appeals. Unlikely though it may be, the possibility remains that a circuit could convey the impression of harmony while masking considerable dissensus by the way in which it applies the not for publication rule. In spite of these restrictions, however, using the coefficient of variation computed over unanimous cases to study dissensus on the courts of appeals has the advantage of reducing the effect of the not for publication rule.

To use this strategy, the data base was modified to include only all published unanimously decided cases. All votes in the data set were scored as either supporting or not supporting the government's position in a criminal appeal. A further distinction was drawn between cases that raised a constitutional claim (most often under the Fourth, Fifth, Sixth, or Fourteenth Amendments) and those that did not. This is, of course, a time-honored classification in the study of appellate courts justified by the intuitive though never demonstrated idea that cases raising constitutional claims are more important than others. To the litigants, obviously, this distinction is insignificant. Nonetheless, to maintain consistency with the literature, each judge's government support score, based on at least five votes, was computed along with the mean, standard deviation, and coefficient of variation for each circuit for the two types of cases. The results are presented in Table 6.2.

As the 1976 article made clear, the coefficient of variation is by no means a perfect measure of disagreement; it is only a more thorough one than the simple dissent rate. The principal difficulty associated with use of the coefficient of variation is that it is not normed: circuits cannot be labeled as high or low in dissensus because such standards do not exist. But comparisons can be drawn between circuits for the same time period and between time periods for the same circuit to determine whether judicial behavior has changed.

The data in Table 6.2 show clearly that the low dissent rate on the courts of appeals masks or hides a substantial amount of disagreement among the judges. There is dissensus in each circuit, indicated by the failure of the government support scores for each judge to cluster tightly about the mean, and, just as obviously, this result was to be expected. The higher the coefficient of variation, the greater the difference of opinion among the judges as to how criminal cases ought to be decided. Over all circuits, the average coefficient of variation for cases presenting a constitutional claim is 20.3 while the comparable rate for cases without such a claim is 19.8. Since constitutional cases are generally thought to present the more difficult questions and allow more room for disagreement, the similarity of the means is somewhat unexpected. Apparently as much masked disagreement occurs in constitutional cases as in nonconstitutional cases, and this was true of seven of the ten circuits as well as for all circuits combined. These averages acquire substantially more meaning if compared to the 1966–70 data. At that time, the average coefficient of variation for constitutional cases was 18.4, not significantly different from the 1980 figure of 20.3. For

Table 6.2. Characteristics of Government Support Scores in Criminal Cases

Circuit	Constitutional Claim Raised	Mean	Standard Deviation	Coefficient of Variation	Number of Judges
1	Yes	.894	.042	4.7	4
	No	.831	.034	4.0	
2	Yes	.814	.158	19.4	14
	No	.786	.273	34.7	
3	Yes	.601	.136	22.6	10
	No	.682	.194	28.5	
4	Yes	.718	.186	25.9	9
	No	.780	.190	24.4	
5	Yes	.711	.124	17.4	29
	No	.810	.110	13.6	
6	Yes	.634	.164	25.9	11
	No	.654	.098	15.0	
7	Yes	.826	.170	20.6	9
	No	.751	.162	21.6	
8	Yes	.827	.084	10.2	9
	No	.907	.066	7.3	
9	Yes	.817	.186	22.8	23
	No	.688	.121	17.6	
10	Yes	.762	.098	12.9	9
	No	.884	.103	11.7	

nonconstitutional cases, however, the average coefficient of variation in 1966–70 was 9.2. If that figure is compared to the 1980 mean of 19.8 one must conclude that judges on the courts of appeals agreed far less on how these cases should be decided in 1980 than in 1966–70. This disagreement was not reflected in an increased dissent rate, however, and becomes visible only when a measure such as the coefficient of variation is applied to all cases, including those decided by a unanimous vote. By the one measure but not the other, the level of disagreement appears to have increased substantially between the two time periods.

A major methodological issue examined in the 1976 article concerned the two measures of disagreement: are they measuring the same concept? At the time, the conclusion was that they were not. The evidence consisted of low Spearman rank-order correlations (rho) between disagreement as measured by the two variables. If the dissent rate and the coefficient of variation were simply two different ways of measuring the same phenomenon, the correlations should be very high. But in 1966–70 they were not; the correlation between the two measures over all circuits using constitutional cases was .052 and in nonconstitutional cases .382. In 1980, these correlations were .542 and .773 respectively. Whereas it appears that in 1966–70 the two measures were tapping different types of disagreement, such was not the case in 1980. Circuits with higher dissent rates also showed greater disagreement in unanimous cases as measured by the coefficient of variation.

Comparing the 1966–70 coefficients with those computed using the 1980 data reveals another striking difference. During the earlier period, the First Circuit appeared riddled by disagreement. In 1980, however, it was a model of harmony. Although that distinction may present an interesting secondary research question, the broader issue is the identification of factors that incline circuits toward dissensus. This topic was not investigated using the 1966–70 data, nor have later projects taken it up directly. Two obvious sources ought to be checked. The first is easily discarded: types of cases heard. There is no reason to believe that circuits with high coefficients of variation heard different types of cases than those with lower coefficients. The second potential source is personnel. A hypothesis worth testing would be whether circuits presenting high coefficients are marked by a bench fairly evenly divided between the political parties.[20] Given all that is known about the recruiting process, party of the appointing president would be the best variable to adopt as a surrogate measure of political ideology. Like all substitutes, it is imperfect in several respects, but it is adequate to test the hypothesis that benches composed of judges with diverse backgrounds will disagree more frequently than will more homogeneous benches.

The literature on small groups reports that people are disinclined to be sole dissenters. If a three-judge bench is divided between conservatives and liberals, and if dissent is suppressed by factors related to small groups, the minority judge on each panel will vote with the majority though truly disagreeing with the decision. This will become clear when that minority judge joins a like-minded individual to form a majority, which might then force another judge to agree without dissent. Such behavior increases the coefficient of variation in the circuit. Complicating factors in this exercise are that panels of the courts of appeals are not always randomly constructed and that ideology has, in the past, been used as the basis for forming panels.[21]

In 1980, most of the circuit benches were fairly evenly divided according to the party of the appointing president. Of the 110 judges in active service 70 (64 percent) had been appointed by a Democratic president. Rank-ordering the circuits by the partisan division on the bench and then computing a rank-order correlation using the coefficient of variation yielded interesting results. For cases presenting a constitutional claim, the rank-order correlation coefficient between partisan division and dissensus as measured by the coefficient of variation is .043. For cases without a constitutional claim, the rho is .558. Although the coefficients show, as expected, that the more narrowly divided is the bench the more likely it is to be in disagreement on the proper disposition of cases even though that disagreement is not carried to the point of filing a dissenting opinion, the expected relationship was substantial only in nonconstitutional cases. The frequent focus on constitutional cases in the literature, in the apparent belief that they are the important cases, suggests that the correlation would be lower in cases not presenting a constitutional claim, but this did not prove to be the case.

Although the data in Table 6.2 can be analyzed in myriads of ways, one conclusion stands out. In the 1976 article, the dissent rate was found to have significantly understated the amount of disagreement on the courts of appeals. The 1980 data show that the dissent rate is the same or a bit lower than it was in 1966–70, but the coefficients of variation tend to be higher. While continuing to present the image of a consensual court, the rotating panel structure of the court has permitted judges to disagree with each other in the general judicial philosophy used to decide cases. All of the arguments presented by Atkins and Green, as well as by Sickels and by Howard to the effect that dissent rates are not always the best measure of disagreement on a court are confirmed by examination of the 1980 data. There are changes, significant and worthy of further investigation, in the parameters of disagreement, but to understand the phenomenon demands an inquiry beyond the use of dissent rates.

1. Robert J. Sickels, "The Illusion of Judicial Consensus: Zoning Decisions in the Maryland Court of Appeals," *American Political Science Review* 59 (1965): 100-104.

2. J. Woodford Howard, Jr., *Courts of Appeals in the Federal Judicial System: A Study of the Second, Fifth, and District of Columbia Circuits* (Princeton: Princeton University Press, 1981), p. 194.

3. Burton M. Atkins and Justin J. Green, "Consensus on the United States Courts of Appeals: Illusion or Reality?" *American Journal of Political Science* 20 (1976): 735-48.

4. Donald R. Songer, "Consensual and Nonconsensual Decisions in Unanimous Opinions of the United States Courts of Appeals," *American Journal of Political Science* 26 (1982): 225-39.

5. On the general subject of bench size and related issues, see Carl Baar, *Judgeship Creation in the Federal Courts: Options for Reform* (Washington, D.C.: Federal Judicial Center, 1981).

6. See *Workload Statistics for the Decade of the 1970s* (Washington, D.C.: Administrative Office of the U.S. Courts, 1980); *Management Statistics for U.S. Courts* (Washington, D.C.: Administrative Office of the U.S. Courts, 1981).

7. P.L. 95-486; 92 Stat. 1629.

8. Stephen L. Wasby, "Of Judges, Hobgoblins, and Small Minds: Dimensions of Disagreement in the Ninth Circuit," Chapter 7 of this volume.

9. Justin J. Green and Burton M. Atkins, "Designated Judges: How Well Do They Perform?" *Judicature* 6 (1978): 358-70; Justin J. Green, "The Influence of Judges Sitting 'By Designation' on Circuit Law," paper delivered at the Annual Meeting of the American Political Science Association, August 31-September 3, 1979, Washington, D.C.; Stephen L. Wasby, " 'Extra' Judges in a Federal Appeals Court: The Ninth Circuit," *Law and Society Review* 15 (1981): 369-84.

10. See *Report on Opinion Publication Plans in the U.S. Courts of Appeals* (Washington, D.C.: Subcommittee on Federal Jurisdiction of the Committee on Court Administration of the Judicial Conference of the U.S., 1971); *Standards for Publication of Judicial Opinions* (Washington, D.C.: Committee on Use of Appellate Court Energies, Advisory Council for Appellate Justice, 1973).

11. Daniel H. Hoffman, "Nonpublication of Federal Appellate Court Opinions," *Justice System Journal* 6 (1981): 405-16; William L. Reynolds and William M. Richman, "Limited Publication in the Fourth and Sixth Circuits," *Duke Law Journal* (1979): 807-41; William L. Reynolds and William M. Richman, "An Evaluation of Limited Publication in the U.S. Courts of Appeals: The Price of Reform," *University of Chicago Law Review* 48 (1981): 573-631.

12. Section 6 of Public Law 95-486, the Omnibus Judgeship Act of 1978, authorized any court of appeals with more than fifteen judges to form administrative units. This section would apply to the Ninth as well as to the Fifth Circuit. See "Attacking the Full Court Press: Section 6 of the Omnibus Judgeship Act of 1978 and the Administrative Accommodation of New Federal Appellate Judges," *Virginia Law Review* 65 (1979): 1499-1519.

13. P.L. 96-452; 94 Stat. 1994. See also Robert A. Ainsworth, "Fifth Circuit

Court of Appeals Reorganization Act of 1980: Overdue Relief for an Overworked Court," *Cumberland Law Review* 11 (1981): 597-617.

14. See R. H. Deane, "Judicial Administration in the U.S. Court of Appeals for the Ninth Circuit," *Golden Gate University Law Review* 11 (1981): 1-20.

15. Steven A. Peterson, "Dissent in American Courts," *Journal of Politics* 43 (1981): 412-34.

16. Hoffman, "Nonpublication," pp. 412, 416; Reynolds and Richman, "Limited Publication," p. 829; Wasby, "Of Judges, Hobgoblins, and Small Minds."

17. Wasby presents supportive figures in "Of Judges, Hobgoblins, and Small Minds."

18. There were not enough criminal cases decided and published by the District of Columbia Circuit in 1980 to permit statistical analysis. Accordingly, that circuit has been omitted from all tabulations.

19. Wasby, "Of Judges, Hobgoblins, and Small Minds"; Howard, *Courts of Appeals,* p. 205. See by contrast Donald R. Songer, "Factors Affecting Variation in Rates of Dissent in the U.S. Courts of Appeals," Chapter 5 of this volume.

20. John W. Patterson and Gregory J. Rathjen, "Background Diversity and State Supreme Court Dissent Behavior," *Polity* 8 (1976): 610-22. Contrast Songer, "Factors Affecting Variation in Rates of Dissent in the U.S. Courts of Appeals."

21. Burton M. Atkins, "Some Theoretical Effects of Decision-Making Rules on the United States Courts of Appeals," *Jurimetrics Journal* 11 (1970): 10-13; Burton M. Atkins, "Decision-Making Rules and Judicial Strategy on the United States Courts of Appeals," *Western Political Quarterly* 25 (1972): 626-42.

7

Of Judges, Hobgoblins, and Small Minds: Dimensions of Disagreement in the Ninth Circuit

STEPHEN L. WASBY

Consistency, we are often told, is the hobgoblin of small minds. Yet we are hesitant to suggest that judges and legal scholars who have complained about doctrinal inconsistency, for example, in the Supreme Court's jurisprudence, are small-minded. Commentators have exhibited concern that the law should be uniform at all levels of the court system and that inconsistency should be avoided. The role of the law as a stabilizing force in society must be recognized, and, unless judicial rulings are reasonably consistent, lawyers will not be able to counsel clients or to keep disputes out of court. That is, of course, not to say that the law should be rigid or mechanical; it need not stand still in order to have a stabilizing effect.

Attention has been focused on intercircuit inconsistency by the Supreme Court's rules (Rule 17, formerly Rule 19), which make conflict between the U.S. courts of appeals one factor to be considered in the decision whether to grant *certiorari*. Attention is further focused on the matter by justices dissenting from the denial of review when there is an intercircuit conflict and arguing that our judicial system requires the capacity to produce a body of uniform national law.[1] Claims that individual U.S. courts of appeals do not maintain sufficient internal uniformity of doctrine have directed attention to intracircuit inconsistency.[2]

There is, however, another view. Its advocates do not make inconsistency a virtue or argue that it does not exist. They either place inconsistency in context by arguing that, particularly over the short term, it is a necessary part of the way the law grows, or—based on intensive study of cases or participants' views—they minimize the seriousness or significance of the problem created by inconsistency. For example, a study conducted for the Commission on Revision of the Federal Court Appellate System (the Hruska Commission, named for its chair, Sen. Roman Hruska) showed relatively few direct intercircuit conflicts in which a court "deals with the same explicit point as some other case and reaches a contradictory result," although indirect conflicts and "side-swipes" did exist, as did both "strong" and "weak" partial conflicts.[3] In another study, the judges of the U.S. Court of Appeals for the Ninth Circuit, which received particular attention during Hruska Commission testimony, indicated that intracircuit inconsistency was far less serious than alleged and was not a major concern.[4]

Those arguing that inconsistency is necessary may accept uniformity as a goal but place emphasis on the need for law to change and for variation to occur in aid of that change. J. Woodford Howard, Jr., has stated the position most effectively: "Uniformity, after all, is not an absolute but an organizational objective to be weighed against competing goals. Perfect harmony, indeed, is an undesirable obstacle to legal growth. Just as the doctrine of *stare decisis* affords appellate judges sufficient leeway to bridge the values of the past and present, so the quest for uniformity contains room for regional experimentation and adaptation of national law to continental diversity."[5] In an adversary common law system, law changes incrementally as courts face cases raising different aspects of recurring problems and as judges distinguish present cases while trying to follow available precedent. The result may be considerable unevenness, particularly in the short term as the law develops in fits and starts. Inconsistency may also be functional in other ways. For example, the intercircuit conflict that results as each lower appellate court develops its own doctrine "bubbles up" to the Supreme Court for resolution, thus providing the high court material through which to state uniform national law. As Justice Stevens has remarked, "Experience with conflicting interpretations of federal rules may help to illuminate an issue before it is finally resolved and thus may play a constructive role in the lawmaking process."[6]

Such nontraditional views should caution us in any discussion of judges' doctrinal inconsistency. They should not, however, prevent us from suspending judgment on whether inconsistency is a virtue or detriment and from further exploring the forms, dimensions, and extent of inconsistency and disharmony, dissensus, and disagreement—the latter terms avoiding the pejorative connotations of "inconsistency."[7]

This chapter provides an examination of disagreement—lack of unanimity in votes or opinion-writing in particular cases—in the U.S. Court of Appeals for the Ninth Circuit from 1970 through 1975. After an initial conceptual discussion of consistency and disagreement and their causes, the Ninth Circuit judges' views on inconsistency are presented, and literature on levels of disagreement and its causes in the U.S. courts of appeals is reviewed. Agreement and disagreement by the different types of judges who decide the Ninth Circuit's cases—active-duty and senior circuit judges, active-duty and senior district judges, and visiting judges from outside the circuit, individually and in combination—are then examined. Finally, the relationship between the court's disposition of district court rulings and disagreement within the court's panels is discussed.

INCONSISTENCY AND DISAGREEMENT

What Is Consistency? In the judicial context, consistency is not an exact concept.[8] In a multimember court, it can refer to consistency across the entire court or within a panel of judges. Focused discussion of consistency requires first that one "identify cases that are similar in ways that are relevant to the issues being adjudicated." Then a baseline, departure from which is inconsistency, must be established. That baseline might be "a distinct line of authority" governing cases: if cases "raise one or more issues that are governed by a line of authority common to [the] case," conflict might occur between the decisions in those cases.[9] U.S. Supreme Court decisions provide an external baseline for examining inconsistency in the U.S. courts of appeals. Although most judges Sheldon Goldman interviewed "strongly suggested that stare decisis, when the precedent involves policy set by the Supreme Court, *is* largely responsible for encouraging decisional consensus on the appellate courts," the Supreme Court often has not spoken to issues faced by the lower appellate courts.[10] This makes its word unavailable either as a source of guidance to the lower courts or as a measure of their inconsistency.

An internal baseline is provided for the courts of appeals by their own *en banc* decisions, which create circuit precedent. Because the appeals courts do not sit *en banc* frequently, circuit precedent is most often provided by one of the court's panels, which are the court of appeals for the cases they decide. When not explicit, circuit precedent may be relatively obvious from the central thrust of a series of incrementally developed panel opinions. Absent clear circuit precedent, a baseline from which to measure inconsistency might be constructed from liberal or conservative trends evident in the judges' voting patterns.[11]

The basic rule is that "once a panel of a circuit formulates a rule of decision in one case, the other judges of the circuit are bound to follow that precedent, right or wrong, in future cases, at least until it is reconsidered by the entire court sitting en banc."[12] Because judges at times dislike circuit precedent, however, they must face squarely "the question of whether to adhere to earlier decisions that they disagreed with."[13] The tradition of adhering to earlier panel decisions is sufficiently strong that "judges have declined to dissent because 'the law of the Circuit has apparently been determined to the contrary, and so I shall join in my brothers' disposition.' "[14] However, at times they "fail to accord to prior decisions . . . willing acceptance and whole hearted enforcement."[15] Judges in the Second, Fifth, and D.C. circuits admitted to fudging on the rule of not overruling another panel "by distinguishing cases, narrowing down rulings, and other tactics."[16]

If inconsistency is departure from circuit precedent, disharmony is seen in judges' voting disagreement and their failure to join a majority opinion even when they agree with the court's disposition of a case. Both concurring and dissenting opinions are indications of disharmony, even though the latter is directed at the results of the decision— with implications for "who gets what, when, and how" in the immediate case—whereas the former does not affect the immediate disposition of a case but may pose questions for the longer-term development of doctrine or may provide signals of internal friction to those observing the court. In any event, taken together, they "understate internal disharmony" because they represent only "the differences judges failed to compose." They also do not measure either "intensity of disagreement among circuit judges nor its reflection in voting blocs, bargaining over the language of opinions, and divergent outcomes among rotating panels."[17]

The possibility of such "divergent outcomes" means that inconsistency may coexist with the absence of disagreement. A panel may thus be unanimous while simultaneously it is inconsistent with the court's overall position—producing "discordant outcomes without dissent."[18]

When two or more unanimous panels consider the same issues, they may produce results pointing in different directions even if homage is paid to the court's precedents, masking disagreement within the larger court. Robert J. Sickels found this situation in zoning appeals cases decided by the Maryland Court of Appeals, which assigns opinion-writing by lot. Such a procedure leaves the court, "by division of labor, . . . in the hands of the judge who writes the opinion rather than the members who subscribe their perfunctory concurrence."[19] Systematic rotation of judges among panels in the U.S. courts of appeals may lead to similarly discordant results with disagreement over both interpretation and application of circuit precedent. If there is departure from systematic rotation in panel assignments, it is possible for the minority position within the court to be dominant in a subject area.[20]

Causes of Inconsistency. Inconsistency, dissensus, disharmony, disagreement—whatever the phenomenon or phenomena are called—have several causes. Principal among them is appellate courts' caseload, reinforced by the number of "extra" judges necessary to dispose of that caseload. The courts' use of rotating rather than fixed panels or *en banc* sittings provides a structural explanation; closely related are behavioral norms deriving from the panel structure. Judges' attitudes, ideologies, or party affiliations that subsume attitudinal differences provide an additional explanation.

Inconsistency in doctrine is particularly likely when a court decides many cases with a common element, such as issues of appellate procedure, standards by which lower court judgments are to be reviewed, or substantive matters such as the "intent to monopolize" standard in antitrust law. Inconsistency in result may stem from a large number of cases in the same subject area, such as labor law, leading to apparently erratic decisions concerning enforcement of National Labor Relations Board (NLRB) orders. High caseloads have, however, been thought a major reason for low dissent rates, in part because there is much "routine litigation" in the workload, particularly for courts without discretionary jurisdiction.[21] Thus "overworked judges, under pressure to deal rapidly with an ever-increasing caseload . . . will be less inclined to indulge in writing numerous dissents."[22] Indeed, the judges of the Second, Fifth, and D.C. circuits thought workload "the chief depressant of dissent."[23] For the fiscal years 1965–71, although there was a high negative correlation $(-.44)$ between a court's dissent rate and the rate at which appeals were terminated—less a matter of work-load than of efficiency—there was "little support" for the hypothesis that circuits with the heaviest workloads would also have the lowest dissent rates.[24]

Courts confronting large caseloads are compelled to draw on judges from other courts for assistance.[25] The Ninth Circuit, which made greatest use of extra judges, used seventy per year during the late 1970s, and almost one hundred later. The presence of such judges "further increases the number of possible panel combinations that may appear"; because panels will be less likely to be aware of each others' decisions and because the extra judges will be less likely to know circuit precedents, intracircuit inconsistency may also increase.[26] This suggestion appears to be borne out because from 1965 to 1969, judges sitting by designation differed from a circuit's regular judges in their support for particular positions: less for labor, more for the government in tax cases, and less for criminal defendants making a constitutional claim. However, when "conflict is measured by dissent, . . . desig-nated judges are disagreeing less, or conforming more to majority sentiment, than the regular judges."[27] District judges filed roughly one-fourth the dissenting opinions and one-seventh the concurring opinions expected on the basis of their panel participation; judges from outside the circuit filed about one-third the expected dissents; and senior circuit judges, though still filing proportionately fewer dissents and only one-half the expected concurring opinions, did so more than did district or visiting judges.[28] These data illustrate the point that "for any judge to file a solitary opinion requires a strong will plus opportun-ity; for a designated judge to do so must require the presentation of the most salient of issues in order to force the creation of an opportunity."[29]

The use of panels and rotation of judges among panels may also contribute to dissensus. Judges dispersed across panels "need not clash over how an issue should be resolved; yet . . . disparate points of view may nevertheless emerge."[30] In addition to "inject[ing] a certain amount of flexibility into the manpower commitments of the admin-istration of appellate justice," rotation dilutes personal conflicts and keeps coalitions "relatively fluid" in panels. It "hinders, if not pre-cludes, effective formation of stable sub-group patterns"; if panel membership were not rotated, each panel would develop "distinctive policy patterns, at odds with the other panels."[31] Personal conflict is avoided but "at the expense of institutional solidarity"; indeed, panel rotation can "breed diverse outcomes" and allow dissensus "to flourish among unanimous panels. . . . The more . . . disagreement is dispersed among panels, the more diffuse becomes circuit policy." More generally, rotation, which "pluralize[s]" the appellate courts, is to those courts "what regionalism is to the whole [judicial system]—a decentralizing and destabilizing force."[32]

"Behavioral norms enforced by peer groups" also affect levels of disagreement. Many circuit judges do not regard this as the major factor, with most judges "not hesitat[ing] to dissent if they thought their protest would influence the Supreme Court or another circuit."[33] Yet because a dissent in the court of appeals is less likely to be used by the court's judges in the future than is a dissent in the Supreme Court, "the suppressed dissent is a more common phenomenon in an intermediate appellate court than in a court of last resort."[34] Also serving to depress dissent is an "unwritten rule . . . that judges must be able to reasonably justify their votes in their written opinions."[35] Dissenting is thus not merely a matter of casting a vote but entails the time-consuming task of writing a justificatory opinion. Similarly, dissent rate would be lowered by the view that judges should discuss a case "in a spirit of 'give-and-take' (or accommodation) in an effort to reach decisional consensus" without making disagreement public.[36] Psychological pressure on a would-be dissenter can serve as an effective reinforcement for these norms: in a three-judge panel, a judge must dissent alone, whereas in a larger court there is greater possibility that a colleague will join in the dissent.[37] As Burton Atkins notes, "The small group setting . . . places behavioral constraints upon the individual and subdues his inclination toward individuality."[38]

What about judges' attitudes? "Attitudes and values defined politically rather than legally" are important for understanding judges' votes in the courts of appeals; circuit judges Goldman interviewed "perceived attitudinal differences concerning various issues as being the cause of conflict in the appellate courts."[39] He found that in fiscal years 1962–64, judges' party affiliations were related to their judicial votes "notably when the issues involved economic liberalism," but demographic variables "such as religion, socio-economic origins, education, and age were . . . almost entirely unrelated directly to voting behavior."[40] However, "negative correlations were found between dissent and voting on civil liberties and on labor issues."[41]

Goldman also found that for 1965–71, "interrelated politically defined attitudes account for much of the overt conflict among courts of appeals judges."[42] In this later period, Democratic and Republican judges differed on civil liberties and criminal procedure in non-unanimous cases, although they had not earlier.[43] Although experience—separate from age—had little effect on dimensions of voting in 1965–71, older judges were "more conservative on the criminal procedures, civil liberties, labor, injured persons, political liberalism, economic liberalism and activism dimensions" than were younger judges.[44] Political party affiliation was the single most important background variable tested on all these dimensions except for activism, for which age was the most important. In the later period, unlike the earlier one, there were "no statistically significant correlations of dissent behavior to voting on any of the issues" so that "political and economic conservatives do not have a greater propensity for dissent than do political and economic liberals."[45] However, judges with previous judicial experience dissented less than those without such experience. Nonetheless, it is likely that differences in dissent rates between circuits are "a result of the different attitudinal predispositions of the judges and the particular combinations of judges on the panels."[46]

THE NINTH CIRCUIT

Inconsistency. The Ninth Circuit has been used as an example of a court in which, according to former Solicitor General Erwin Griswold, a prior decision on a question "makes no difference" because another panel "may take a different view of the problem," even after the problem was "quite specifically pointed out to them." Indeed, alleged Griswold, "in the Ninth Circuit very little attention was paid to the question of intracircuit conflicts," with "another panel ten days later deciding essentially the same question the other way without any reference to the first case."[47]

Although most Ninth Circuit judges I interviewed differed with Griswold about the magnitude of inconsistency, they felt that intracircuit inconsistency occurred more frequently in some areas of the law than in others.[48] Judges' attitudes or ideologies were thought to be the principal cause of inconsistency in the Ninth Circuit. Most of the ideological disagreement to which attention was called was not on partisan Democratic-Republican grounds—although some judges said they could tell when "staunch Republicans" were on the panel in NLRB cases—but the result of "strong philosophical disagreements." Such disagreements were reinforced because, although many judges were content to adhere closely to existing circuit precedent, others were "advocates, always trying to make a point, trying to move the court over to their position, to change the law of the circuit."

For example, the presence on a panel of one or two judges who, according to their critics, "want[ed] to reverse all criminal cases" led to "trouble like a conjunction of stars" requiring an *en banc* sitting of the court. "Some judges have higher thresholds of indignation" than others, particularly in the area of search and seizure: "Some feel all wiretapping is evil and resolve all cases against the government"; others resolve all cases for the government, "which is trying to protect us," or, as stated by a self-styled "strict constructionist" judge, some want to "help defendants and punish the police or punish defendants and help the police." When judges have "different notions of justice" that "reflect different approaches in society," they cannot be convinced to change their minds about such notions, which also serve to color their perceptions about facts and how they apply the law to the facts.

Other frequently mentioned major causes of inconsistency were the size of the court's caseload, which often led to different panels dealing with the same issues, and the increased number of judges needed to process that caseload, which created difficulty in coordinating the flow of information within the court. As one judge put it, "The bigger the court, the more difficult it is to arrive at consensus." Ninth Circuit judges generally agreed that the participation of district judges and of the circuit's own senior appellate judges did not contribute to inconsistency; opinion concerning visiting judges was divided.[49] District judges, if contributing to inconsistency at all, did so "no more than [did] the mingling of the court's own judges" or only "idiosyncratically" or in "aberrational circumstances." District judges might dissent, but such dissents did not "contribute to differences between panels." A minority of circuit judges, however, were critical of district judges as unaware of trends in circuit law and thus "out of step." One judge, who felt the court lost "harmony of decision and integrity of precedent" when a "whole lot of strangers are dabbling in writing law," said district judges' presence also created "uncertainty" about circuit precedent.

Disagreement. Prior studies reveal very low levels of disagreement in the U.S. courts of appeals. In fiscal years 1962–64, the proportion of nonunanimous decisions ranged from 2.8 percent in the Sixth Circuit to 15.5 percent in the District of Columbia Circuit.[50] The District of Columbia Circuit again had the highest rate of disagreement (13.2 percent) in 1965–71; it was the only circuit in which more than 10 percent of the decisions were nonunanimous. The Seventh Circuit had a disagreement rate of just under 10 percent, and three others had rates of disagreement of roughly 7.5 percent; the rest disagreed less than 5 percent of the time.[51] These figures are small in absolute terms and certainly small by comparison with the U.S. Supreme Court, less than half of whose decisions were unanimous.

Another study showed dissents in only 6.2 percent of cases across all circuits in 1965–69.[52] The frequency of separate concurring opinions was even lower than the frequency of dissents; they appeared in only 2.9 percent of all cases, with "the rate of concurrence . . . almost perfectly correlated with the rate of dissent"—parallel to the finding that in the Second Circuit "the bulk of concurring opinions were written by the most frequent dissenters."[53]

Informal norms may provide an explanation for differences between dissent rates and rates of concurring opinions. For a judge who disagrees with his colleagues to register a dissent may not be considered inappropriate, particularly if principle is involved, but to rob a major opinion of some of its force through a separate concurring opinion may not be well regarded, and for a judge to divide a two-judge majority between two opinions is particularly disliked. A separate concurrence thus breaks unity far more in a three-judge panel than in a larger court such as the U.S. Supreme Court. This may explain why, in the Second Circuit, "the judges either settle their differences or, failing this, dissent," with partial dissents preferred over concurring opinions.[54]

The information presented here on the Ninth Circuit for calendar years 1970–75 is based on rulings by that court's three-judge panels; *en banc* rulings and the small number of decisions by two-judge panels are excluded. During 1970–75, three-judge panels of the U.S. Court of Appeals for the Ninth Circuit decided more than seven thousand cases. The great majority of the court's panels contained at least two circuit judges, whose votes were thus determinative in most of the court's cases. The Ninth Circuit's work was, however, no longer performed only by the court's own circuit judges, including senior circuit judges. District judges and senior district judges, who sat on well over half the court's panels, performed a significant and increasing role, although visiting judges played only a small if nonnegligible role. Statistics for the immediately preceding five years show that this general picture of participation by extra judges was true of other U.S. courts of appeals as well.[55]

The data base includes published decisions for 1970–75 and "Not for Publication" rulings for 1973–75. For 1970–72, published rulings include virtually all cases except those on preliminary motions and some other decisions such as affirmances of denied preliminary injunctions; even brief Memorandum Orders were published. It was not until late 1972 that the court adopted rules calling for the designation of certain cases as not for publication.

Because data from published cases alone would show a substantial decrease in cases decided after 1972, data on unpublished opinions after that time must be provided to present a more complete picture of the court's work. The court's calendaring procedures did not intentionally assign less important cases—those in which the opinions are more likely to be designated "Not for Publication"—to panels containing district or visiting judges. Thus it is possible that extra judges might participate more in one type than in the other, making it even more important to include both types of cases in the data base. Identification of circuit precedent is more difficult, and the possibility of the development of intracircuit inconsistency greater, when there is a decrease in the number of published opinions. This is true because it is in those opinions that doctrine is most clearly developed and because of the possibility that inconsistencies will be "buried" in unpublished rulings.[56]

In the Ninth Circuit, a case is designated "Not for Publication" by the panel deciding it, although the panel may defer to the opinion-writer's wishes in deciding whether or not to publish. Thus if a district judge writing for a panel is seized by the urge to see his or her name in "Fed Second" and other panel members defer to the "writing judge," allowing the case to be published, publication may be more, rather than less, likely for cases in which extra judges participate. Indeed, examination of the Ninth Circuit's publication record for 1973–75 shows that when a panel contained a senior circuit judge, cases were more likely to be published than if the panel contained three active-duty circuit judges. Similarly, cases decided by panels including senior district judges were also more likely to be published than cases decided by panels including active-duty district judges. The cases least likely to be published were those on which a visiting judge served.

In the following analysis, several practices have been followed. One is that concurrences are counted with disagreements. Although dissents—of which there are proportionately more than of concurrences—are stronger statements of disagreement that concurring votes and opinions, both break the unanimity of a three-judge panel. A second is that, despite the judge's recognition that inconsistency occurs more frequently in some areas of law, such as search and seizure, than in others, no decomposition of the cases by subject matter has been attempted. The principal reason is that, to provide sufficient instances of panels composed of particular combinations of judge-types in a particular year, extremely broad categories would have to be used. Few panels sit together for a substantial number of cases in any substantive categories of law where disagreement is meaningful to the judges. We also consider judges fungible within a given category of judges. That a particular judge might account for a nonnegligible proportion of the participation by a category, for example, senior district judges or visiting judges, is not factored into the analysis. Such differences may account for some of the year-by-year variation evident in the data, but this is not likely because of the number of different judges who participated in the Ninth Circuit's cases.

Disagreement: An Overall View. In the Ninth Circuit for 1970–75, disagreement was registered in only 6.4 percent of all cases, both published and unpublished; the rate was somewhat lower at the end of the period than at the beginning. (Although Ninth Circuit judges easily recognized that disagreement in the courts of appeals is lower than in the Supreme Court, many did not think the level was low, an indication of the importance of one's perceptions of the level of disagreement.) Once the court began regular use of unpublished opinions, there was a much higher rate of disagreement—more than 10 percent in both 1973 and 1974—in published cases, while the disagreement rate for unpublished cases was substantially less (3.3 percent in 1973, 1.3 percent in 1974). This pattern was like that in the 1978–79 reporting year for all circuits; there was much more dissidence in published than in not for publication opinions, with separate opinions in 12.4 percent of published cases (range: 2.8–21.1 percent) and 0.5 percent of the unpublished opinions (range: 0–1.5 percent).[57] Most Ninth Circuit disagreements were dissents, with a ratio of roughly 3:1 or 4:1. Over the six-year period, the proportion of concurrences to total disagreements in published cases was roughly one-fourth in the first four years but rose to just over two-fifths in 1975. Concurrences accounted for between 25 and 30 percent of all disagreements in unpublished cases for 1973–75.

Reversing our focus, we find that cases in which disagreement was registered were more likely to be published than were cases in which the panel unanimously agreed on a single opinion. In 1973, although three-fifths of all cases decided by panels of three circuit judges were unpublished, three-fifths of the cases in which such panels disagreed were published. In 1974, with two-thirds of their decisions unpublished, all cases in which disagreement was registered were published. The pattern for cases decided by panels containing a senior circuit judge is not dissimilar. Roughly half of all the cases were unpublished for the three years, but of the cases in which there was disagreement, from three-fourths to just under 90 percent were published. For cases on which district judges, senior district judges, and visiting judges served, in all three years only a relatively small percentage containing disagreement were not published.

Differences between the rates of disagreement appearing in published and unpublished cases may result in large measure from a Ninth Circuit rule. One criterion is that publication should not occur unless an opinion "is accompanied by a separate concurring or dissenting expression, and the author of such separate expression desires that it be reported or distributed to regular subscribers" (Rule 21(b) (6)). Thus disagreement would make publication more likely, but, as the latter clause indicates, a judge writing a separate opinion might not press for publication, and some disagreement does appear in unpublished cases.

Variation was evident in the forms of disagreement among categories of judges. Roughly one-third of the disagreements circuit judges registered in published cases were concurrences; for unpublished opinions, the proportion was only slightly lower. Only one-fifth of senior circuit judges' disagreements took the form of separate concurrences. (For unpublished opinions, except for those of circuit judges, the number of disagreements was too small for percentages to be meaningful.) Roughly one-fourth of disagreements by district judges and senior district judges combined were concurring opinions; district judges were somewhat more likely to dissent and senior district judges somewhat more likely to concur, making the latter more like circuit judges in this regard. Almost all visiting judges' disagreements were dissents.

Circuit judges disagreed in 3 percent of their sittings; the chief judge, Richard Chambers, had a slightly higher disagreement rate, fluctuating around 4 percent. Rates varied from year to year for the other categories of judges. Senior circuit judges registered disagreements in just over 1 percent of their sittings in 1971 but in over 5 percent of their sittings in 1974. District judges' disagreements rose to under 5 percent of their sittings in 1975 but with only one other exception were just under 3 percent. Senior district judges' disagreements fell in the latter half of the period; after being over 4 percent of their sittings from 1970 to 1972, the figure dropped to nearly 3 percent in 1973 and 1974, then to just over 1 percent in 1975. In part a function of a small number of sittings, the fluctuation for visiting judges was particularly great. They registered no disagreements in two years (1970 and 1974) but disagreed almost 10 percent of the times they sat in 1972.

The rate of disagreement as a percentage of sittings in published cases rose over the period for circuit judges and senior circuit judges and for district judges but not for senior district judges or for visiting judges. For circuit judges, the rate of disagreement increased from roughly 3 percent to just under 5 percent in 1973 and to almost 7 percent in 1974; for senior circuit judges it rose over 5 percent in 1973 and over 9 percent in 1974 before falling to only 3 percent in 1975, roughly the same level as before the practice of not publishing cases. Starting in 1973, district judges' disagreement rate was roughly twice pre-1973 levels and in 1975 increased to almost 10 percent.

If we look at specific combinations of categories of judges, we find that for the entire six-year period, there was disagreement in only slightly over 5 percent of the cases decided by panels of three circuit judges. Their highest level of agreement was in 1972 (97.2 percent of the cases), the lowest level in 1970 (91.8 percent agreement). For 1973–75, there was less disagreement in unpublished cases than in published ones—2.3 percent against 8.7 percent.

The overall level of agreement for the six years was roughly the same for all combinations of judges other than three circuit judges, but there are some minor differences between them (see Table 7.1). Although the agreement level was exactly the same for panels of two circuit judges and a senior circuit judge as for panels of three circuit judges, it was slightly lower for other combinations and lowest (just under 92 percent) for panels with two circuit judges and a visiting judge. There are, however, somewhat greater differences across dif-

Table 7.1. Percentage of Agreement in the U.S. Court of Appeals for the Ninth Circuit

Year	C-C-C	%	C-C-SCJ	%	C-C-DJ	%	C-SCJ-DJ	%	C-C-SDJ	%	C-SCJ-SDJ	%	C-C-VJ	%	OTHER	%	TOTAL	%
								Published Opinions										
1970	402/36	91.8	66/2	97.1	303/18	94.4	2/0	100	75/9	89.3	1/0	100	47/3	94.0	1/0	100	897/68	93.0
1971	416/30	93.3	239/12	95.2	184/13	93.4	62/3	95.4	50/4	92.6	22/2	91.7	55/4	93.2	51/3	94.4	1079/71	93.8
1972	281/8	97.2	191/15	92.7	205/20	91.1	64/8	88.9	81/4	95.3	19/5	79.2	38/6	86.3	30/5	85.7	909/71	92.7
1970-72	1099/74	93.7	496/29	94.2	692/51	92.6	128/11	91.4	206/17	91.7	42/7	83.3	140/13	90.7	82/8	90.2	2885/210	92.7
1973	120/7	94.5	73/8	90.1	131/30	81.4	43/4	91.4	83/8	91.2	40/4	90.9	27/6	81.8	17/0	100	534/67	88.9
1974	81/9	90.0	63/9	87.5	158/24	86.8	54/6	90.0	91/12	88.3	26/5	83.8	19/6	76.0	17/4	81.0	509/75	87.2
1975	53/6	89.8	74/4	94.9	169/15	91.8	44/9	83.0	91/9	90.0	40/1	97.6	56/6	90.3	37/2	94.9	564/52	91.2
1973-75	254/22	91.3	210/21	90.0	458/69	84.9	141/19	86.5	265/29	89.1	106/10	90.6	102/18	82.4	71/6	91.5	1607/194	87.9
TOTAL	1353/96	92.9	706/50	92.9	1150/120	89.6	269/30	88.8	471/46	90.2	148/17	88.5	242/31	87.2	153/14	90.8	4492/404	91.0

Table 7.1. Continued

Year	C-C-C	%	C-C-SCJ	%	C-C-DJ	%	C-SCJ-DJ	%	C-C-SDJ	%	C-SCJ-SDJ	%	C-C-VJ	%	OTHER	%	TOTAL	%
							Not for Publication Decisions											
1973	190/7	96.4	68/4	94.4	216/6	97.3	43/1	97.7	102/3	97.1	18/0	100	31/2	93.9	8/0	100	676/23	96.7
1974	172/0	100	66/2	97.0	286/2	99.3	82/2	97.6	136/3	97.8	23/1	95.8	49/1	98.0	13/0	100	827/11	98.7
1975	70/3	95.9	85/0	100	236/11	95.5	60/0	100	107/4	96.4	46/0	100	67/3	95.7	22/0	100	693/21	97.1
TOTAL	432/10	97.7	219/6	97.3	738/19	97.4	185/3	98.4	345/10	97.1	87/1	98.9	147/6	95.9	43/0	100	2196/55	97.6
GRAND TOTAL	1784/106	94.4	921/55	94.4	1,884/139	93.1	457/32	93.5	800/53	93.8	239/18	93.0	385/34	91.9	196/17	92.0	6656/456	93.6

Key: C = Circuit judge
SCJ = Senior circuit judge
DJ = District judge
SDJ = Senior district judge
VJ = Visiting judge

Note: The figures are for the number of cases in which there was agreement over the number of cases in which there was disagreement. Hence for 1970 published cases decided by three circuit judges, there were 402 cases in which the panels agreed and 36 in which they did not, for a total of 438 (91.8 percent agreement).

ferently composed panels on a year-by-year basis. For example, in 1970, compared to only 7.2 percent disagreement for panels of three circuit judges, disagreement occurred in just over 10 percent of the cases when a senior district judge sat with two circuit judges, and there was only 2.9 percent disagreement when a senior circuit judge sat with two circuit judges. In 1972, panels of three circuit judges registered less than 3 percent disagreement, those with two circuit judges and a district judge had a much higher disagreement rate (8.9 percent), and disagreement occurred in 13.7 percent of the cases when a visiting judge sat with two circuit judges. Disagreement was also high when there were two extra judges on a panel instead of only one. Combinations of a circuit judge, senior circuit judge, and district judge registered disagreement more than 10 percent of the time they sat together; disagreement exceeded one-fifth when a circuit judge and a senior circuit judge sat with a senior district judge, somewhat higher than the rate for 1970–72 (one-sixth of their cases).

In 1973, when either a district judge or a visiting judge joined two circuit judges, higher levels of disagreement (11.6 and 12.1 percent respectively) were likely than for three circuit judges, with disagreement registered disproportionately in published cases—just under 20 percent for both panel combinations. The pattern was similar in 1974, when, although the number of cases was small, for panels of two circuit judges and a visiting judge, disagreement occurred in almost one-fourth of the cases. In that year, the combination showing the highest overall disagreement rate was that of circuit judge, senior circuit judge, and senior district judge; they disagreed in just over 10 percent of all cases and in 16.2 percent of published ones. That this category of panel registered very little disagreement the following year, 1975, with none in unpublished cases, is illustrative of year-by-year fluctuation.

Published cases for 1973–75 decided by panels of three circuit judges showed lower percentages of disagreement than those decided by other frequent combinations. The highest level of disagreement (17.6 percent) was found in panels with two circuit judges and a visiting judge, with panels of two circuit judges and a district judge close behind (15.1 percent). Panels of two circuit judges and a senior district judge registered only 10.9 percent disagreement, still more than that by panels of three circuit judges. Also registering more than 10 percent disagreement in published cases during this period were panels of a circuit judge, senior circuit judge, and district judge (13.5 percent).

Disposition of Cases. We now turn to the relation between disposition of cases and disagreement and to the question of whether some categories of judges participate more in reversals than do others. In the Second, Fifth, and District of Columbia circuits in the mid-1960s, dissents were "more likely when Courts of Appeals disturbed (14%) than affirmed (6%) decisions below."[58] In another study, neither the hypothesis that senior circuit judges, district judges, and visiting judges would be less likely to participate in courts of appeals rulings vacating or reversing the court below nor the hypothesis that district judges would be less likely to reverse their own colleagues was sustained; there was "no notable tendency for panels composed solely of circuit judges to reverse the court below, compared to panels including a designated judge. Nor is there clear evidence of reluctance on the part of designated judges to vacate or reverse a judgment,"[59] although there was a slight tendency for panels with a senior circuit judge to be more likely to reverse and those with a district judge to be somewhat less likely to reverse.

A court of appeals has available a variety of dispositions in addition to "Affirm" and "Reverse." In tabulating the data, I have combined "Affirm" and "Affirm and Remand" (designated affirmances) and "Reverse," "Reverse and Remand," and "Remand" (designated reversals). "Affirm in part, Reverse in part" has been added to the reversals because they indicate at least some disagreement with the district court, although others have assigned such partial affirmances a weight midway between affirmances and reversals and still others have counted them as affirmances.[60] Instances in which the court vacated or vacated and remanded court rulings are also added to reversals in the data presented in Table 7.2. The court might also dismiss appeals, deny petitions for rehearing, and grant or deny enforcement of Labor Board orders, shown separately in the table.

Disagreement is registered in a higher percentage of reversals than affirmances, both overall and generally year by year for the various combinations of judges. Most exceptions are found in combinations of judges accounting for only small numbers of cases. Published and not for publication rulings are combined here, but published opinions contain roughly twice the proportion of reversals that unpublished rulings contain.[61]

For the six-year totals, for all combinations of judges, the rate of disagreement was usually twice as high or higher for cases in which the

Table 7.2. Disposition of Cases, U.S. Court of Appeals for the Ninth Circuit

Disposition	C-C-C	%	C-C-SCJ	%	C-C-DJ	%	C-SCJ-DJ	%	C-C-SDJ	%	C-SCJ-SDJ	%	C-C-VJ	%	OTHER	%	TOTAL	%
Affirm[a]	1255/51	96.1	640/26	96.1	1337/75	94.7	330/10	97.1	548/25	95.6	164/12	93.2	288/16	94.7	128/7	94.8	4690/222	95.5
Reverse[b]	340/47	87.9	180/23	88.7	400/55	87.9	84/19	81.6	181/19	90.5	42/6	87.5	81/13	86.2	47/8	85.5	1335/190	87.5
Vacate[c]	50/3	94.3	25/1	96.1	43/3	93.5	4/0	100	27/4	87.1	11/0	100	8/3	72.7	5/0	100	173/14	92.5
Re + Va[d]	390/50	88.6	205/24	89.5	443/58	88.4	88/19	82.2	198/23	89.6	53/6	89.8	89/16	84.8	52/8	86.7	1508/204	88.1
Dismiss	70/1	98.6	37/0	100	40/3	93.0	17/1	94.4	13/0	100	7/0	100	3/1	75.0	7/0	100	194/6	97.0
EO[e]	49/3	94.2	33/4	89.1	53/3	94.6	21/2	91.3	36/4	90.0	12/0	100	5/0	100	8/1	88.9	217/15	93.5
Petition																		
Denied	20/1	95.2	6/1	83.3	11/0	100	1/0	100	5/1	83.3	3/0	100	0/1	-0-	1/1	50.0	47/5	90.3
TOTAL	1,784/106	94.4	921/55	94.4	1,884/139	93.1	457/32	93.5	800/53	93.8	239/18	93.0	385/34	91.9	196/17	92.0	6,656/452	93.6

Note: For explanation of presentation of figures, see note to table 7.1.
[a]Includes affirm and remand.
[b]Includes remand, reverse and remand, and affirm in part/reverse in part.
[c]Includes vacate and remand
[d]Reverse and vacate combined
[e]Enforcement of order granted or denied.

court reversed than when it affirmed the lower court. In reversals, panels of two circuit judges and either a senior circuit judge or senior district judge registered disagreement less often than did panels of three circuit judges or two circuit judges and a district judge. Panels of a circuit judge, senior circuit judge, and district judge showed the greatest rate of disagreement in reversals (18.4 percent), more than six times their disagreement rate in affirming the lower court. Panels of two circuit judges and a district judge in 1971 and panels of two circuit judges and a senior circuit judge in 1974 were the only combinations deciding more than a small number of published cases in which the pattern of higher disagreement in reversal cases was not borne out.

It has been strongly suggested that district judges are more likely to affirm than to reverse the trial court because of their "institutional loyalty" to the district court and their own sensitivity to being reversed, although senior district judges are thought to be more neutral toward district judges than are their active-duty colleagues.[62] Thus we need to examine what categories of judges are most likely to disagree in reversals. Circuit judges' suggestions that when a panel reversing the trial court registers disagreement, extra judges are more likely to dissent (thus voting in the direction of affirming their district court colleagues) than to join the majority are not borne out. In 1970–72, district judges on nonunanimous panels did not lean more to affirmance or reversal in dissent than when they were part of the majority. In published cases in 1974, such district judges did behave somewhat as it was suggested they would, that is, they were somewhat more likely to affirm than were their circuit judge colleagues, but in 1973 and 1975, when they dissented in nonunanimous reversals, they were somewhat more likely to reverse their district court colleagues than were dissenting circuit judges with whom they served. (Among the unpublished opinions in 1975, the three dissenters would have affirmed, with the majority more likely to reverse—only weak support for the judges' suggestions.)

Behavior of senior district judges shows support for the hypothesis only in 1974 published cases, but the number of cases is very small. In the other years, when differences existed, a dissenting senior district judge was more likely to reverse than were dissenting appellate colleagues. Visiting judges either did not dissent in reversals or their participation was too infrequent to allow a test of the hypothesis except in 1972, when they showed a slight tendency to be more likely than circuit judges to affirm in dissent.

A hypothesis is that former district judges among the circuit judges will sympathize with district judges more than will appellate judges without such prior experience and thus will be less likely to reverse; a competing hypothesis is that former district judges now on the appellate court, having had a greater chance to acclimate themselves to court of appeals work, will be less deferential to district judges than will district judges sitting with the appellate court by designation. For 1970–72, we find no differences between Ninth Circuit judges who were former district judges and their colleagues who lacked district court experience. In 1973 published cases, the former district judges were more likely to affirm the trial court when they dissented than were their colleagues when they were in dissent. (In unpublished opinions for 1973–75, no pattern was visible.)

One must be careful not to make sweeping statements on the basis of this relatively limited set of data from several years of cases from a single appellate court. Nevertheless, such in-depth examination is important—indeed, necessary—for a more complete picture of appellate court inconsistency and disagreement. This study of the U.S. Court of Appeals for the Ninth Circuit shows a perspective from inside the court that what intracircuit inconsistency exists is concentrated in several areas of the law rather than affecting (and infecting) all areas of the law and is not a major problem. As one would expect from previous studies, the level of disagreement in the court is also low. Yet there is noticeable variation in rates of disagreement from one category of judge or combination of categories to another and fluctuation from one year to another. No particular category or combination stands out as having a particularly high disagreement rate, although some combinations registered more disagreement than did panels of three circuit judges—perhaps an indication of a modestly disruptive effect of the presence of extra judges. Because of the expectation that district judges' votes would be skewed in the direction of affirmance, an important finding is that they did not disproportionately vote to affirm their district court colleagues.

Adoption of the position that the law can develop only or largely through disagreement and "inconsistency" leads one to view the picture presented here not as demonstrating major difficulties of integrating a court with many participants, but perhaps instead indicating a leavening effect assisting in the law's development. There is, however, enough disagreement and inconsistency that we can say, first, that this large appellate court does not feel—and is not—burdened by an overweening concern with uniformity; second, that the judges' minds thus are not "small"; and, last, that at least certain hobgoblins have not been bothering the Ninth Circuit, however much they have been haunting the court's critics.

I wish to acknowledge the assistance of Becky Colford, John Rink, Jesse Brown, George Dirks, Susan Hickman, and Michael Wepsiec in coding and creating the tables. Financial assistance for this project from the Office of Research and Projects, Southern Illinois University at Carbondale, is also gratefully acknowledged. Finally, I wish to thank Joel B. Grossman for his comments and Sheldon Goldman for his helpful suggestions.

1. See *Maryland v. Marzullo*, 435 U.S. 1011 at 1013 (1975); *Brown Transport Corp. v. Atcon, Inc.*, 439 U.S. 1014 at 1015-26 (Justice White), 1026-33 (Chief Justice Burger).

2. See Commission on Revision of the Federal Court Appellate System, *Hearings: Phase One* (Washington, D.C., 1973), and *Hearings: Second Phase, 1974-1975* (Washington, D.C., 1975), passim.

3. Commission on Revision of the Federal Court Appellate System, *Structure and Internal Procedure: Recommendations for Change* (Washington, D.C., 1975), p. A-59. In a "strong" partial conflict, a court decides a case "in the same general area of the law as some other case and . . . the implications of the doctrine followed in one case would compel an opposite result in the other" but "the points involved are not exactly the same."

4. Stephen L. Wasby, "Inconsistency in the United States Courts of Appeals: Dimensions and Mechanisms for Resolution," *Vanderbilt Law Review* 32 (1979): 1343-73.

5. J. Woodford Howard, Jr., *Courts of Appeals in the Federal Judicial System: A Study of the Second, Fifth, and District of Columbia Circuits* (Princeton: Princeton University Press, 1981), p. 81.

6. John Paul Stevens, remarks at the American Judicature Society banquet, San Francisco, August 6, 1982, p. 14.

7. See Burton M. Atkins and Justin J. Green, "Consensus on the United States Courts of Appeals: Illusion or Reality?" *American Journal of Political Science* 20 (1976): 735-48.

8. See Commission on Revision of the Federal Appellate Court System, *Structure and Internal Procedure*, p. A-8.

9. Arthur D. Hellman, "Central Staff in Appellate Courts: The Experience of the Ninth Circuit," *California Law Review* 68 (1980): 959.

10. Sheldon Goldman, "Conflict and Consensus in the United States Courts of

Appeals," *Wisconsin Law Review* (1968): 477; Howard, *Courts of Appeals,* pp. 57-59, 65-67.

11. See John P. McIver, "Scaling Judicial Decisions: The Panel Decision-Making Process of the U.S. Courts of Appeals," *American Journal of Political Science* 20 (1976): 749-61.

12. Alvin B. Rubin, "Views from the Lower Court," *UCLA Law Review* 23 (1976): 452.

13. Marvin Schick, *Learned Hand's Court* (Baltimore: Johns Hopkins University Press, 1970), p. 309.

14. Ibid., p. 114.

15. Rubin, "Views from the Lower Court," p. 452. Schick notes an instance in which all three panel members went along with an earlier 2-1 ruling although all three agreed with the earlier minority position. Schick, *Learned Hand's Court,* p. 114. See *Dickinson* v. *Mulligan,* 173 F.2d 738 (2d Cir. 1949), rev'd sub nom. *Dickinson* v. *Petroleum Conversion Corp.,* 339 U.S. 508 (1950).

16. Howard, *Courts of Appeals,* p. 210.

17. Ibid., pp. 193-94.

18. Ibid., p. 194. See also Justin J. Green, "Parameters of Dissensus on Shifting Small Groups," Chapter 6 of this volume.

19. Robert J. Sickels, "The Illusion of Judicial Consensus: Zoning Decisions in the Maryland Court of Appeals," *American Political Science Review* 69 (1965): 101.

20. See Burton M. Atkins and William Zavoina, "Judicial Leadership on the Courts of Appeals: A Probability Analysis of Panel Assignments in Race Relations Cases on the Fifth Circuit," *American Journal of Political Science* 18 (1975): pp. 701-11; Howard, *Courts of Appeals,* pp. 235-55, esp. 247-53.

21. Howard, *Courts of Appeals,* p. 193.

22. Sheldon Goldman, "Conflict on the U.S. Courts of Appeals 1965-1971: A Quantitative Analysis," *University of Cincinnati Law Review* 42 (1973): 639.

23. Howard, *Courts of Appeals,* p. 205.

24. Sheldon Goldman, "Voting Behavior on the United States Courts of Appeals Revisited," *American Political Science Review* 69 (1975): 493, n. 9.

25. See Stephen L. Wasby, " 'Extra' Judges in a Federal Appeals Court: The Ninth Circuit," *Law and Society Review* 15 (1980-81): 376.

26. Burton M. Atkins, "Decision-Making Rules and Judicial Strategy on the United States Courts of Appeals," *Western Political Quarterly* 25 (1972): 630. But see Wasby, "Inconsistency," pp. 1360-63.

27. Burton M. Atkins and Justin J. Green, "Problems in the Measurement of Conflict on the United States Courts of Appeals," paper delivered at the Annual Meeting of the American Political Science Association, August 29-September 2, 1974, Chicago, pp. 20, 22.

28. Justin J. Green and Burton M. Atkins, "Designated Judges: How Well Do They Perform?" *Judicature* 61 (1978): 368-69.

29. Ibid., p. 368.

30. Atkins and Green, "Consensus," p. 740.

31. Atkins, "Decision-Making Rules," p. 629.

32. Howard, *Courts of Appeals*, pp. 190, 194, 220.

33. Ibid., p. 205.

34. Paul Carrington, "Crowded Dockets and the Courts of Appeals: The Threat to the Functions of Review and the National Law," *Harvard Law Review* 84 (1969): 562.

35. Goldman, "Conflict and Consensus," p. 478.

36. Ibid., p. 479.

37. See Atkins and Green, "Consensus," p. 738, n. 2.

38. Burton M. Atkins, "Judicial Behavior and Tendencies towards Conformity in a Three Member Small Group: A Case Study of Dissent Behavior on the U.S. Court of Appeals," *Social Science Quarterly* 54 (1973): 43.

39. Goldman, "Voting Behavior Revisited," p. 495; Goldman, "Conflict and Consensus," p. 475.

40. Sheldon Goldman, "Voting Behavior on the United States Courts of Appeals, 1961-1964," *American Political Science Review* 60 (1966): 382.

41. Goldman, "Voting Behavior Revisited," p. 495, n. 12.

42. Goldman, "Conflict 1965-1971," p. 656.

43. Goldman, "Voting Behavior Revisited," p. 497.

44. Ibid., p. 499.

45. Ibid., p. 495.

46. Goldman, "Conflict 1965-1971," pp. 656-57.

47. Commission on Revision of the Federal Court Appellate System, *Hearings: Phase One*, pp. 10, 28, 468.

48. During the spring of 1977, I conducted interviews with fifteen Ninth Circuit appellate judges (all but one of the eleven active-duty judges then serving), five senior circuit judges, and ten district judges from California and Oregon. Material appearing in quotation marks without attribution is drawn from the interview transcripts.

49. For a more complete picture see Wasby, " 'Extra' Judges," pp. 373-81.

50. Goldman, "Conflict and Consensus," p. 464.

51. Goldman, "Conflict 1965-1971," p. 638.

52. Atkins and Green, "Consensus," p. 742.

53. Atkins and Green, "Problems," p. 17; Schick, *Learned Hand's Court*, p. 316.

54. Schick, *Learned Hand's Court*, p. 313.

55. Green and Atkins, "Designated Judges."

56. James N. Gardner, "Ninth Circuit's Unpublished Opinions: Denial of Equal Justice," *American Bar Association Journal* 61 (1975): 1224-27; see also Daniel N. Hoffman, "Nonpublication of Federal Appellate Court Opinions," *Justice System Journal* 6 (1981): 415-16.

57. William L. Reynolds and William M. Richman, "Limited Publication in the Fourth and Sixth Circuits," *Duke Law Journal* (1979): 829; William L. Reynolds and William M. Richman, "An Evaluation of Limited Publication in the United States Courts of Appeals: The Price of Reform," *University of Chicago Law Review* 48 (1981): 613.

58. Howard, *Courts of Appeals*, p. 42.

59. Green and Atkins, "Designated Judges," p. 366.

60. For the latter, see Reynolds and Richman, "Evaluation," p. 824, n. 71. They also indicated a "nonaffirmance" rate by adding these cases to reversals. In the Fourth Circuit, in 1978-79, the nonaffirmance rate in published cases was 42 percent (28.9 percent when partial reversals are not counted as reversals); in the Sixth Circuit, the nonaffirmance rate in published cases was 37 percent (32 percent).

61. In the Fourth Circuit, more than one-fourth of the published opinions (28.9 percent) were reversals; for unpublished opinions the rate was only 4 percent. In the Sixth Circuit, the ratio was smaller but the direction was the same: in published opinions almost one-third (32 percent) reversals, but in unpublished opinions only 12 percent reversals. See Reynolds and Richman, "Limited Publication," p. 823.

62. See Green and Atkins, "Designated Judges," p. 365; Wasby, " 'Extra' Judges," pp. 379-80.

8

A Microlevel Analysis of Appeals Court Conflict: Warren Burger and His Colleagues on the D.C. Circuit

CHARLES M. LAMB

In this chapter, as in Stephen Wasby's, one court of appeals is examined in detail to promote an understanding of specific aspects of judicial conflict. Conflict is operationally defined and measured here in terms of voting disagreement. The magnitude of judicial conflict thus increases in direct proportion to increases in the percentage of cases decided nonunanimously. No attempt is made to develop and test an overarching theory of judicial conflict, which ideally should include a number of variables, as other contributors to this book explain in their chapters. Rather, the goal is to look at some largely unexplored dimensions of conflict in a court of appeals that has witnessed a very high level of dissent over time, while simultaneously recognizing some problems associated with investigating appeals court voting behavior at the microlevel.[1]

Political science literature on the courts of appeals was surveyed to determine which of these courts has experienced the greatest magnitude of disagreement over time. Burton Atkins found that the rate of conflict on the District of Columbia Circuit between 1956 and 1962 made it the best candidate for quantitative investigation. Sheldon Goldman's research also indicates greater conflict on the D.C. Circuit than on any other between 1962 and 1971. Both Atkins and Goldman additionally concluded that criminal justice cases stimulated more conflict on the D.C. Circuit than did any other single cluster of issues.[2] Their conclusions are consistent with those of Donald Songer in Chapter 5 of this volume.

Table 8.1. Conflict in *En Banc* and Three-Judge Criminal Justice Panels, 1956-1969

Year	Total Number of *En Banc* Decisions	Percent Decided Nonunanimously	Total Number of Dissenting Votes in *En Banc* Decisions	Percent of Dissenting Votes in *En Banc* Decisions	Total Number of Three-Judge Panel Decisions	Percent Decided Nonunanimously
1956	3	66.7	5	18.5	19	52.6
1957	4	100.0	15	41.7	24	29.2
1958	4	100.0	13	36.1	25	52.0
1959	6	83.3	12	22.2	27	18.5
1960	2	100.0	7	38.9	23	30.4
1961	7	85.7	17	27.0	17	23.5
1962	6	100.0	15	27.8	39	15.4
1963	9	55.6	10	12.3	43	18.6
1964	5	100.0	17	37.8	31	48.4
1965	8	100.0	28	39.4	28	42.9
1966	2	50.0	2	11.8	28	39.3
1967	3	100.0	7	29.2	27	18.5
1968	1	100.0	2	25.0	36	30.6
1969	1	100.0	4	44.4	18	38.9
Totals	61	86.9	154	28.3	385	32.8

Because of these findings, criminal justice cases decided by the D.C. Circuit between 1956 and 1969 were selected as the general focus of this chapter. The broader objective is to probe the relationship between voting conflict and (1) lower court reversals and (2) appeals court outputs in a way that has received little attention in literature on appeals courts. These were also the years when Warren E. Burger served on the D.C. Circuit before his elevation to the Supreme Court. As a more specific focus, to clarify the lower court experience of the chief justice, emphasis is placed on the relationship between voting conflict and judges' background traits and on voting disagreement between Burger and his colleagues over time and on five major criminal justice issues.

APPROACH, DATA, AND THEIR LIMITATIONS

The microlevel approach relied on in this study has both advantages and disadvantages. A principal advantage is that it may be used to explore detailed aspects or extreme degrees of conflict, particularly that involving specific issues within a broader data set. Such amplification is not possible in macrolevel studies and is useful for in-depth analysis of prominent appeals court judges. A disadvantage, however, is that the data base is small and is spread over fourteen years during which the D.C. Circuit experienced five turnovers in personnel. The small number of observations in certain years and the absence of one natural court limit the testing of some possible hypotheses and the application of certain statistics. Inferential statistics and the reporting of levels of significance are not used in this chapter because the complete population is the data base and there is no generalizing to other courts. Any statistic that rests for its interpretation on a level of significance attempts to determine how often a certain pattern will be present in a population based on the analysis of a sample. If, however, one has the entire population, drawing statistical inferences is not essential.

Table 8.1 allows a detailed description of some of the data which Atkins, Goldman, and Songer analyzed primarily at the macrolevel. Because of the focus on Burger, the data base consists of all criminal justice cases in which he participated over the fourteen-year period, including unanimous and nonunanimous three-judge and *en banc* panel decisions. Defining the focus in this manner results in a data set of 61 *en banc* and 385 three-judge decisions.[3] Column 3 shows that court members were divided in 86.9 percent of the *en banc* panels—a striking level of disagreement for any court, even surpassing the overall dissent rate on the Supreme Court for any term on which data are available.[4] One could argue that since complex, controversial issues are more often adjudicated *en banc,* conflict in those cases is naturally more discernible than on three-judge panels, but that argument is inadequate to account for the extremely high rate of dissent found here. Yet, though conflict was a normal occurrence in these *en banc* decisions, the size of dissenting groups was frequently small (column 5). In contrast, conflict occurred in 32.8 percent of all three-judge panels (column 7). This figure is also very high for a court of appeals, in which split decisions typically occur in less than 10 percent of all cases.[5] It is relevant to recall here that in the research reported in Chapter 5 Songer discovered an overall dissent rate of more than 22 percent in all criminal cases decided by the D.C. Circuit from 1959 to 1970, but after Burger left the court the dissent rate dropped to 13.4 percent.

Consistent with this chapter's approach, two other points should be mentioned about Table 8.1. Since the magnitude of conflict is almost three times more likely to occur in *en banc* than in three-judge panels, one might conclude that this finding is related to small group studies which suggest that judges may behave differently in different environments or that the size and composition of panels may affect voting. Among other things, the literature indicates that when the *en banc* procedure is employed, judges may feel more at ease in dissenting if they can gain the support of at least one colleague.[6] Yet such a conclusion here is fraught with difficulties. Although the data confirm findings that frequent use of the *en banc* procedure tends to underscore intracourt conflict,[7] small group dynamics cannot explain the oscillations in magnitude of conflict because different judges were usually interacting on different three-member panels. To draw a small group inference, the same judges must serve on each panel and all variables must be controlled except size of group. Instead of a small group explanation, these variances undoubtedly reflect the mathematical probability that as the size of the decision-making group increases, the likelihood increases that at least one judge will dissent. Second, Table 8.1 indicates considerable conflict fluctuation longitudinally. The D.C. Circuit decided anywhere from 50 to 100 percent of its *en banc* criminal justice cases nonunanimously in any given year. (The percent of dissenting votes out of all votes cast also varied but not as markedly.)

Major oscillations in magnitude of conflict on three-judge panels are also evident, ranging from 15.4 to 52.6 percent. Although the data set is small, Table 8.1 suggests that conflict may be dynamic rather than static longitudinally. As explained in other chapters of this volume, a number of factors may account for this finding.

Several hypotheses or expectations involving the general and specific foci of this chapter are investigated in the following pages. At the same time, the limitations on analysis imposed by the small data set and the mixture of *en banc* and three-judge panels continue to be mentioned periodically.

CONFLICT WHEN OVERRULING DISTRICT COURTS

One widely cited study focusing in part on the courts of appeals reached an important finding which surprisingly had not been tested again in published form with respect to the appeals courts prior to this book. Richard J. Richardson and Kenneth N. Vines analyzed a sample of civil liberties decisions announced by three circuits.[8] Although the authors did not explain whether their data included three-judge or *en banc* decisions or both, they concluded that there was considerably greater conflict (three to six times as much) on a court of appeals that reversed than on one that affirmed district courts. This finding is tested here with criminal justice data, the hypothesis again being that there was a far greater magnitude of conflict on the D.C. Circuit when it reversed the district court. The theory behind this hypothesis is that nonunanimous reversals are manifestations of a conflict situation within an appellate court. Judges experience obvious choice points and may decide to move in different directions for various reasons, including dissimilar attitudes, values, and role conceptions. Unanimous affirmances, on the other hand, strongly suggest the absence of meaningful choice points; therefore, a substantial level of conflict would not be theoretically expected.[9] To be cautious, I have excluded from the data base cases affirmed in part and reversed in part, remanded without a specific statement of affirmance, dismissed as frivolous or on related grounds, vacated judgments, and sentences set aside without reversal. On these grounds, 118 of 446 cases (26.5 percent) were excluded. Of these cases, by far the largest number involved decisions affirming in part and reversing in part, for they are usually extremely difficult to classify objectively and consistently as either affirmances or reversals.

Table 8.2 allows a reexamination of the finding of Richardson and

Table 8.2. Reversals, Affirmances, and Conflict

	Reversals				Affirmances			
	Three-Judge Panels		En Banc Panels		Three-Judge Panels		En Banc Panels	
	Number	Percent	Number	Percent	Number	Percent	Number	Percent
Unanimous	29	53.7	2	6.9	195	71.2	3	10.7
Nonunanimous	25	46.3	27	93.1	79	28.8	25	89.3
Totals	54	100.0	29	100.0	274	100.0	28	100.0

Vines. It shows that 46.3 percent of the 54 three-judge reversals but only 28.8 percent of the 274 three-judge affirmances were decided nonunanimously, whereas 93.1 percent of the 29 *en banc* reversals and 89.3 percent of the 28 *en banc* affirmances were decided non-unanimously. Thus the hypothesis is supported only for three-judge panel decisions. Richardson and Vines found that district court reversals tend to be prolibertarian. The data here support this finding.[10] The nature of the data, however, warns against any conclusion being drawn. Because of the constitutional prohibition against double jeopardy, a vast majority of these criminal cases were appealed from antidefendant decisions. A reversal, consequently, is almost by definition prodefendant, which is not true of the more general category of civil liberties decisions examined by Richardson and Vines.

CONFLICT MAGNITUDE AND COURT OUTPUT

Although reversing lower courts may cause judicial conflict, some consequences of conflict may be related to court output. Two general hypotheses selected here relate magnitude of conflict to the time required for reaching decisions and the volume of the court's outputs. Neither has been directly tested for the courts of appeals, but research on the Supreme Court indicates that one effect of a high level of conflict is a delay in decision making because judges tend to devote more time to writing dissenting and concurring opinions.[11] Hence the first hypothesis is that the greater the magnitude of conflict, the longer the time judges will take from oral argument until final decisions are announced. The second hypothesis, which logically follows, is that there will be a substantial decrease in the total number of decisions announced by the court in years of greater conflict. If these hypotheses

Table 8.3. Conflict in Three-Judge Panels, Time Required for
Decision, and Number of Decisions, 1956-1969

Percent Non-unanimous Decisions	Days to Decision (Mean)		Days to Decision (Median)		Total Decisions	
	Unani-mous	Non-unanimous	Unani-mous	Non-unanimous	Unani-mous	Non-unanimous
52.6 (1956)	46.8	188.0	21.0	188.0	9	10
52.0 (1958)	28.1	106.9	21.0	99.0	10	10
48.4 (1964)	80.3	174.3	57.0	185.0	15	15
42.9 (1965)	85.8	150.3	54.0	107.0	15	11
39.3 (1966)	101.3	190.0	67.0	161.0	14	12
38.9 (1969)	70.3	214.8	68.5	221.5	10	6
30.6 (1968)	139.9	211.5	109.5	201.0	22	11
30.4 (1960)	62.2	119.3	36.0	129.0	16	6
29.2 (1957)	33.5	122.9	25.0	57.0	13	7
23.5 (1961)	61.7	88.7	41.0	80.0	13	6
18.6 (1963)	35.5	104.4	28.0	104.5	32	8
18.5 (1967)	92.2	189.8	79.0	190.0	22	5
18.5 (1959)	56.9	87.0	39.0	65.0	17	5
15.4 (1962)	63.5	105.8	53.5	91.0	28	5
Average	68.4	146.7	50.0	134.2		

Note: In thirty-two three-judge panel decisions, no date of oral argument is provided by the *Federal Reporter, Second Edition.* These cases were therefore excluded from the data in this table.

contain any validity, it should be obvious from ranking years of greatest conflict, derived from Table 8.1.

Table 8.3 is designed to examine these propositions for three-judge panel decisions. (Reflecting one disadvantage of a microlevel study such as this one, the small number of *en banc* decisions precludes a similar analysis of them.) The table shows the mean and median number of days required for three-judge decisions handed down at different levels of conflict and the total number of three-judge decisions each year. Surprisingly little support for the two hypotheses is evident. Although in each year substantially more time was necessary to hand down nonunanimous decisions, the length of time required varied greatly by year almost irrespective of the magnitude of conflict. In none of the four years in which conflict rose above 40 percent did the mean number of days needed to reach a decision rank in the top four, and in only one (1956) did the median number of days rank in the top four. In contrast, 1967 witnessed only an 18.5 percent rate of dissent, but the median and mean number of days necessary for decisions ranked third and fourth, respectively, out of fourteen years.

Concerning the total number of three-judge decisions each year, the data suggest a weak relationship between magnitude of conflict and the number of unanimous decisions announced, but for nonunanimous decisions the hypothesis is clearly not confirmed. Indeed, ironically, the relationship between magnitude of conflict and number of non-unanimous decisions announced each year appears to be roughly the opposite of what was hypothesized. Of the seven years of greatest conflict, in only one (1969) was the number of nonunanimous decisions generally as low as anticipated. In light of these findings, additional testing of both hypotheses with a larger data set would seem worthwhile.

Another point of interest is that the longest periods of delay for nonunanimous three-judge decisions occurred in 1969, Burger's final year on the D.C. Circuit. In that year the magnitude of conflict was not substantially higher than the average for all fourteen years when the data in Tables 8.1 and 8.3 are compared (38.9 percent versus 32.8 percent), but an average of 214.8 days and a median of 221.5 days were required to announce the 1969 decisions. Of the seven nonunanimous three-judge decisions handed down that year, Burger dissented in the last four, and in three he authored a dissenting opinion. At least two explanations are plausible concerning these delays in expediting the court's business. First, Richard Nixon's nomination of Burger as chief justice on May 21, 1969, may have had some effect on slowing the process since two of Burger's last four decisions were announced after his nomination and an average of 211.5 days was required in those cases. Perhaps Burger was preoccupied by the prospect of assuming his new duties as chief justice. Second, relevant here is the very critical tone of Burger's dissent in *Frazier* v. *United States*,[12] one of his last opinions on the D.C. Circuit, which required 298 days for decision. *Frazier* was announced after Burger had been invited to the White House and knew he might be elevated to the Supreme Court.[13] Hence Burger may have reserved a great deal of time so he could carefully mold a final jab toward D.C. Circuit liberals (in this case David L. Bazelon and Spottswood W. Robinson), who had regularly disagreed with him on criminal justice issues. To draw on the concept of Walter F. Murphy, in *Frazier* Burger seemed to be using a sanction against his colleagues through a strongly worded dissent.[14] Burger could write a stinging dissent knowing he was probably leaving the court and need not worry about alienating his D.C. Circuit colleagues for purposes of future coalition-building. Not coincidentally, perhaps, Burger's *Frazier* opinion was also emphasized during Senate confirmation hearings as being consonant with the "law and order" stance that Nixon had successfully taken in the 1968 presidential campaign and similar views by conservative Senate Judiciary Committee members.

JUDICIAL CONFLICT AND BACKGROUND TRAITS

The more specific focus on conflict between Burger and his appeals court colleagues begins with a hypothesis suggested by social background theory, the purpose of which is to determine whether background characteristics affect judicial decision making. The fundamental theoretical link in the paradigm is the notion that certain background traits are independent variables that help explain judges' behavior, including the propensity of one judge to agree or disagree with his brethren. Sheldon Goldman has conducted the most extensive background research on the courts of appeals. Two of his main conclusions were that appeals court judges who are Democrats and either Catholic or Jewish are more liberal than judges who are Republicans and Protestants. Other research focusing specifically on criminal justice cases is largely consistent with Goldman's findings. Among others, Stuart S. Nagel has shown that judges who are Democrats are more likely to vote in favor of criminal defendants than judges who are Republicans. S. Sidney Ulmer and Nagel have additionally provided evidence that Catholic judges are more inclined to support defendants than are Protestant judges.[15] One would therefore hypothesize that Burger, a Republican Protestant, would be in greatest voting conflict with judges who were Democrats and either Catholic or Jewish.

Table 8.4 categorizes the D.C. Circuit judges who served between 1956 and 1969 according to these background traits. The purpose is to determine whether any patterns emerge when these two background characteristics are related to magnitude of agreement and disagreement. Put otherwise, one may investigate the hypothesized relationship by calculating the percentage of times that each judge voted with Burger as shown through a four-cell matrix using the party and religion variables. The data include all nonunanimous three-judge and *en banc* decisions.

It is obvious from Table 8.4 that Burger was in most agreement

Table 8.4. Background Traits and Voting Agreement with Burger in Nonunanimous Decisions, 1956-1969

Protestant		Catholic or Jewish	
Democrats			
Henry W. Edgerton	28.1 (18/64)	David L. Bazelon	19.3 (21/109)
Carl E. McGowan	47.6 (10/21)	Charles Fahy	36.2 (29/80)
Wilbur K. Miller	63.0 (46/73)	Harold Leventhal	50.0 (6/12)
E. Barrett Prettyman	86.3 (44/51)	Edward A. Tamm	94.7 (18/19)
Spottswood W. Robinson	22.2 (2/9)	J. Skelly Wright	25.0 (10/40)
George Thomas Washington	51.7 (30/58)		
Republicans			
Walter M. Bastian	75.4 (43/57)	John A. Danaher	87.7 (57/65)

Sources: The data on political party and religious identification are taken from *Judges of the United States; Who's Who in America; The American Bench;* the *Dictionary of American Judges;* and U.S. Senate, Committee on the Judiciary, *Legislative History of the United States Circuit Courts of Appeals and Judges Who Served during the Period 1801 through May 1972* (Washington, D.C.: U.S. Government Printing Office, 1972).

over time with four judges: Edward A. Tamm, John A. Danaher, E. Barrett Prettyman, and Walter M. Bastian. Given the background literature, one would have anticipated the high level of consensus between Burger and Bastian, but certainly not between Burger and Tamm. Burger agreed with the court's other two Republicans at an average rate of 81.5 percent but with the eleven Democrats at only 47.6 percent. By contrast, Burger's average agreement was 53.5 percent with the other seven Protestants but 52.1 percent with the six Catholic or Jewish judges. Therefore, although only two other Republicans served on the court, the data suggest that party was clearly more related to conflict than was religion. The picture becomes muddied, however, when party and religion are both related to conflict. Of the Democrats, Burger agreed 49.8 percent of the time with Protestant judges and 45.0 percent with Catholic or Jewish judges. Yet these averages should not disguise the fact that of the four judges with whom Burger experienced the greatest magnitude of conflict in a substantial number of cases, three were Democrats and either Catholic or Jewish (Bazelon, Charles Fahy, and J. Skelly Wright).

To relate only two background variables to voting conflict and consensus clearly is an elementary approach. It does not pretend to be methodoligically sophisticated or to consider a comprehensive list of background traits such as that developed by C. Neal Tate.[16] Yet the data demonstrate, as one would anticipate, that Burger was in strong consensus with Republican judges and most likely to be in greatest conflict with colleagues who were Democrats and either Catholic or Jewish. Overall, the findings are mixed and only partially support Songer's macrolevel conclusion in Chapter 5 regarding the relationship between conflict and judges' political party identifications.

CONFLICT, JUDGES, AND ISSUES

Microlevel research implies analysis that goes beyond general levels of disagreement shown in Table 8.4. It is entirely possible that such data may mask important fluctuations in conflict between Burger and his colleagues over time and on specific issues. Indeed, beginning with C. Herman Pritchett's *The Roosevelt Court,* political scientists have compared aggregated and disaggregated data to describe oscillations in voting agreement among judges longitudinally and on particular issues. When substantial fluctuations occur, a microlevel approach clarifies change over time and indicates which issues are most related to variation in conflict. The data in Table 8.4 were therefore more closely examined for both three-judge and *en banc* panels.

Table 8.5 breaks down the data by year. During Burger's initial two years on the D.C. Circuit he experienced strong to moderate conflict with Bazelon, Henry W. Edgerton, and Fahy. The only judge he voted consistently with was Judge Prettyman. This pattern suggests support at the appeals court level for small group studies demonstrating that newly appointed Supreme Court justices do not tend to align with colleagues at either extreme of the ideological spectrum.[17] Between 1958 and 1964 consensual changes in voting relations appear. Burger's voting became more harmonious with that of Danaher, Wilbur K. Miller, and George T. Washington. Conflict with Bazelon, Edgerton, and Fahy also diminished somewhat.

In contrast, dramatic changes in voting patterns emerged from 1965 through 1969. A very high magnitude of conflict is clearly evident during these years as the cleavage between Burger and Bazelon, Wright, and Fahy became severe. This was the first period in Burger's lower court career in which he maintained conflictual voting relations with more than half of his brethren. So pronounced was disagreement between Burger and the Bazelon-Wright duo that it surpassed such

Table 8.5. Voting Agreement Between Burger and his Colleagues in Nonunanimous Criminal Justice Cases, 1956-1969

	1956	1957	1958	1959	1960	1961	1962	1963	1964	1965	1966	1967	1968	1969	Totals
Bastian															
Three-judge				2/2	1/1		2/2	3/3	1/1	2/2			2/2		13/13
En banc	2/2	2/4	1/4	4/5	2/2	5/6	3/6	5/5	1/5	4/4		1/1			30/44
Bazelon															
Three-judge	0/10	0/2	2/9	1/2	0/2	0/1	0/4	0/3	0/3	0/5	0/5	0/3	0/4	0/3	3/56
En banc	0/2	2/4	3/4	2/5	0/2	2/6	4/6	0/5	4/5	0/8	1/1	0/3	0/1	0/1	18/53
Danaher															
Three-judge		1/1			1/1	2/2	1/1	1/1	3/3	1/1	1/1		1/1		12/12
En banc	1/2	2/4	2/4	5/5	2/2	6/6	6/6	5/5	2/5	8/8	1/1	3/3	1/1	1/1	45/53
Edgerton															
Three-judge		0/4	0/4	0/1	0/1	0/2		0/2		0/1	0/9	0/2	0/1		0/27
En banc	0/2	3/4	3/4	3/5	0/2	2/6	4/6	0/5	3/3						18/37
Fahy															
Three-judge		1/3	0/3	0/3	0/4	0/1	0/1	0/2	0/2	1/4	3/4		1/6		6/33
En banc	0/2	2/4	3/4	3/5	0/2	2/6	4/6	5/5	4/5	0/6	0/1	0/1			23/47
Leventhal															
Three-judge											1/1		1/1		2/2
En banc										0/4	1/1	2/3	1/1	0/1	4/10
McGowan															
Three-judge									1/1	0/1	1/2	2/3	0/1		2/5
En banc									2/2	2/8	1/1	2/3	1/1	0/1	8/16

Table 8.5. Continued

	1956	1957	1958	1959	1960	1961	1962	1963	1964	1965	1966	1967	1968	1969	Totals
Miller															
Three-judge		0/1	1/3	1/3	1/1	1/1	1/1	1/1	6/9	2/3		1/1		1/1	16/25
En banc	2/2	2/4	1/4	3/5	2/2	3/6	2/6	5/5	1/5	8/8				1/1	30/48
Prettyman															
Three-judge	10/10	3/3	3/3		2/2					1/1		0/1			19/20
En banc	1/2	3/4	3/4	5/5	2/2	6/6	5/5		0/3						25/31
Robinson															
Three-judge												1/2	0/1	0/4	1/7
En banc													1/1	0/1	1/2
Tamn															
Three-judge										1/1	1/1		4/4	2/3	8/9
En banc										4/4	1/1	3/3	1/1	1/1	10/10
Washington															
Three-judge				0/1	0/1	0/1	1/2	1/1	0/3	1/3					3/12
En banc	1/2	2/4	3/4	3/5	1/2	3/6	4/6	5/5	4/5	0/6	1/1				27/46
Wright															
Three-judge							0/1	0/3	3/8	0/2		1/2	0/1	0/1	4/18
En banc		2/4	3/4				0/1	5/5	1/2	0/8	0/1	0/3	0/1	0/1	6/22

Table 8.6. Summary Data on Conflict in Five Criminal Justice Issues, 1956-1969

	Arrests	Searches and Seizures	Effective Assistance of Counsel	Unnecessary Delays	Insanity Defense
Percent of cases decided nonunanimously	32.3 (10/31)	66.7 (22/33)	45.8 (11/24)	72.2 (26/36)	46.2 (24/52)
Voting divisions in *en banc* panels	No *en banc* panels	5-4 7-2 8-1	5-4 5-4 6-3	5-4 5-4 5-4 5-4 6-3 6-3 7-2 7-2	5-4 5-4 5-4 6-3 6-3 4-2 5-3 7-2 7-2 7-2 7-2 8-1 8-1
Years in which conflict was greatest	1958-59 1964-66	Generally constant	1956-59	1958 1964	1957 1961
Judge(s) with whom Burger experienced greatest conflict[a]	Bazelon (0/6)	Bazelon (1/17) Edgerton (1/5) Fahy (2/5)	Bazelon (1/7) Edgerton (1/6) Fahy (1/5)	Bazelon (5/17) Fahy (6/15) Miller (5/11)	Wright (1/6) Miller (4/12) Bazelon (7/19)
Judge(s) with whom Burger experienced greatest consensus[a]	Insufficient data	Prettyman (13/13) Bastian (5/5)	Prettyman (4/5) Miller (4/5)	No agreement rate above 55 percent	Prettyman (9/9) Danaher (16/18) Bastian (8/13) Fahy (8/13)

[a]A minimum of at least five joint participations in nonunanimous decisions is used in this table.

Supreme Court rivalries as those between Louis Brandeis and James C. McReynolds or Hugo Black and Owen Roberts.[18] A corresponding high degree of consensus characterized Burger's voting relations with four other judges—Danaher, Bastian, Tamm, and Miller.

Voting on specific criminal justice issues was also investigated to delve further into conflict between Burger and his colleagues. The analysis has two main objectives: to compare the magnitude of conflict between Burger and his colleagues across major criminal justice issues, and to determine whether Burger was in conflict with the same judges on specific issues as in criminal justice generally. One disadvantage of this microlevel approach is that when the 174 nonunanimous cases are disaggregated into discrete categories, the number in each is too small for analysis except on five issues: arrests, searches and seizures, unnecessary delays prior to preliminary hearings, effective assistance of counsel, and the insanity defense.[19] The data are summarized in Table 8.6

Table 8.6 shows considerable variance in magnitude of conflict across issues. Search and seizure provoked more than twice as much disagreement as arrest questions. Conflict in effective assistance cases was high but falls between that generated by the first two issues. *En banc* panels were rarely used in these three issues but always resulted in a divided court. Importantly, Burger experienced conflict and consensus with essentially the same judges as indicated in Table 8.5. By contrast, an extremely high 72.2 percent disagreement rate was present in unnecessary delay cases, and the nine *en banc* decisions were substantially divided. Levels of conflict between Burger and his colleagues were somewhat different in unnecessary delay cases, however, with Burger agreeing far more often with Edgerton, Washington, and even Bazelon. At the same time, Burger's level of consensus with more conservative court members declined.[20] A somewhat similar pattern emerges for criminal insanity cases. Of fifty-two panels, at least one dissent occurred in twenty-four, and conflict was evident in all but two of eleven *en banc* panels. For the first time Burger experienced his highest magnitude of conflict not with Bazelon but with Wright and Miller. Meanwhile, relative consensus existed between Burger and Edgerton, Fahy, and Washington, again atypical except in unnecessary delay cases. Overall, therefore, the data in Table 8.6 suggest notable variations in magnitude of conflict depending on the issue and in patterns of disagreement between Burger and several of his colleagues.

This chapter has investigated conflict on the D.C. Circuit between 1956 and 1969 in criminal justice cases. Emphasis has been placed on one possible cause of conflict (reversing lower court decisions), two possible effects of conflict (delays and decreases in decisional outputs), one possible cause of conflict among individual judges (background differences), and conflict between Warren Burger and his colleagues over time in criminal justice litigation generally and in five major issues.

It was first hypothesized that when the D.C. Circuit reversed a district court, intracourt conflict would be substantially higher than when the lower court was affirmed. The hypothesis was confirmed for three-judge but not for *en banc* decisions. Second was the expectation of a relationship between greater magnitude of conflict and (1) greater time required for the court to reach a decision and (2) decreases in total outputs. Since the size of the *en banc* data base was small, this hypothesis was tested only with three-judge decisions, and surprisingly neither expectation was confirmed. Additional research involving both hypotheses would seem worthwhile.

Concerning the chapter's more specific focus, it was first suggested that there would be a relationship between magnitude of conflict between Burger and his brethren when two background characteristics—political party identification and religion—were examined. Relying on a simple test of the hypothesis, the findings were mixed although Burger was in very high agreement with other Republican judges and usually in greatest conflict with judges who were Democrats and either Catholic or Jewish. When the data were examined by year and disaggregated into three-judge and *en banc* panels, there was considerable variance in magnitude of conflict between Burger and other judges over time and in specific criminal justice issues. Perhaps this type of microlevel research will be most justified in the future to clarify the behavior of prominent appeals court judges. Especially for those ultimately elevated to the Supreme Court, comparative institutional and individual research involving both levels of federal appellate courts may provide some new insights into judicial process and behavior.

I wish to thank the Research Foundation of the State University of New York for helping to finance this project and Sheldon Goldman, Justin J. Green, Donald R. Songer, and S. Sidney Ulmer for their comments on an early draft of the chapter.

1. On the need for research at the microlevel, see James L. Gibson, "From Simplicity to Complexity: The Development of Theory in the Study of Judicial Behavior," *Political Behavior* 5 (1983): 7-49.

2. Burton M. Atkins, "Decision-Making Rules and Judicial Strategy on the United States Courts of Appeals," *Western Political Quarterly* 25 (1972): 632-35; Sheldon Goldman, "Voting Behavior on the United States Courts of Appeals, 1961-1964," *American Political Science Review* 60 (1966): 377-78; Sheldon Goldman, "Voting Behavior on the United States Courts of Appeals Revisited," *American Political Science Review* 69 (1975): 493; Sheldon Goldman, "Conflict on the U.S. Courts of Appeals 1965-1971: A Quantitative Analysis," *University of Cincinnati Law Review* 42 (1973): 641.

3. On the research design for this chapter, see Charles M. Lamb, "Exploring the Conservatism of Federal Appeals Court Judges," *Indiana Law Journal* 51 (1976): 260-63.

4. See, e.g., C. Herman Pritchett, *The Roosevelt Court: A Study of Judicial Politics and Values, 1937-1947* (New York: Macmillan, 1948), p. 25; Glendon Schubert, *The Judicial Mind: The Attitudes and Ideologies of Supreme Court Justices, 1946-1963* (Evanston: Northwestern University Press, 1965), p. 45.

5. See Songer, "Factors Affecting Variation in Rates of Dissent in the U.S. Courts of Appeals," Chapter 5 of this volume.

6. See, e.g., S. Sidney Ulmer, *Courts as Small and Not So Small Groups* (New York: General Learning Press, 1971), pp. 4-7 and the research cited therein. See also Burton M. Atkins, "Judicial Behavior and Tendencies towards Conformity in a Three Member Small Group: A Case Study of Dissent Behavior on the U.S. Court of Appeals," *Social Science Quarterly* 51 (1973): 44-53 and the research cited therein.

7. See, e.g., J. Woodford Howard, Jr., *Courts of Appeals in the Federal Judicial System: A Study of the Second, Fifth, and District of Columbia Circuits* (Princeton: Princeton University Press, 1981), chap. 7 and the research cited therein.

8. Richard J. Richardson and Kenneth N. Vines, *The Politics of Federal Courts: Lower Courts in the United States* (Boston: Little, Brown, 1970), pp. 135-36; Richard J. Richardson and Kenneth N. Vines, "Review, Dissent and the Appellate Process: A Political Interpretation," *Journal of Politics* 29 (1967): 606-9.

9. See, e.g., Sheldon Goldman, "Backgrounds, Attitudes and Voting Behavior of Judges: A Comment on Joel Grossman's *Social Backgrounds and Judicial Decisions,*" *Journal of Politics* 31 (1969): 214-20 and the research cited therein.

10. Although only 2.6 percent of the 274 three-judge affirmances were decided in favor of defendants, 94.4 percent of the 54 three-judge reversals were prodefendant. Similarly, only 3.6 percent of the 28 *en banc* affirmances were prodefendant, and 86.2 percent of the 29 *en banc* reversals were decided in favor of defendants.

11. See, e.g., Walter F. Murphy, *Elements of Judicial Strategy* (Chicago: University of Chicago Press, 1964), pp. 44-45.

12. 419 F.2d 1161 (1969).

13. See, e.g., James F. Simon, *In His Own Image: The Supreme Court in Richard Nixon's America* (New York: David McKay, 1973), p. 75.

14. Murphy, *Elements of Judicial Strategy,* pp. 54-56.

15. Goldman, "Voting Behavior Revisited," pp. 498, 503-4; Stuart S. Nagel, *The Legal Process from a Behavioral Perspective* (Homewood, Ill.: Dorsey, 1969), pp. 227, 230; S. Sidney Ulmer, "Social Background as an Indicator to the Votes of Supreme Court Justices in Criminal Cases: 1946-1956 Terms," *American Journal of Political Science* 18 (1973): 624-30.

16. See C. Neal Tate, "Personal Attribute Models of the Voting Behavior of U.S. Supreme Court Justices: Liberalism in Civil Liberties and Economics Decisions, 1946-1978," *American Political Science Review* 75 (1981): 355-67.

17. See, e.g., J. Woodford Howard, Jr., *Mr. Justice Murphy: A Political Biography* (Princeton: Princeton University Press, 1968), pp. 231-64; S. Sidney Ulmer, "Toward a Theory of Sub-Group Formation in the United States Supreme Court," *Journal of Politics* 27 (1965): 133-52. Prior research on the D.C. Circuit by Atkins and Lamb, cited in notes 2 and 3, provides sufficient grounds for classifying the attitudes of Burger and his colleagues during these years. Generally, in criminal justice cases, the attitudinal rankings show that Bastian, Danaher, Miller, Prettyman, and Tamm tended to be conservative. Bazelon, Edgerton, Fahy, Wright, and Washington were liberal. The remainder of the judges possessed more moderate attitudes, with Burger being moderately conservative.

18. See, e.g., Pritchett, *Roosevelt Court,* pp. 242-46. Concerning conflict between Burger and Bazelon, see Charles M. Lamb, "When Judicial Agreement Seems Impossible: Warren Burger, David Bazelon, and the D.C. Court of Appeals," *Journal of Political Science* 11 (1984): 75-82.

19. For a substantive analysis of the cases in these areas, see Charles M. Lamb, "The Making of a Chief Justice: Warren Burger on Criminal Procedure, 1956-1969," *Cornell Law Review* 60 (1975): 743-88; Charles M. Lamb, "Warren Burger and the Insanity Defense—Judicial Philosophy and Voting Behavior on a U.S. Court of Appeals," *American University Law Review* 24 (1974): 91-128.

20. See note 17.

III
The State Supreme Courts

9

Dissent in State Supreme Courts: Patterns and Correlates of Conflict

HENRY R. GLICK and
GEORGE W. PRUET, JR.

The presence of dissent on collegial courts, especially the U.S. Supreme Court, has long been a research interest in political science. In a shorthand way, the level of dissent reveals the amount of conflict and consensus on appellate courts. Certainly the lack of dissent does not guarantee that judges always agree on issues and solutions to cases,[1] but formal dissents are a clear indicator that judges seriously disagree on basic features of cases. High levels of dissent also have led social scientists to doubt the power of *stare decisis* or other legal doctrines to account for most judicial decisions. Judges who respond to the same cases and have access to the same legal sources but consistently reach different conclusions are influenced by something other than law. High levels of dissent have provided the crucial raw materials for systematic empirical research demonstrating that small group interaction, judges' backgrounds and attitudes, and their social and political environments substantially influence judicial decision making.

In addition to focusing on individual judges and courts, dissent can be viewed as a reflection of conflict in society. There is a link between the amount of political conflict within a society and the presence of conflict within that society's political institutions. In this sense, courts are not isolated parts of government, immune to the influence of political pressures, but are components of the broader political system. Similar to other political institutions, they respond to various political influences and concerns. From this perspective, conflict exhibited by an appellate court is analogous to conflict found in a legislature or in the executive branch.

This chapter focuses on conflict and consensus on state supreme courts revealed through variations in levels of dissent. Instead of studying dissents and particular decisions of one or a few appellate courts, we are concerned with the level and causes of dissent on all fifty state supreme courts. Our primary objective is to describe current levels of dissent in the fifty states, to compare current and past levels of dissent, and to examine several hypotheses concerning the social conditions that often are believed to produce differences in the level of dissent. The main theme of this chapter is that although courts are more insulated from political and social pressures than legislatures and the rest of government, state courts respond to and reflect conflict in state political and social systems.

DISSENT IN STATE SUPREME COURTS

Most research on dissent has studied the U.S. Supreme Court, mainly because it is the highest court in the land but also because it regularly produces many decisions with dissents, typically at least 50 percent since the 1943 term.[2] Usually researchers are able to find only a handful of state supreme courts and an occasional federal court of appeals in which levels of dissent are high enough to attract attention or to serve for background and attitude studies of decision making.[3] The most important studies of dissent including all fifty state supreme courts were conducted using data from the early to mid-1960s, but during this period, there was not much variation in dissent.[4] Fewer than ten states produced dissents in 20 percent or more of their cases, and only the supreme courts in Michigan, Pennsylvania, and New York produced dissents at or above the 40 percent mark.[5]

These high dissent rates were not typical of supreme courts in most states and could create a misleading impression that conflict is common in state supreme courts. As stated earlier, an important question is whether the level and variation of dissents have changed very much since earlier fifty-state studies. Other research suggests that dissent is on the rise,[6] but there have been no recent fifty-state surveys. The level of dissent informs us about conflict on courts, but the amount of dissent also has implications for future small group and other research on judicial decision making. Higher levels of dissent on more courts present both more opportunities and compelling reasons for additional comparative research.[7]

Research on state court decision making is important also because state courts hear the vast majority of all cases decided in the United States. For instance, the federal courts combined decide approximately 240,000 cases per year while state courts in Florida decide almost 3 million and those in New York decide nearly 4 million annually. State supreme court workloads vary from several hundred to several thousand cases each year. Although the percentage of highly controversial state supreme court decisions is much smaller than that in the U.S. Supreme Court, the odds are extremely high that when citizens go to court, either in civil or criminal cases, they go to a state court. The likely impact of state courts on most Americans looms very large in judicial politics. Decision making on these courts deserves more attention.

LEVEL OF DISSENT

To begin the analysis of dissent in the fifty states, Table 9.1 presents the percentage of state supreme court cases in which there were dissents for five periods beginning in 1916. Data for 1916, 1941, and 1966 were obtained from earlier research.[8] Data for 1974–75 and 1980–81 were added to bring the analysis up to date. Dissents for two years for each of the latest periods (1974–75 and 1980–81) were compared and averaged to avoid the possibility that an individual year might not reflect the time studied.[9]

Table 9.1 reveals that very high levels of dissent still are the exception in the fifty states. Only thirteen states had dissent rates at or above 25 percent, although three others were very close. Comparisons across the years, however, show considerable growth in the level of dissent. In 1974–75, only eight state supreme courts produced dissents in 25 percent or more of their cases. In 1966, there were seven, in 1941, five, and in 1916 only two states had dissent levels at or above 25 percent.

The mean percentage of cases involving dissents also has risen from approximately 12 percent in 1941 and 1966 to nearly 15 percent in 1974–75 and to over 18 percent in 1980–81. Variation among states in dissent rates increased a little in 1980–81, but since the standard deviations from 1966 on are similar, the figures suggest a general upward shift in the level of dissent in most of the states. Comparison of individual states between 1966 and 1980–81 confirms a general pattern toward more dissents: thirty-eight state supreme courts experienced

Table 9.1. Percentage of Decisions with Dissents in State Supreme Courts

Rank in 1980-81	State	Mean 1980-81	Mean 1974-75	1966	1941	1916
		High Dissent Courts, 1980-81 (Dissent ⟩ 25 percent)				
1	California	54.8	18.8	32.3	16.7	5.3
2	Louisiana	43.1	42.3	12.7	0.9	12.8
3	Florida	42.2	61.5	28.2	17.7	4.1
4	Idaho	40.1	19.9	9.0	35.6	12.2
5	Oklahoma	37.6	24.7	26.5	19.7	0.1
6	Ohio	36.8	27.4	34.9	14.1	14.8
7	Pennsylvania	32.8	39.2	41.0	5.0	1.5
8	New Jersey	30.6	1.6	7.1	30.2	14.0
9	Washington	30.2	25.3	11.5	28.7	10.0
10	Missouri	27.6	12.3	4.1	0.7	17.4
11	Kentucky	27.1	4.3	8.1	3.0	0.1
12	Arkansas	26.4	19.1	13.6	14.3	9.6
13	New York	25.3	26.9	41.0	15.8	34.1
		Low Dissent Courts, 1980-81 (Dissent ⟨ 25 percent)				
50	Hawaii	2.4	11.8	–	–	–
49	Maine	2.5	4.6	4.2	7.0	2.5
48	Rhode Island	2.6	3.2	1.4	5.4	6.5
47	Vermont	3.1	3.8	5.9	1.7	5.4
46	Delaware	4.0	4.1	3.4	15.4	15.0
45	New Hampshire	5.0	7.8	7.3	1.4	3.3
44	Massachusetts	5.7	11.0	1.2	0.6	0.0
43	Nevada	6.0	4.4	9.8	6.8	11.4
42	Mississippi	6.1	6.6	3.9	8.0	0.1
41	Connecticut	7.4	3.4	3.6	3.9	11.9
40	Arizona	8.3	7.0	6.1	1.8	8.3
39	Virginia	8.5	3.3	7.4	19.6	0.1
38	Iowa	9.1	12.0	19.7	14.4	5.2
37	North Dakota	9.2	13.2	8.4	15.1	10.0
36	Minnesota	10.0	5.2	6.8	10.8	5.9
35	West Virginia	10.1	15.7	10.7	14.3	4.8
34	Colorado	10.7	12.5	9.8	26.3	18.5
33	New Mexico	10.7	6.2	6.0	10.3	6.2
32	Tennessee	11.2	6.0	3.0	2.3	1.6
31	North Carolina	11.4	18.3	2.4	17.8	13.2
30	Nebraska	11.4	13.0	11.2	7.1	36.5
29	Alabama	14.3	16.5	1.7	4.1	6.1
28	Wisconsin	15.1	8.8	8.0	3.9	8.6
27	Indiana	15.3	28.8	11.5	5.7	7.1
26	South Carolina	17.0	9.4	3.4	8.3	17.0
25	Montana	17.3	6.5	11.9	16.1	0.1

Table 9.1. Continued

Rank in 1980-81	State	Mean 1980-81	Mean 1974-75	1966	1941	1916
		Low Dissent Courts, 1980-81 (Dissent ⟨ 25 percent)				
24	Illinois	17.3	14.6	7.2	15.7	15.0
23	Maryland	18.5	9.9	5.4	8.6	5.6
22	Georgia	18.7	18.0	8.3	7.2	5.8
21	Oregon	18.9	16.5	9.1	12.2	9.1
20	Texas	19.2	13.0	19.1	3.4	5.7
19	South Dakota	21.1	23.4	24.3	12.0	18.6
18	Kansas	21.9	5.2	12.1	13.4	8.5
17	Wyoming	22.2	16.4	9.7	4.3	2.6
16	Michigan	24.0	29.5	46.5	19.0	9.6
15	Alaska	24.6	12.5	–	–	–
14	Utah	24.9	20.1	11.7	33.0	7.7
		$\bar{x} = 18.4$	$\bar{x} = 14.91$	$\bar{x} = 12.3$	$\bar{x} = 11.7$	$\bar{x} = 8.9$
		S.D. = 12.27	S.D. = 11.53	S.D. = 11.13	S.D. = 8.80	S.D. = 7.66

Note: Includes *per curiam* but not memorandum decisions.
Source: West's Regional Reporters, 1974, 1975, 1980, and 1981, and Henry Robert Glick and Kenneth N. Vines, *State Court Systems* (Englewood Cliffs, N.J.: Prentice-Hall, 1973), p. 79.

increased levels of dissent between 1966 and 1981 and only ten experienced decreased levels of dissent.[10]

On a number of state supreme courts, levels of dissent rose dramatically between 1966 and 1980–81, suggesting that important changes have occurred in state judicial politics. For example, the New Jersey Supreme Court, described in the 1970s as very harmonious and cohesive,[11] increased its level of dissent from 7.1 percent in 1966 (1.6 percent in 1974–75) to slightly more than 30 percent in 1980–81. Courts in about a dozen other states have doubled or nearly tripled their rates of dissent since the 1960s.

Yet there are a few large changes in the opposite direction. A remarkable decrease occurred in the Michigan Supreme Court, often described as a partisan, contentious, and divided court.[12] In 1980–81, it had a dissent rate of 24 percent and ranked sixteenth, compared with its rank as number one in dissents in 1966 at 46.5 percent. The New York and Pennsylvania supreme courts, also often described as very contentious with high levels of dissent, have decreased their levels in 1966 of around 40 percent to 25.3 and 32.8 percent, respectively, in 1980–81.

Table 9.2. Intercorrelations of State Supreme Court Dissent Rates

	1980-81	1974-75	1966	1941	1916
1980-81	–	.65	.59	.36	.07
1974-75	.65	–	.65	.18	.10
1966	.59	.65	–	.22	.15
1941	.36	.18	.22	–	.18
1916	.07	.10	.15	.18	–

Despite increases in levels of dissent in 1980–81, caution must be used in describing or identifying trends in state supreme court dissent. For instance, previous correlations among levels of dissent revealed practically no relationships among the states in the three periods 1916, 1941, and 1966.[13] Table 9.2 reproduces these correlations plus the relationships for 1974–75 and 1980–81. Unlike the earlier figures, however, dissent rates in 1966, 1974–75, and 1980–81 are moderately related ($R = .59$ to $.65$), and the 1980–81 and 1941 dissents also are somewhat related. Therefore, dissent rates in many of the states are shifting in the same general direction and in corresponding proportions. The sharp downward shifts that occurred in Michigan, Pennsylvania, and New York are exceptions to the overall pattern of moderate to high increases in the rate of dissents.

The moderately high positive correlations between the 1966, 1974–75, and 1980–81 rates suggest that there may be common forces responsible for increasing levels of dissent. Perhaps the levels of state political conflict generally were higher, or the recent creation of intermediate appellate courts in states previously without them gave more state supreme court judges time for the luxury of writing more dissents. Besides identifying patterns of supreme court dissent, an interesting line of research would be to relate patterns of conflict in state supreme courts to other indicators of conflict in state and national politics, such as in legislative voting, conflict among political parties and interest groups, and between legislatures and governors, and in other areas of state politics. Political scientists increasingly appreciate the connections between courts and other aspects of political and social systems, but there still is a tendency to concentrate on the inner workings of courts and the behavior of small groups of judges rather than to adopt a broader perspective on the causes of dissent and political conflict generally. A broader focus on judicial dissent as part of social and political conflict would enlarge our understanding of the links between judicial and other forms of political behavior.

FACTORS AFFECTING DISSENT

There are many possible influences on conflict and dissent in appellate courts. Some have been studied extensively in the past, and our research compares current relationships with those previously uncovered. The influence of three major factors is reported here: the social and economic diversity of the states, the level of other political conflict and complexity in the states, and the impact of state court structure and organization. We have selected several specific indicators to represent the influence of these three sets of variables.

Social and Economic Complexity and Political Competition. Our first hypothesis is that state social, economic, and political heterogeneity, complexity, and competition contribute to higher dissent rates. Therefore, conflict should be greatest in states that have diversified economies, varied populations, substantial urban-rural differences, two-party competition, the largest budgets, and the highest increases in expenditures. These economic, social and political cleavages should produce much more conflict in the states' political institutions, including the courts.[14]

It is not necessary to elaborate on each independent variable that may be related to levels of dissent. Most of the indicators of complexity are self-explanatory from Table 9.3. Several that may not be are percentages of private and criminal litigation in 1980, integration, and education and welfare spending. The percentage of private and criminal litigation is a measure of the complexity and controversial nature of a supreme court's docket. Private litigation includes cases such as divorce, contract disputes between individuals, wills and estates, suits for injuries, and landlord-tenant cases.[15] We hypothesize that private litigation as well as criminal appeals generally are viewed as less controversial by most judges and that large percentages of these cases in a court's docket will depress dissent. Although criminal appeals raise questions of procedure and constitutional protections, we believe they generally are not controversial in the states because there are so many of them in nearly every state and they often are desperate efforts to obtain a release from jail, a new trial, or a stay of execution. On average, state

Table 9.3. Correlations of Social and Political Factors and Court
Structure with State Supreme Court Dissent, 1980–81
(Zero Order Correlations)

	All States	States with Intermediate Appellate Courts	States without Intermediate Appellate Courts
Social and Economic Complexity			
Urbanization, 1980	.21	.30	−.22
Percent change in urbanization, 1970-80	−.13	−.16	.16
Percent nonagricultural employment, 1980	.10	−.03	−.46[a]
Median income	−.14	.07	−.12
Percent black population	−.13	−.17	.22
Percent private litigation	−.27	−.19	.01
Percent criminal cases	.06	−.05	−.04
Integration	.01	.11	−.27
Political Complexity and Competition			
Total state expenditures, 1978	.48[a]	.48[a]	−.08
Percent change in total expenditures, 1968-78	.03	−.14	.23
Percent Democratic vote for governor	.05	−.08	.01
Percent majority party lower house, 1978	.04	−.05	.06
Education/welfare expenditures	−.17	−.06	−.54[a]
Complexity of Court Structure			
Multiple court locations	−.20	−.09	−.26
Number of judges	.31[a]	.33	−.08
Jurisdiction of supreme court	.30[a]	−.05	−[b]
Presence of intermediate appellate court	.25	−	−
Caseload, 1980-81	.12	.07	.01

[a]Significant at .05 level.
[b]Correlation not computed because states without intermediate appellate courts do not provide supreme court discretion to hear cases.

supreme courts uphold convictions three-fourths of the time. Consequently, we hypothesize that state supreme courts will come to view these cases as relatively trivial and unimportant. Integration is a composite measure of state social and economic complexity designed to tap features of states in the postindustrial period. Education and welfare expenditures measure the commitments of the states to important and often controversial policies. The highest expenditures for these purposes tend to be in the richer, urban-industrial states with greater amounts of political competition and social heterogeneity.[16] We expect support for them to parallel high levels of dissent.

Social, economic, and political diversity may affect dissent directly and indirectly. Direct influences may occur through judges' backgrounds and attitudes.[17] Supreme court judges often live in different parts of a state and in varied communities, they have had different personal and political experiences, and they may even feel that they represent different constituencies.

Previous research has discovered that diversity among state supreme court judges is an important contributor to the level of dissent as well as to the direction of decisions.[18] This research should be updated and retested, especially since the level of dissent is much higher and involves more courts. It is important to know whether diversity among judges still affects the level of dissent or whether dissent is increasing generally, regardless of variations among judges. This research question, however, was beyond the scope of the present study.

Court Structure. The structure of state courts influences their behavior. Earlier studies have shown that certain characteristics of state judiciaries are associated with the presence of conflict. One structural characteristic found to be associated with dissent is the number of justices involved in making collective decisions.[19] As the number of justices on a court increases, so should the likelihood of conflict and its expression in the form of dissent.

Probably the structural variable that has been most closely associated with the occurrence of dissent is the presence of an intermediate appellate court, which usually results in many socially and politically trivial appeals being decided before they reach the supreme court. Therefore, many cases that would have been settled by the supreme court, typically with unanimous agreement, are removed so it can address the more legally complex and politically controversial appeals. States that do not provide this filter place a heavier burden on their courts of last resort. In other words, as these supreme courts are swamped by a large number of trivial legal issues, the proportion of cases with potential for dissent is reduced and there is less time to deal with complex cases that would likely lead to conflict and dissenting votes.

An additional structural variable included here is the number of locations where supreme courts meet. Some state supreme courts hear cases in different parts of the state, and the judges move several times each year. State supreme court judges also sometimes live and maintain their offices in different cities rather than in the state capitol or supreme court building. We hypothesize that there will be more dissent in these states because the judges may not be able to develop cohesive social or work groups.

Another explanatory variable that we have introduced is a measure of the discretionary jurisdiction of state supreme courts. One explanation for the high rates of dissent exhibited by the U.S. Supreme Court is its wide discretion in determining the cases it will hear. In line with this reasoning, all of the fifty state supreme courts were coded for their discretionary jurisdiction with a score of zero given to courts with no discretion and a score of five given to those with nearly complete discretion. We would expect supreme courts with substantial discretion to exhibit higher levels of dissent than courts that have little to say about what cases are to be decided.

A final structural variable is caseload. The reasoning is straightforward. We hypothesize that the larger the caseload, the less likely it is that disagreement will be expressed because there is much internal and external pressure to complete the court's business. Smaller caseloads provide judges more time and opportunity to express dissents.[20]

FINDINGS

Table 9.3 presents the correlations between each of the three sets of predictors and dissent in 1980-81. Correlations were computed for all fifty states and for states with and without intermediate appellate courts. The presence of intermediate appellate courts received special attention because much previous research has found that these courts are related to levels of supreme court dissent as well as to the kinds of issues that state supreme courts are likely to hear.[21]

Several measures of state complexity are related to levels of dissent in the way we hypothesized. Most of our indicators, however, have little impact. The only variable reflecting social and economic complexity that has any appreciable effect on dissent in all fifty states is the percentage of private litigation. Increases in private litigation tend to depress dissent somewhat. Among the political variables, total state expenditures are correlated most clearly with levels of dissent. The percent of change in total state expenditures between 1968 and 1978, however, had no impact. As suggested earlier, we believe that high state expenditures stimulate substantial political competition over the fruits of government. Although total state expenditures are related somewhat to certain other characteristics of the states, such as population size and social complexity, the level of expenditures taps the high stakes of state politics and its accompanying competition.[22] It also correlates with dissent in the fifty states much more highly than any other indicator of state social, economic, or political complexity. High expenditures probably reflect a complex political environment in the state with multiple political issues, demands for government resources, and disagreement over how these issues ought to be resolved and funds allocated. Some of these disputes become court cases, but more likely, judges in these states have been affected by years of state political competition. Two measures of the complexity of court structure are modestly related to dissent. Courts with more members and those with some control over their workload are somewhat more likely to produce more conflict. Judges on these courts probably select a larger percentage of controversial and unusual cases. Too much cannot be made of this finding, however, because the correlations are low.

Several predictors in Table 9.3 are similar to those used previously to explain levels of dissent in 1966.[23] They are used here partly to note any changes in relationships since 1966. A few changes appear in the correlations, although none is a very powerful indicator of dissent. For instance, the correlation between urbanism in 1960 and dissents in 1966 was .28 whereas the correlation for urbanism in 1980 and dissents in 1980-81 was .21. The effect of the percentage of black population also remained very small. For 1966 dissents, percentage of black population correlated $-.11$ and in 1980–81 it was $-.13$. In 1966, interparty competition correlated .16 with dissents, and in 1980–81 Democratic votes for governor and party dominance of the lower house of the legislature correlated .05 and .04 with dissents, respectively. Despite some changes, none of these environmental variables has any appreciable impact on the overall level of dissents on state supreme courts.

An interesting pattern emerges when we examine the relationships between our predictors and dissent for states with and without intermediate appellate courts. The correlation between percent urban population and dissent in all fifty states is .21. For states with intermediate appellate courts it is .30, but in states without intermediate appellate courts it is $-.22$. A similar pattern occurs for nonagricultural employment, integration, and education and welfare expenditures. The correlations are low and usually positive for all fifty states and for those with intermediate appellate courts but increase notably and are negative for states without intermediate appellate courts. Private litigation tends slightly to depress dissent in all states but has no effect on supreme courts that have no intermediate appellate courts below them.

These results generally are similar to earlier correlations between environmental variables and supreme court dissents in states with intermediate appellate courts. In 1966, three environmental variables (percent urban population, 1960; percent foreign born, 1960; and percent black population, 1960) had a multiple correlation of .29 with dissent on all fifty supreme courts. But the multiple correlation between this same set of variables and dissent increased to .51 when examining only those states with an intermediate appellate court.[24] These findings suggest that an intermediate appellate court generally is necessary to permit social and economic complexity to have a noticeable impact on levels of dissent. Perhaps supreme court judges in some urban, non-agricultural states without intermediate appellate courts have so much routine work that dissents rarely seem worthwhile. Table 9.3 suggests that dissent rates are not dependent upon the size of caseloads, but perhaps the mundane content of their work generally discourages dissent.

Despite the continued effect of intermediate appellate courts on levels of dissent, chances are that the impact of this variable will decline in coming years. State trends are toward the creation of intermediate courts. About two-thirds of the states had them in 1983, and as more states adopt them in the future there probably will be very little difference among the states on this variable. Rates of dissent may climb in many more states, but the presence of intermediate appellate courts will no longer account for differences in levels of dissent.

To examine the combined effects of the independent variables on dissent, we selected those with the highest and most significant associations with dissent for additional regression analysis. Table 9.4 presents the standardized regression coefficients (betas) for the largest correlations previously examined. The coefficients in Table 9.4 present the impact of each of these predictors while controlling simultaneously for the impact of the others. When all states are examined, total state expenditures is the single best predictor of dissent. Other variables have little independent effect. Collectively, however, these four predictors account for almost a third of the variation in rates of dissent ($R^2 = .28$).

Table 9.4. Combined Effects of Variables with Highest Correlations
with Dissent, 1980–81 (betas)

All States	
Total state expenditures, 1978	.38[a]
Number of judges	.18
Percent private litigation	− .10
Jurisdiction of supreme court	.05
$R^2 = .28$	
States with Intermediate Appellate Courts	
Total state expenditures, 1978	.41[a]
Number of judges	.28
Urbanization, 1980	.10
$R^2 = .32$	
States without Intermediate Appellate Courts	
Education/welfare expenditures	− .40[a]
Nonagricultural employment	− .23
Integration	− .01
Multiple court locations	− .02
$R^2 = .33$	

[a]Significant at .05 level.

For states with intermediate appellate courts, total expenditures
also is the single best predictor, and the number of justices contributes
some explanation. Urbanization has very little independent impact on
dissent when controlling for state expenditures and number of judges.
Education and welfare expenditures best account for dissents in states
without intermediate appellate courts. The direction of the correlations
in these states is perhaps the most interesting finding. It suggests that in
states without intermediate appellate courts, there may be potential
dissenters waiting to break free were it not for their obligation to hear all
cases appealed in these states. All predictors collectively explain one-
third of the variance in dissent in states both with and without intermediate appellate courts.

This chapter has described current levels of dissent in all fifty state
supreme courts, compared them with past conflict levels, and examined the impact of a number of environmental and structural variables
on levels of dissent. An important discovery is that dissent rates are
increasing in the states. This finding is a boon for researchers in judicial
politics and should lead to the development of broader theories and

models linking state court decision making to additional patterns of state politics.

Many independent variables and hypotheses could be examined to explain rates of dissent. Three major categories of variables are the social, economic, and political environments of the states; the characteristics of the judges; and the structure, organization, and work of state court systems. Several variables are related to levels of dissent, although many others, especially indicators of political party conflict, are not. We need to collect more precise and perhaps more relevant indicators of political conflict in the states. Many commentators, for example, have lamented the decline of party competition and the meaning of party organization in state politics. If party no longer is very important, perhaps we need to find other variables that do relate to conflict and tie them to patterns of dissent. Diversity in judges' backgrounds also needs to be examined, for it has been a long time since these variables have been studied in relation to levels of dissent in the states.

Court organization continues to be an important factor related to levels of dissent. The presence of an intermediate appellate court appears to free judges from many mundane tasks and to give them more time and stimulation to focus on more controversial issues and to write dissenting opinions. Without intermediate appellate courts, social and economic diversity does not appear to have much of a chance to affect the expression of conflict. The trend is for states to create intermediate appellate courts, which may lead to more incentives and opportunities for judges to write dissenting opinions. Thus the pattern of increasing judicial conflict through formal dissents may continue.

Finally, research on state court dissent is only one part of the comprehensive research needed on the work of state supreme courts. The presence of fairly high rates of dissent on many courts presents new opportunities to examine the impact of numerous environmental, personal, and structural factors on the direction of judicial decisions. For example, many of the earlier background and attitude studies should be retested on a variety of state supreme courts to determine the effect of personal characteristics on decision making and the basis of divisions while controlling for numerous differences in state political and social environments. This work would help students of courts to build more general theories about judicial behavior.

We appreciate the comments of Joel Grossman and the volume editors on an early draft of this chapter and the research assistance of Stephanie Larson and Lesa Hawkins.

1. Robert J. Sickels, "The Illusion of Judicial Consensus: Zoning Decisions in the Maryland Court of Appeals," *American Political Science Review* 59 (1965): 100-104.

2. See the Prologue to this volume.

3. Richard J. Richardson and Kenneth N. Vines, *The Politics of Federal Courts: Lower Courts in the United States* (Boston: Little, Brown, 1970), pp. 138-41; Glendon Schubert, *Quantitative Analysis of Judicial Behavior* (Glencoe, Ill.: Free Press, 1959), pp. 129-42; Daryl R. Fair, "An Experimental Application of Scalogram Analysis to State Supreme Court Decisions" *Wisconsin Law Review* (1967): 449-67; S. Sidney Ulmer, "The Political Party Variable in the Michigan Supreme Court," *Journal of Public Law* 11 (1962): 352-63.

4. Bradley C. Canon and Dean Jaros, "External Variables, Institutional Structure, and Dissent on State Supreme Courts," *Polity* 4 (1970): 185-200; John W. Patterson and Gregory J. Rathjen, "Background Diversity and State Supreme Court Dissent Behavior," *Polity* 8 (1976): 610-22.

5. Henry Robert Glick and Kenneth N. Vines, *State Court Systems* (Englewood Cliffs, N.J.: Prentice-Hall, 1973), p. 79.

6. Robert A. Kagan, Bliss Cartwright, Lawrence M. Friedman, and Stanton Wheeler, "The Evolution of State Supreme Courts," *Michigan Law Review* 76 (1978): 995-98.

7. Few state intermediate appellate courts have high levels of dissent. Cases sometimes are rotated among individual judges with little group interaction among them in making decisions. See John L. Wold, "Going through the Motions," *Judicature* 62 (1978): 62.

8. Glick and Vines, *State Court Systems*, pp. 77-82.

9. For the years 1974 and 1975, the level of dissent changed by as much as 5 percent in only one state. For 1980 and 1981, however, the levels of dissent changed in three states by as much as 20 percent, and in five others the differences were up to 15 percent. It is not possible to say that either of these years is typical of these few courts, but averaging the two years in each period smooths out the variation and prevents either grossly over or underestimating levels of dissent in a few states. The data also suggest that recent dissent behavior may be more erratic and subject to idiosyncratic conditions of individual state politics than was behavior in earlier years. Despite this shortcoming, the simple bivariate correlation between 1980 and 1981 dissent rates is .97.

10. Data were also collected on the percentage of cases involving two or more dissents for 1980 to determine whether individual lone dissenters were responsible for high dissent rates. The percentage of cases accounted for by lone dissenters varied widely. With the exception of Missouri (ranked tenth), however, where all but 2 percent of the dissents were the result of loners, dissent rates generally did not reflect an overwhelming amount of isolated dissenting. State rankings changed little regardless of which dissent rate was used.

11. Henry Robert Glick, *Supreme Courts in State Politics: An Investigation of the Judicial Role* (New York: Basic Books, 1971), pp. 100-106.

12. See Schubert, *Quantitative Analysis*, pp. 129-42; Ulmer, "Political Party Variable."

13. Glick and Vines, *State Court Systems*, p. 80.

14. See Paul K. Warr, "Socioeconomic-Political and Incremental Variables, and Levels of State Supreme Court Dissent, 1966-1981," paper delivered at the Annual Meeting of the Midwest Political Science Association, April 21-23, 1983, Chicago.

15. See also Burton M. Atkins and Henry R. Glick, "Environmental and Structural Variables as Determinants of Issues in State Courts of Last Resort," *American Journal of Political Science* 20 (1976): 97-114.

16. Sarah McCally Morehouse, *State Politics, Parties and Policy* (New York: Holt, Rinehart and Winston, 1981), pp. 363-65 and 405-12. The integration measure includes a variety of socioeconomic variables. The highest loading variables on this factor are per capita income, percent of the population over age twenty-five, percent of employed persons in finance and insurance, percent of urban population, percent of employed professionals, percent of population of foreign white stock, and retail trade sales per capita, all in 1967. The change in the welfare and education expenditures variable is measured as the change in spending for these purposes from 1968 to 1972.

17. See Burton M. Atkins, "Judicial Behavior and Tendencies towards Conformity in a Three Member Group: A Case Study of Dissent Behavior on the U.S. Court of Appeals," *Social Science Quarterly* 54 (1973): 41-53; Stuart S. Nagel, "Political Party Affiliation and Judges' Decisions," *American Political Science Review* 55 (1961): 843-50; John R. Schmidhauser, *"Stare Decisis,* Dissent, and the Backgrounds of the Justices of the Supreme Court of the United States," *University of Toronto Law Review* 14 (1962): 209.

18. Nagel, "Political Party Affiliation"; S. Sidney Ulmer, "Dissent Behavior and Social Backgrounds of Supreme Court Justices," *Journal of Politics* 32 (1970): 580-98.

19. Burton M. Atkins and Justin J. Green, "Consensus on the United States Courts of Appeals: Illusion or Reality?" *American Journal of Political Science* 20 (1976): 97-114; Thomas G. Walker, "Behavioral Tendencies in the Three-Judge District Court," *American Journal of Political Science* 17 (1973): 407-13; Stephen L. Wasby, "Extra Judges in the Court Nobody Knows: Some Aspects of Decision-Making in the United States Courts of Appeals," paper delivered at the Annual Meeting of the American Political Science Association, August 31-September 3, 1979, Washington, D.C.

20. See Kagan, Cartwright, Friedman, and Wheeler, "Evolution of State Supreme Courts," pp. 966-73.

21. Glick and Vines, *State Court Systems*, p. 81; Atkins and Glick, "Environmental and Structural Variables"; Canon and Jaros, "External Variables."

22. We have examined the intercorrelations among all of our independent variables for multicollinearity. None of the variables is highly intercorrelated.

23. Glick and Vines, *State Court Systems*, p. 81.

24. Ibid

10

Measuring Leadership through Opinion Assignment in Two State Supreme Courts

VICTOR E. FLANGO, CRAIG R. DUCAT,
and R. NEAL McKNIGHT

In 1976, the senior authors created an empirical typology of judicial leadership based upon the ratio of nonunanimous decisions and dissent rates of individual justices.[1] At that time, the authors promised to validate the technique using opinion assignment and bloc analysis. This chapter takes the first step toward fulfilling that promise by using opinion assignment to measure leadership on two state supreme courts.

LEADERSHIP AND VOTING CONSENSUS

Following the general idea of the earlier study, the basic premise of this study is that the chief justice, as formal leader of a state supreme court, is an important determinant of productivity. Productivity on a court means deciding the maximum number of cases possible consistent with giving each case due consideration. It also means reaching consensus whenever possible so that the development of the law is unambiguous. This conception assumes that effective leadership results in minimum conflict and a high degree of cohesiveness, satisfaction, and productivity.[2]

Not only the chief justice but most justices desire to increase the impact of their decisions and to avoid the adverse effects of visible conflict. Other things being equal, they would prefer unanimous decisions. J. Woodford Howard gives several examples of the sacrifice of deeply held views to group and institutional interests. Consensus decision making may indeed be the relevant model for most judicial decisions. S. Sidney Ulmer thus notes, "An obvious fact about collegial courts is that they tend strongly not only toward conformity but also toward unanimity."[3] Although the dissent rate in state supreme courts appears to be increasing, the proportion of unanimous to non-unanimous decisions is still high.[4] The traditional explanation for this high degree of consensus is that "dissent detracts from the prestige of the court and undermines its institutional solidarity."[5] Dissent is thought to create uncertainty in the law and thus reduce the impact of judicial decisions.[6]

With all the inhibitions against dissent, perhaps it is surprising that there is so much dissent on state supreme courts. Because of the strictures against dissent, nonunanimous decisions have taken on an importance of their own. Burton M. Atkins and Justin J. Green contend that the "nonunanimous decision has, perhaps by default, emerged as the primary measure of conflict on appellate courts." Sheldon Goldman claims that decisions that contain dissents "are manifestations of direct and open conflict within the courts."[7] Yet decisions that do not contain dissent need not imply consensus. Some justices find dissents distasteful because they involve criticizing a colleague's work directly.[8] Voting consensus may even be an artifact of large caseloads and consequently of the time justices have available to write dissenting opinions. Many state appellate courts deal with heavy caseloads by assigning cases to a single judge, who researches and writes the opinion of the court. The result is single-judge decision making and a false facade of consensus.[9] Consensus in a large percentage of cases could be a result of court structure (the absence of an intermediate appellate court to screen out the more routine appeals) or court jurisdiction (mandatory jurisdiction that forces the court of last resort to consider each case). In sum, the absence of dissent may indicate an "illusion of consensus," not agreement.[10]

OPINION ASSIGNMENT

To surmount the methodological problems caused by an artificially high proportion of unanimous decisions, opinions will be used to measure leadership in this chapter.[11] For decisions on the merits, justices must vote for the majority or dissent, and so a certain amount of voting agreement is inevitable. Judges who vote together may not do so for the same reasons. As Walter F. Murphy writes, "The fact that two or more Justices vote together is rather weak evidence that their votes are 'the result of interaction; standing alone, voting records tell us very little about the force or direction of any interpersonal influence that may exist."[12] To join an opinion coalition, however, each justice must make a conscious decision either to join or write an opinion or to concur in the result.[13]

The opinion coalition is an important stage of decision making. A decision on the merits of a case determines which litigant wins, but the majority opinion provides legal justification for the decision and establishes precedent for future decisions. To a large extent, the content of an opinion depends upon the opinion-writer. Danelski's comments on the selection of an opinion-writer in the U.S. Supreme Court are applicable to the selection of spokesmen in other courts as well. The opinion-writer may determine the value of a decision as precedent (for example, the opinion may be placed on one ground rather than another, two grounds instead of one, or deal narrowly or broadly with the issues), could affect the acceptability of the decision to the public, may retain the court's majority in close cases, and may persuade dissenting associates to join the court's opinion.[14]

Most research on opinion assignment, like that on most judicial behavior, has focused upon the U.S. Supreme Court. Thus conclusions about opinion assignment may be generalizable only to courts in which the chief justice assigns the opinions, if he is in the majority. If not, of course, the most senior associate justice in the majority makes the assignment. The justice assigned to write the majority opinion prepares a draft and circulates it. Yet because justices receiving the draft may either join the opinion, request that changes be made, or write their own opinions, the opinion majority is often smaller than the decisional majority.

Stanford S. McConkie claims that Hawaii is the only state that follows the opinion assignment practice of the U.S. Supreme Court precisely. Elliot E. Slotnick counts four states that follow the federal method of assignment.[15] Both authors agree that in more than a quarter of the states the chief justice assigns opinions in all cases, whether in the majority or not.[16] Murphy notes ways the chief justice of the U.S. Supreme Court could use his opinion-assignment authority to encourage consensus. He may, for example, select a wavering member of a coalition to write an opinion or may use the assignment of an opinion to reward past cooperation.[17]

More than two-thirds of the states use an automatic method of opinion assignment. Justices either draw cases by lot or, more often, receive them by rotation. Assignments are usually made when briefs come in, although several courts wait until the postargument conference.[18] In less than half of the twenty states in which assignment is made on a rotating basis, the assignment holds only if the justice to whom the case is assigned is in the majority. In Indiana, for example, the reporting justice writes the opinion unless outvoted, in which case the dissenting opinion becomes the majority opinion. In Kansas and New Mexico, which use a rigid rotational method of assignment, one justice has written both the majority and dissenting opinions.[19] In many states that use the rotational system, some exercise of discretion by the chief justice is permitted. For example, one justice from a New England state explained that although opinions were distributed "by lot," the "chief justice reserves a certain number of cases for assignment by him to a justice who is specifically qualified for that particular case."[20]

Advocates of the rotational method of assignment claim that it distributes cases equitably in the long run, limits perceptions that any particular justice receives more than his or her share of routine or time-consuming cases, precludes the development of special experts on the courts, and relieves the chief justice of the responsibility for balancing the workload.[21] Advocates of assignment by the chief justice claim that method is more flexible and permits more rational assignments based upon judges' interests and expertise.[22]

The American Bar Association once favored opinion assignment by the presiding justice rather than a rotational method of assignment so that the views of a justice as expressed in conference, his interest in the problem, and his grasp of issues could be considered. The American Bar Association's recent *Standards Relating to Appellate Courts* states only that "responsibility for preparing opinions should be assigned among the judges participating in the decision through procedures supervised by the judge who presides in the decision conference." The ABA Report warns, however, against unwise specialization, one-person decisions, and the vulnerability of the court if an "expert" in a particular field of law leaves the court. Most state supreme court justices disagree with the recommendation.[23]

In sum, a chief justice who is an extraordinary leader can make the court perform more effectively and efficiently by using selective opinion assignment. A court without an extraordinary leader may be better served by a rotational method of assignment. Slotnick concludes that nondiscretionary assignment methods best maintain social cohesion, but the chief justice's discretion in assigning opinions can best accomplish the efficient disposition of the workload.[24] An exploration of the effect of methods of opinion assignment on leadership is one objective of this chapter.

LEADERSHIP AND OPINION ASSIGNMENT

There are almost as many definitions of leadership as there are people who have attempted to define the concept. Leadership has been defined as a formal position in an organization, as charismatic personality, as the exercise of influence, as power, and as the instrument of goal achievement.[25] We can accept Ulmer's definition of leadership as "a process of exerting influence on that behavior, in an organized group, which leads to the establishment and achievement of goals."[26] This definition neither specifies how influence is exercised nor suggests that only one person can be a leader. One person may perform leadership functions in one situation or at one time and be a nonleader in other situations or at other times.[27]

In this chapter, several indicators will be used to identify leaders. Of course, the chief justice occupies the formal leadership position, and there is nothing to prevent the chief justice from being the actual leader of the court. Leadership, however, is treated not as an assumption but as a hypothesis to be tested.

The actual or informal leader of the court is defined as the court member who attracts the most justices to join his opinion coalition. It is not unreasonable to assume that a justice would join in opinions he finds attractive, whether the basis of the attraction is similar values, the brilliance of the opinion, or other factors. Conversely, a justice who can attract others to join his opinions exerts influence over them. Indicators of actual leadership attempt to tap the charismatic, influence, and power dimensions of leadership. Specific indicators will be explained as they are introduced.

Operationally, all indicators of informal leadership are based on majority opinion coalitions. In this respect we differ from Ulmer, who did not distinguish between majority and dissenting opinions. Yet even Ulmer conceded that a majority opinion is special because it becomes law.[28] Only the majority opinion provides the rationale for the court's decision and becomes precedent for future decisions.

In addition to the formal leader (the chief justice) and the informal leader (the justice with whom other members of the court most often agree), the concept of a rival leader will be explored. This alternative leader would be expected to lead the opposition in dissent. If successful, this justice would become the new informal leader on the court. Indicators of alternative leaders are the same as the ones used to identify actual leaders, except that the indicators are based upon dissenting opinion coalitions only.

THE MICHIGAN SUPREME COURT, 1956-1962

The Michigan Supreme Court uses a rotational method of opinion assignment. A justice is assigned to write an opinion for the case, but other justices may also write opinions. Differences among opinions are discussed at conference and reconciled if possible. If consensus is not possible, the opinion with the most signatures becomes the majority opinion. Thus the majority opinion-writer is not known until after conference. Justices must support opinions without knowing "whether the opinion will be a dissent, a concurrence, or the opinion of the court."[29]

It is appropriate that we begin our analysis of leadership where Ulmer started in 1963—the Michigan Supreme Court. Ulmer chose to analyze five hundred opinions written between 1958 and 1960. Because our "courts" are defined by change in chief justice, we chose the time period that John R. Dethmers was chief justice—1956 to 1962. This period has been studied by Glendon Schubert as well as by Ulmer.[30] Although our time period is longer than Ulmer's, our sample of cases (221) is smaller because it does not include unanimous decisions. Cases involving dissent exaggerate the amount of conflict on the court and thus highlight situations in which leadership is exercised.[31]

One disadvantage of defining a court by the tenure of the chief justice rather than by a change in court membership is that any justice who served during the tenure of the chief justice, no matter how briefly, could be included in the analysis. Between 1956 and 1962, fourteen justices served on the Dethmers court. Justices Paul L. Adams, Emerson R. Boyles, Neil E. Reid, Edward M. Sharpe, and Otis M. Smith, however, participated in fewer than ten cases in which there was a dissenting opinion and therefore are excluded from our analysis.

Before beginning our examination of leadership, we attempted to gain an understanding of the basic structure of the Dethmers court

Table 10.1. Principal Components Analysis of the Dethmers Court

Dethmers	.77	.19	−.09	.16
Carr	.87	.16	−.13	.03
Kelly	.75	.18	−.03	.19
Smith	−.30	.04	.22	−.79
Black	−.75	.40	−.10	.29
Edwards	−.06	.08	.91	−.08
Voelker	.10	.87	.28	−.02
Kavanagh	−.13	−.28	.50	.65
Souris	−.24	−.78	.35	.28

through bloc analysis. Our earlier examinations of leadership revealed that after Dethmers assumed the chief justiceship, both his own dissent rate and the proportion of decisions on the Michigan Supreme Court that were nonunanimous increased, indicating that Dethmers was a weak leader.[32] The chief justice along with Justices Leland W. Carr and Harry F. Kelly were the only Republicans on the bench during this period. A principal components analysis with an orthogonal rotation revealed four dimensions to the court. The loadings are listed in Table 10.1.

The Republicans and Justice Eugene F. Black load highest on the first dimension. Yet Justice Black has an opposite sign, which indicates agreement on the issues involved but disagreement with the Republican bloc with respect to how they should be decided. The other dimensions are fragmented but show agreement between George Edwards and Thomas M. Kavanagh on the third dimension and disagreement between Talbot Smith and Kavanagh on the fourth dimension. The second dimension shows modest disagreement between Black and Theodore Souris. It also reveals that John D. Voelker and Souris related to other members of the court in opposite ways, but it does not describe their relationship with each other because they did not sit together on the Dethmers court. The replacement of Voelker with Souris did affect relationships within the court. This is about as far as principal components analysis can take us, however, for it can describe voting blocs but not explain their causes. We must go beyond agreement scores and factor loadings to determine leadership within blocs.

Measures of Majority Leadership. Ulmer uses one summary indicator of leadership, the percentage of a judge's total opinion output that became majority opinions.[33] He contends that this percentage singles

Table 10.2. Majority Opinions in the Dethmers Court

	Majority Opinions	Total Opinions	Percentage Majority	Rank Order
Kavanagh	24	32	75	1
Voelker	12	18	67	2
Edwards	32	54	59	3
Dethmers	21	38	55	4
Carr	33	72	46	5.5
Smith	22	48	46	5.5
Kelly	22	52	42	7
Souris	11	29	38	8
Black	29	78	37	9

Table 10.3. Opportunity to Write Majority Opinions in the Dethmers Court

	Majority Opinions	Total Opinions	Percentage Majority	Rank Order
Souris	11	39	28	1
Carr	33	121	27	2
Edwards	32	130	25	3
Kavanagh	24	101	24	4
Black	29	138	21	5
Voelker	12	66	18	6
Smith	22	128	17	7
Dethmers	21	137	15	8.5
Kelly	22	144	15	8.5

out those justices most successful in attracting majority support for their opinions. Applying this index to our data, we find, like Ulmer, that Kavanagh scores highest, as shown in Table 10.2.

This measure, however, does not take into account the number of opportunities the writer had to write a majority opinion. The opinion assignment ratio, the percentage of times a justice wrote an opinion when that justice was part of the majority, may also be useful as a summary measure of leadership.[34]

This ratio in Table 10.3 indicates that Souris and Carr were most successful in writing the majority opinion when they were in the majority. Souris wrote the largest percentage of opinions when he was in the majority, but this percentage is based on a comparatively small sample of opinions.

Table 10.4. Majority Opinion-Writer and Voting Split in the
Dethmers Court

Majority Opinion-Writer	Number of Opinions When Vote Was				Shapley-Shubik Index
	7-1	6-2	5-3	4-4	
Kavanagh	1	5	11	2	.193
Carr	6	5	6	6	.191
Smith	4	4	10	2	.188
Black	3	6	9	2	.186
Kelly	3	5	2	3	.185
Souris	0	4	5	0	.184
Voelker	0	5	5	0	.183
Edwards	4	11	9	0	.175
Dethmers	6	5	4	2	.175

The discussion of the opinion assignment ratio generates a related question: does choice of opinion-writer vary by closeness of the vote? Do some justices write the opinion more frequently when the vote is close and others when the majority coalition is large?

Table 10.4 indicates that Chief Justice Dethmers and Justice Carr each wrote more opinions than any other court members when only one justice dissented. It appears that the chief justice wrote most of his opinions when the opinion coalition was large, that is, when only one or two justices dissented. Justice Edwards wrote proportionately more opinions when the vote was split six to two. Five-to-three voting divisions saw the majority opinion most often written by one of the Democratic justices—Kavanagh, Smith, Black, and Edwards. Justice Souris did not write opinions when the vote was evenly split or when the majority coalition was seven. Justice Carr wrote a large number of opinions when the opinion coalition was large but also when the vote was evenly split. This indicates Justice Carr's ability to hold a coalition together and suggests that he could attract at least one Democrat to the Republican bloc.

The Shapley-Shubik index defines power in groups as the probability that an individual is the one who casts the decisive vote.[35] Justices who dissent are given no credit; only justices who join in the majority share in the power. Applying this index to opinion coalitions, rather than voting blocs, still means that smaller opinion coalitions give the opinion-writer more power than larger coalitions. Table 10.4 reveals Justices Kavanagh and Carr as most powerful.

Table 10.5. Support for Majority Opinion-Writers in the Dethmers Court

Majority Opinion-Writer	Number of Opinions	Number of Agreements	Number of Dissents	Percentage Support	Rank Order
Voelker	12	52	25	67.5	1
Kavanagh	24	98	52	65.3	2
Carr	33	122	77	61.3	3
Smith	22	88	57	60.7	4
Edwards	32	123	80	60.6	5
Dethmers	21	78	51	60.5	6
Souris	11	41	28	59.4	7
Black	29	105	82	56.1	8
Kelly	2.2	71	57	55.5	9

The next indicator measures leadership by the number of justices the opinion-writer attracts to his opinions. This measure should show the differential success of opinion-writers in attracting support, but because our sample contains only nonunanimous decisions it is not possible for any opinion-writer to have a support score of 100 percent.

On an eight-justice court with all justices participating, the opinion-writer would need the support of seven justices in each case for which he wrote the majority opinion to be supported 100 percent. Support from six justices in all cases would mean a support score of 87.5 percent, the theoretical upper limit of this index in the Michigan Supreme Court, where the sample consists of nonunanimous cases. The theoretical lower limit of the index is 50 percent, a score below which the justice would no longer be the majority opinion-writer. This index in Table 10.5 shows Voelker and Kavanagh as the justices most likely to put together opinion coalitions and Kelly and Black as the justices who attracted the least support. There is very little difference among the scores of the remaining justices.

Table 10.6 is a matrix of support for the opinion-writer that Ulmer labeled an Inter-individual Solidarity Index (ISI).[36] Each cell entry is essentially a percentage figure showing the magnitude of support for the opinion-writer. For example, Justice Carr participated in twenty decisions when Chief Justice Dethmers wrote the opinion. Eighteen of these twenty times Carr joined the Dethmers opinion, hence the entry 90 percent in the Dethmers-Carr cell of Table 10.6. Conversely, Dethmers was in the majority the thirty-two times when Carr wrote the

Table 10.6. Inter-Individual Solidarity Index, Majority Opinions in the Dethmers Court

Majority Opinion-Writer	Percentage Support for Majority Opinion-Writer									Average Support	Rank Order
	De	Ca	Ke	Sm	Bl	Ed	Vo	Ka	So		
Smith	82	14	36		95	100	85	94	100	75.7	1
Voelker	8	9	83	100	100	100		100	X	70.3	2
Kavanagh	66	50	56	65	84	75	72		55	65.4	3
Edwards	48	38	52	86	70		84	69	70	64.6	4
Souris	22	18	18	100	80	100	X	90		61.1	5
Black	57	31	62	69		68	92	75	20	59.2	6
Dethmers		90	90	43	43	61	29	53	13	52.7	7
Carr	100		97	50	39	46	25	30	28	51.9	8
Kelly	77	86		28	42	31	50	70	28	51.5	9

opinion, joining the majority opinion each time. Because the chief justice supported Carr more than Carr supported him, we conclude that Carr was the more influential of the two.

Ulmer rank-ordered each justice's support patterns and used the sums of rows as one indication of the relative influence of each justice. From these rankings, Ulmer concluded that Kavanagh was the de facto leader of the Dethmers court.[37]

Ulmer's practice of creating a matrix of support for each opinion-writer, rank-ordering justices in order of support for the opinion-writer, and then averaging the rank orders to determine leadership seems unduly complex. Perhaps it is necessary to use this procedure to amplify small differences among justices which result when both unanimous and nonunanimous opinions were used to measure leadership. In this chapter either means or medians of support for the opinion-writer are taken directly from the ISI and those figures rank-ordered. Using this approach, Smith, with an average support score of 76 percent, emerges as the de facto leader of the Dethmers court. (If medians of support for opinion-writers are used to rank-order justices, however, Voelker appears as the actual leader.)

Considering only first- and second-order support relationships, Figure 10.1 is a sociogram of opinion relationships in the Dethmers court. It shows that Justice Smith received the most first and second choices. It also demonstrates that Kavanagh was not the first choice (did not receive the most support) of any other justice, whereas Voelker, for example, was the first choice of Kavanagh, Smith, Black, and

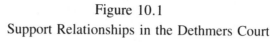

Figure 10.1

Support Relationships in the Dethmers Court

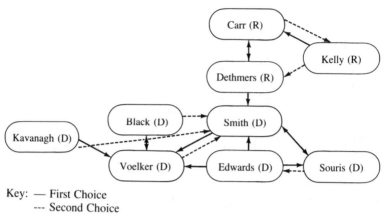

Key: — First Choice
     --- Second Choice

Edwards. Figure 10.1 also reveals that the chief justice was the link between the Republican bloc of Dethmers, Carr, and Kelly and the Democratic group.

Ulmer rank-ordered each justice on the court to determine which opinion-writer each justice supported most often. This technique, in effect, forces each justice to support some opinion-writer most. Even if a justice joined in the opinions of a particular opinion-writer less than 50 percent of the time, he still could join the opinions of that justice proportionately more often than those of the other justices.

It seems to us that support scores should be read horizontally rather than vertically and that a minimum threshold of support for the majority opinion-writer be set. For example, if we arbitrarily set a support score of 90 percent agreement with the majority opinion-writer, the sociogram in Figure 10.1 changes as depicted in Figure 10.2.[38] The court is divided into two separate blocs, with Chief Justice Dethmers the leader of the Republican bloc and Justice Smith the leader of the Democratic bloc. In sum, different procedures and different measures yield slightly different results. The task now is to see how these measures of majority leadership interrelate.

Rank-order correlations among the five measures in Table 10.7 reveal that the Inter-individual Solidarity Index, support index, and majority opinions are related to each other but not to the opinion assignment or Shapley-Shubik indices. The opinion assignment ratio

Figure 10.2

Opinion Support in the Dethmers Court (over 90%)

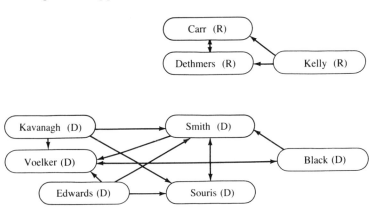

was designed to measure equitability of opinion assignment, not leadership. The Shapley-Shubik index is a measure of power, and although leadership is a component of power, it is not the equivalent of power. Of the three interrelated measures, the Inter-individual Solidarity Index seems to be a better indicator than the two more condensed summary indices because it shows support percentages for each pair of justices.[39]

Alternative Leadership. The concept of leadership, we believe, is large enough to encompass leadership in opposition as well as in majority. Rather than dissent alone, the alternate leader will attempt to forge a minority coalition. This minority opinion coalition has the potential for becoming a majority coalition if it can attract "swing" justices to particular opinions if membership on the court changes.[40]

   In many respects, leadership in opposition may be a more difficult posture to maintain than majority leadership. By definition, leadership in dissent means losing the opportunity immediately to influence the development of the law. There may be more payoff to a "swing" justice in joining the majority and trying to influence the opinion rather than joining a minority. This "chameleon effect" may be the reason some justices, who do not feel strongly about the issue in question, vote with the majority. On the other hand, relative support given to the dissent opinion-writer may more accurately indicate leadership than support given to the majority opinion-writer.[41]

   Table 10.8 contains the ISI for the Dethmers court based upon

Table 10.7. Interrelationship of Leadership Measures in the Dethmers Court

Ulmer's Rank[a]	Majority Opinions	Support Index	ISI	Opinion Assignment	Shapley-Shubik
Kavanagh	Kavanagh	Voelker	Smith	Souris	Kavanagh
Voelker	Voelker	Kavanagh	Voelker	Carr	Carr
Dethmers	Edwards	Carr	Kavanagh	Edwards	Smith
Smith	Dethmers	Smith	Edwards	Kavanagh	Black
Carr	Carr	Edwards	Souris	Black	Kelly
Edwards	Smith	Dethmers	Black	Voelker	Souris
Kelly	Kelly	Souris	Dethmers	Smith	Voelker
Black	Souris	Black	Carr	Dethmers	Edwards
—[a]	Black	Kelly	Kelly	Kelly	Dethmers

	ISI	Support Index	Majority Opinion	Opinion Assignment	Shapley-Shubik
ISI	X				
Support Index	.61	X			
Majority Opinion	.42	.80	X		
Opinion Assignment	.10	.23	00	X	
Shapley-Shubik	.08	.33	−.05	.22	X

[a]Justice Souris was not included in Ulmer's sample.

Table 10.8. Inter-Individual Solidarity Index, Dissenting Opinions in the Dethmers Court

Dissent Bloc Writer	Percentage Support for Dissent Opinion-Writer									Average Support	Rank Order
	De	Ca	Ke	Sm	Bl	Ed	Vo	Ka	So		
Smith	0	0	0		37	62	100[a]	36	100	41.8	1
Black	6	0	9	51		29	100	70	44	38.6	2
Voelker	0	0	0	60[a]	100	60[a]		25[a]	X	35.0	3
Souris	12	6	0	78	23	77	X	35		33.0	4
Kavanagh	29	33	14	0	67	29	50[a]		20	31.5	5
Kelly	84	100		4	7	4	0	5	14	27.2	6
Edwards	13	6	6	8	31		60	22	86	25.5	7
Carr	78		76	3	0	3	9	0	0	21.1	8
Dethmers		93	56	0	0	0	0	0	0[a]	18.6	9

[a]Percentage based upon five opinions or less.

Figure 10.3
Opinion Support in Dissent (over 80%)

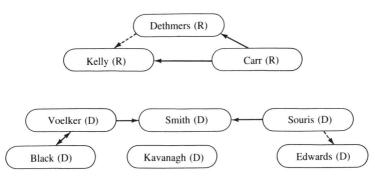

Key: — 90% or more agreement
     --- 80% or more agreement

support for opinion-writers in dissent. Table 10.8 is analogous to Table 10.6 and may be interpreted similarly. For example, Justice Carr participated in fifteen cases in which the chief justice wrote the dissenting opinion. Carr joined Dethmers in the dissenting opinion fourteen of these fifteen times, hence the entry of 93 percent in the Dethmers-Carr cell. Conversely, Carr and Dethmers shared thirty-six opinions when Carr wrote the dissenting opinions. Dethmers joined Carr in twenty-eight of these, hence the entry of 78 percent in the Carr-Dethmers cell.

If support scores of all the justices are used to evaluate leadership in dissent, Justice Smith was the leader even though not one Republican ever joined him in a dissenting opinion. According to the ISI, Chief Justice Dethmers attracted the least support in dissent.

Because the Republican and Democratic opinion coalitions are not connected, there is no need to consider Republican rankings in identifying leaders of the Democratic opinion coalitions and vice versa. Figure 10.3 is a sociogram of opinion support relationships in dissent. In dissent, Chief Justice Dethmers was the de facto leader of the Republicans and Justice Smith was the de facto leader of the Democrats. The Republican bloc was the same in dissent as it was in the majority, but the Democratic coalition broke down. Justice Smith received the support of Voelker and Souris and was still the de facto leader. Voelker and Black formed a dissenting pair, and Kavanagh became an isolate. To the extent that Kavanagh was unable to attract the support in dissenting opinions that he did for majority opinions, credence is lent to the conclusion that the ISI is a better indicator of leadership than percentage of majority opinions.

Using a different data set than Ulmer, confined to nonunanimous decisions over a longer time span, and some different indicators of leadership, we find that Kavanagh and Voelker emerge as high on our ranking as they did on his. By our modified measure, however, Justice Smith was the leader of the court because he was leader of the majority voting bloc. Dethmers, Carr, and Kelly rank lower because they could not attract enough Democratic votes to put together as many majority opinion coalitions. Perhaps our use of nonunanimous decisions emphasized the cleaveage, but it did occur along party lines.

This study introduces the concept of leadership in opposition. On that measure, too, Justice Smith is the leader. Justice Black is also shown to be a strong leader of the opposition, which may explain why he loads on the first dimension of the principal components analysis with the Republican bloc, but with an opposite sign.

PENNSYLVANIA SUPREME COURT, 1961-1971.

Pennsylvania provides a contrast to Michigan in that the chief justice assigns opinions in Pennsylvania. For this illustration, we chose the court of Chief Justice John C. Bell, who assumed the office in August 1961. Our earlier examination of leadership considered Bell a social leader because, although his own dissent rate decreased after he became chief justice, the proportion of nonunanimous decisions on the court increased from 28 to 31 percent.[42] Between 1961 and 1971, eleven justices served on the Pennsylvania Supreme Court, but Justices Anne X. Alpern, Alexander Barbieri, and Earl S. Keim participated in too few cases to be included in the analysis. The data base consists of 1,422 nonunanimous cases.

Before beginning our analysis of leadership on the Pennsylvania Supreme Court, we will again attempt to get an overall picture of the bloc structure of the Bell court using principal components analysis rotated to an orthogonal solution. Table 10.9 reveals three dimensions to the Bell court. Justices Michael J. Eagen, Henry X. O'Brien, and Samuel J. Roberts form a voting bloc on one dimension, the disagreement between Chief Justice Bell and Justice H. B. Cohen forms a second dimension, and Justice Benjamin R. Jones loads alone on the third dimension. Justice Michael Musmanno loads nearly equally on

Table 10.9. Principal Components Analysis of the Bell Court

Bell	−.29	−.73	−.05
Musmanno	−.44	.42	−.37
Jones	−.10	.06	.94
Cohen	−.14	.71	.01
Eagen	.50	.13	.02
O'Brien	.68	.02	−.05
Roberts	.72	−.15	−.05

Table 10.10. Majority Opinions in the Bell Court

	Majority Opinions	Total Opinions	Percentage Majority	Rank Order
O'Brien	164	186	88	1
Eagen	202	245	82	2
Jones	197	245	80	3
Musmanno	105	163	64	4
Bell	146	245	60	5.5
Cohen	169	283	60	5.5
Pomeroy	35	62	56	7
Roberts	194	373	52	8

all three dimensions but does not fit on any one of the three very well. Justice Thomas W. Pomeroy replaced Justice Musmanno on the bench.

Measures of Majority Leadership. The proportion of each justices' opinions that were majority opinions is listed in Table 10.10. Justice O'Brien had the highest percentage of majority opinions. In addition, over 80 percent of the opinions written by Justices Eagen and Jones were majority opinions.

The opinion assignment ratio is an inappropriate measure of leadership in a court where the chief justice assigns the opinions. The reader may be interested to know, however, that Roberts ranked highest on this indicator and Pomeroy lowest.

Table 10.11 breaks down opinion-writers according to closeness of the vote. The Shapley-Shubik index shows Justice Musmanno as the most powerful court member. Twenty-seven percent of Musmanno's opinions (twenty-six of ninety-six) had two dissenters, and another 16 percent (fifteen of ninety-six) were written with only a four-person majority. Justices Eagen, Jones, and Cohen wrote a high proportion of

Table 10.11. Majority Opinion-Writer and Voting Split in the Bell Court

Majority Opinion-Writer	Number of Opinions When Vote Was				Shapley-Shubik	Rank Order
	6-1	5-1	5-2	4-3		
Musmanno	28	27	26	15	.197	1
O'Brien	53	45	26	13	.191	2.5
Roberts	60	55	37	12	.191	2.5
Bell	59	39	22	12	.189	4
Jones	70	53	34	13	.187	5.5
Eagen	73	66	26	8	.187	5.5
Pomeroy	8	13	2	0	.144	7
Cohen	68	40	28	20	.127	8

Table 10.12. Support for Majority Opinion-Writer in the Bell Court

Majority Opinion-Writer	Number of Opinions	Number of Agreements	Number of Dissents	Percentage Support	Rank Order
Bell	146	590	179	77	1.5
Eagen	202	831	244	77	1.5
O'Brien	164	658	222	75	3.5
Roberts	194	764	252	75	3.5
Jones	197	761	268	74	5
Cohen	169	680	254	73	6.5
Pomeroy	35	132	48	73	6.5
Musmanno	105	390	155	72	8

Table 10.13. Inter-Individual Solidarity Index, Majority Opinions in the Bell Court

Majority Opinion-Writer	Percentage Support for Majority Opinion-Writer								Average Support	Rank Order
	Be	Mu	Jo	Co	Ea	O'B	R	Po		
Eagen	66	62	89	70		96	73	81	76.7	1
O'Brien	64	72	76	74	87		69	91	76.1	2
Bell		56	82	62	88	93	70	76	75.3	3
Jones	66	47		85	90	83	59	96	75.1	4
Roberts	60	80	73	49	86	93		82	74.7	5
Pomeroy	52	X	97	87	76	89	45		74.3	6
Cohen	53	69	87		81	91	48	82	73.0	7
Musmanno	49		58	53	89	92	86	X	71.2	8

Key: X = did not sit on the bench together.

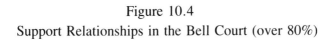

Figure 10.4

Support Relationships in the Bell Court (over 80%)

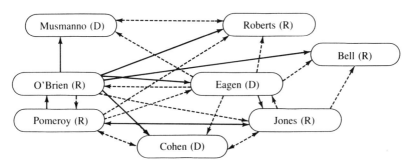

Key: — 90% or more agreement
     --- 80% or more agreement

majority opinions when there was a single dissenter. Justice Pomeroy's opinions nearly always had only one dissenter. This result could be interpreted to mean either that Pomeroy's opinions attracted a strong majority of support or that he was assigned to write the opinion only when strong majority coalitions existed. The latter explanation is more plausible because Pomeroy was the "freshman" on the Bell court and may have been assigned the easier opinions.

The next measure of leadership, as portrayed in Table 10.12, is the differential success of opinion-writers in attracting support. Bell's 146 opinions produced 590 agreements and 179 dissents from his colleagues, who had to choose whether to join his majority opinions. There is only a 5 percentage point difference between Musmanno, who received the least support, and Eagen and Bell, who received the most.

ISI rankings for the Bell court are presented in Table 10.13. Justice Eagen is revealed as the majority opinion leader, and bloc-partner O'Brien is the second most influential majority opinion leader.

The sociogram presented in Figure 10.4 shows that all justices, even Musmanno, are connected. One reason for the apparent connectedness is the high degree of support given to all justices by Justice O'Brien. Comparing both opinion agreement above 90 percent and above 80 percent, Justice Jones emerges as the majority leader.

Unlike the Michigan Supreme Court studied, the justices of the

Table 10.14. Interrelationship of Leadership Measures in the Bell
Court

Justice	Inter-Individual Solidarity Index	Support Index	Majority Opinion	Opinion Assignment	Shapley-Shubik
Eagen	1	1.5	2	5.5	5.5
O'Brien	2	3.5	1	7	2.5
Bell	3	1.5	5.5	3.5	4
Jones	4	5	3	3.5	5.5
Roberts	5	3.5	8	1	2.5
Pomeroy	6	6.5	7	8	7
Cohen	7	6.5	5.5	2	8
Musmanno	8	8	4	5.5	1

Pennsylvania Supreme Court were not easily divided into subgroups. A comparison of Tables 10.7 and 10.13 shows more consensus in the Pennsylvania Supreme Court than in the Michigan Supreme Court. Only 6 percentage points separated Eagen, the justice who received the most support in the majority, from Musmanno, whose opinions received the least support. In contrast, the spread between Justice Smith and Justice Kelly on the Michigan Supreme Court was 24 percentage points.

The rank order of justices in the Bell court on five measures of leadership in the majority is displayed in Table 10.14. Even a casual inspection of these data reveals the same pattern that we discovered in Michigan. The ISI, support, and majority opinion indicators are interrelated; the others are not. Again, the ISI appears to be the best indicator of leadership in the majority. The opinion assignment measure is inappropriate when opinions are assigned by the chief justice, power as measured by the Shapley-Shubik index is not equivalent to leadership, and the support index failed to distinguish leaders from followers.

Alternative Leaders. Leadership in dissent for the Bell court as measured by the ISI is reported in Table 10.15. Justice Jones most frequently led dissenting opinion coalitions. All justices received support in dissent, unlike the situation in the Dethmers court, on which two separate blocs were formed. Musmanno received more support in dissent than he did in the majority but was not a leader in the sense of forming dissenting coalitions. Indeed, Musmanno was selected to illustrate the concept of nonleader or "outsider" on the court.[43]

Table 10.15. Inter-Individual Solidarity Index, Dissenting Opinions in the Bell Court

Dissent Bloc writer	Percentage Support for Dissent Opinion-Writer								Average Support	Rank Order
	Be	Mu	Jo	Co	Ea	O'B	R	Po		
Jones	43	13		33	20	12	13	40	24.8	1
O'Brien	7	50a	0	47	20		44	0	24.0	2
Roberts	35	40	13	6	24	26		16	22.8	3
Eagen	19	0	29	25		28	47	11	22.7	4
Musmanno	10		10	20	12	20	55	X	21.1	5.5
Pomeroy	33	X	60	0	10	11	13		21.1	5.5
Bell		49	21	16	5	16	19	25	20.1	7
Cohen	15	9	40		38	20	2	9	19.0	8

aPercentage based on five opinions or less.

No sociogram of opinion leadership in dissent is presented because no percentage support scores reached the threshold of 90, 80, or even 70 percent. In brief, leadership in dissent was very similar to leadership in the majority in the Bell court.

In this chapter, we have attempted to explore the concept of leadership. Like Ulmer, we have assumed that each justice is trying to "lead"—to persuade others to his point of view.[44] We have also assumed that every justice is industrious and desires to write at least his fair share of opinions. Opinions were not distinguished by subject-matter area. A justice who writes a disproportionate number of opinions in one subject area would be an expert but not a leader. Although expertise may be a consideration in opinion assignment, a leader should be able to attract support in a variety of subject-matter areas.

Our major departure from previous studies of court leadership was the identification of leaders in the majority and leaders of the opposition, which required a separate analysis of majority opinions and dissenting opinions. The results from our two case studies are mixed. In the Michigan Supreme Court, the concept of leader of the opposition is viable. Justice Black was a strong leader of the opposition, which is obscured if agreement in majority opinions is mixed together with agreement in dissent. Justice Smith, however, was a leader both in the majority and in dissent. In Pennsylvania, Justice Eagen emerged as the actual leader in the Bell court, and Justice Jones was the leader in dissent. Support for the opinion-writer was much more evenly distributed in Pennsylvania than it was in Michigan.

Leadership is closely related to means for measuring it. The early part of this chapter makes a case for distinguishing opinion behavior from decisional behavior and for basing the study of leadership only on nonunanimous opinions. We believe that use of nonunanimous opinions highlights conflict situations in which leadership can be identified and measured.

The Inter-Individual Solidarity Index proved to be the best measure of leadership in this study. Leadership may be a component of power, but the Shapley-Shubik index of power was not related to our other measures of leadership. Similarly, the opinion assignment ratio, though measuring equitability of opinion assignment, was not found to be a good measure of leadership in this research. All measures of leadership revealed a higher degree of consensus in the Bell court than in the Dethmers court. During the period of study, the Bell court contained three Democrats and five Republicans and the Dethmers court contained three Republicans and six Democrats.

This study is a preliminary look at leadership in state supreme courts because many more courts in many more states should be analyzed before our hypotheses can be tested thoroughly. The research agenda on leadership in state supreme courts is large, and we will be pleased if our reexamination spurs renewed interest in this topic.

1. Craig R. Ducat and Victor E. Flango, *Leadership in State Supreme Courts: Roles of the Chief Justice*, Sage Professional Papers in American Politics 04-030 (Beverly Hills: Sage, 1976).

2. David J. Danelski, "The Influence of the Chief Justice in the Decisional Process of the Supreme Court," in Sheldon Goldman and Austin Sarat, eds., *American Court Systems: Readings in Judicial Process and Behavior* (San Francisco: W. H. Freeman, 1978), pp. 506-19.

3. J. Woodford Howard, Jr., "On the Fluidity of Judicial Choice," *American Political Science Review* 62 (1968): 43-56; S. Sidney Ulmer, *Courts as Small and Not So Small Groups* (New York: General Learning Press, 1971), p. 13.

4. Henry R. Glick and George W. Pruet, Jr., "Dissent in State Supreme Courts: Patterns and Correlates of Conflict," Chapter 9 of this volume. See also Bradley C. Canon and Dean Jaros, "State Supreme Courts—Some Comparative Data," *State Government* 42 (1969): 260-64.

5. Ulmer, *Courts,* p. 13.

6. Henry Robert Glick, *Supreme Courts in State Politics: An Investigation of the Judicial Role* (New York: Basic Books, 1971), p. 95.

7. Burton M. Atkins and Justin J. Green, "Consensus on the United States Courts

of Appeals: Illusion or Reality?" *American Journal of Political Science* 20 (1976): 735; Sheldon Goldman, "Conflict and Consensus on the United States Courts of Appeals," *Wisconsin Law Review* (1968): 463.

8. Glick, *Supreme Courts*, p. 97. Ulmer, however, has suggested that dissent reduces individual tensions by providing an outlet for frustrations. See S. Sidney Ulmer, "Dissent Behavior and the Social Background of Supreme Court Justices," *Journal of Politics* 32 (1970): 588.

9. Kenneth N. Vines and Herbert Jacob, "State Courts and Public Policy," in Herbert Jacob and Kenneth N. Vines, eds., *Politics in the American States: A Comparative Analysis,* 3d ed. (Boston: Little, Brown, 1976), p. 262.

10. Robert J. Sickels, "The Illusion of Judicial Consensus: Zoning Decisions in the Maryland Court of Appeals," *American Political Science Review* 59 (1965): 100-104.

11. Glendon Schubert used voting data when studying decision making of U.S. Supreme Court justices, but he used opinion data when studying decision-making behavior of High Court justices in Australia because opinion data "afford a better sample of such observations than do votes" ("Opinion Agreement among High Court Justices in Australia," *Australian and New Zealand Journal of Sociology* 4 [1968]: 4).

12. Walter F. Murphy, "Courts as Small Groups," *Harvard Law Review* 79 (1966): 1566.

13. S. Sidney Ulmer, "Leadership in the Michigan Supreme Court," in Glendon Schubert, ed., *Judicial Decision-Making* (Glencoe, Ill.: Free Press, 1963), p. 16. Justices may use the concurring opinion to explain why they joined the majority or may reply to arguments made in dissent.

14. Danelski, "The Influence," p. 514.

15. Stanford S. McConkie, "Decision-Making in State Supreme Courts," *Judicature* 59 (1976): 343; Elliot E. Slotnick, "Who Speaks for the Court? The View from the States," *Emory Law Journal* 26 (1977): 111.

16. Even in states where the chief justice assigns opinions, he may choose to do so on a rotating basis, as is the practice in Wyoming. In California, the opinion is assigned before the conference and is reassigned only if the justice to whom it was assigned is in the minority. See Robert L. Dudley, "Coalition Building on the California Supreme Court: Votes on Access and the Merits," Chapter 12 of this volume.

17. Walter F. Murphy, *Elements of Judicial Strategy* (Chicago: University of Chicago Press, 1964), p. 48.

18. Thomas B. Marvell, *Appellate Courts and Lawyers: Information Gathering in the Adversary System* (Westport, Conn.: Greenwood Press, 1978), p. 105.

19. McConkie, "Decision-Making," p. 343.

20. Slotnick, "Who Speaks for the Court?" p. 113.

21. ABA Committee, "Report on Internal Operating Procedures of Appellate Courts," cited in B.E. Witkin, "A Syllabus for Panel Discussion at the Appellate Judges' Conference of the Section of Judicial Administration," American Bar Association, August 6, 1968, Montreal, Canada, p. 544, reprinted in *Federal Rules Decisions* 63 (1974): 515. `

22. See Marvell, *Appellate Courts and Lawyers*, p. 105. For a discussion of the

relative merits of the two assignment methods, see National Center for State Courts, *The Appellate Process in Alabama* (Williamsburg, Va.: National Center for State Courts, 1973), pp. 127-31; George Rose Smith, "The Appellate Decisional Conference," *Arkansas Law Review* 28 (1975): 425, 431-33; and Robert A. Leflar, *Internal Operating Procedures of Appellate Courts* (Chicago: American Bar Association, 1976), pp. 39, 40.

23. ABA Committee, "Report"; American Bar Association, *Standards Relating to Appellate Courts* (Chicago: American Bar Association, 1977), p. 90.

24. Slotnick, "Who Speaks for the Court?" p. 138.

25. Ralph M. Stogdill, *Handbook of Leadership* (New York: Free Press, 1974), chap. 2, pp. 7-16.

26. Ulmer, "Leadership in the Michigan Supreme Court," p. 15.

27. Sidney Verba, *Small Groups and Political Behavior: A Study of Leadership* (Princeton: Princeton University Press, 1961), p. 118.

28. Ulmer, "Leadership in the Michigan Supreme Court," p. 24.

29. Ibid., p. 17.

30. Glendon Schubert, *Quantitative Analysis of Judicial Behavior* (Glencoe, Ill.: Free Press, 1959), pp. 129-41; see also S. Sidney Ulmer, "The Political Party Variable in the Michigan Supreme Court," *Journal of Public Law* 11 (1962): 352-62.

31. A very high proportion of unanimous decisions does not permit the measurement of leadership. For example, we examined all opinions of the Bernstein and Hays courts in Arizona. Because each justice voted with the majority at least 96 percent of the time, a determination of leadership in the remaining 4 percent of the cases would have been a fruitless exercise.

32. Ducat and Flango, *Leadership in State Supreme Courts*.

33. Ulmer, "Leadership in the Michigan Supreme Court," pp. 17-18.

34. Slotnick uses the opinion assignment ratio to measure equitability of opinion assignment but not as an indicator of leadership. See Elliot E. Slotnick, "Who Speaks for the Court? Majority Opinion Assignment from Taft to Burger," *American Journal of Political Science* 23 (1979): 63.

35. L. S. Shapley and Martin Shubik, "A Method for Evaluating the Distribution of Power in a Committee System," *American Political Science Review* 48 (1954): 787-92.

36. Ulmer, "Leadership in the Michigan Supreme Court," pp. 17-18.

37. Ibid.

38. Harold J. Spaeth and Michael F. Altfeld, "Influence Relationships within the Supreme Court: A Comparison of the Warren and Burger Courts," paper delivered at the Annual Meeting of the American Political Science Association, September 1-4, 1983, Chicago, considered an agreement score of one standard deviation above the mean as a threshold level to distinguish influential and noninfluential relationships. The authors acknowledge that "unfortunately, there is no theory from which we can derive a threshold level." In other words, any threshold level is somewhat arbitrary.

39. Ibid., p. 12. Spaeth and Altfeld also found the dyadic matrices to be the best measure of influence in the U.S. Supreme Court.

40. In contrast to people seeking leadership is the "outsider," a justice who would find himself in a leadership role only by chance. The outsider is expected to dissent regardless of whether anyone else joins the opinion. Unlike the justices seeking leadership roles, the outsider would not compromise to build a winning opinion coalition. Because this role is the antithesis of leadership, it will be discussed separately from the leadership roles. See the discussion of the outsider in Victor E. Flango, Craig R. Ducat, and Neal McKnight, "A Preliminary Look at Leaders, Alternative Leaders, and Non-Leaders in State Supreme Courts," paper delivered at the Annual Meeting of the Southern Political Science Association, October 28-30, 1982, Atlanta.

41. Michael F. Altfeld and Harold J. Spaeth, "Measuring Influence on the U.S. Supreme Court," paper delivered at the 1983 Meeting of the Midwest Political Science Association, Chicago, define both leadership and influence as components of power and restrict their study of influence to special opinions—those that do not constitute the opinion of the court.

42. Ducat and Flango, *Leadership in State Supreme Courts.*

43. Craig R. Ducat and Victor E. Flango, "The Outsider on the Court," *Journal of Politics* 47 (1985): 282-89.

44. Ulmer, "Leadership in the Michigan Supreme Court," p. 26.

11

A Longitudinal Study of the Docket Composition Theory of Conflict and Consensus

JOHN A. STOOKEY

The study of conflict and consensus on state supreme courts has been informed by two major theories: docket composition and justice composition.[1] The docket composition theory suggests that variation in conflict (usually measured as dissent rate) is a function of the types of issues a court must hear. That is, the dissent rate is likely to be higher on courts that are faced with controversial and complex issues than on courts that are confronted with relatively simple issues. The justice composition theory, on the other hand, posits that the conflict rate is determined by the degree of ideological and role heterogeneity among members.

Although John W. Patterson and Gregory J. Rathjen, Dean Jaros and Bradley C. Canon, and Henry R. Glick and Kenneth Vines,[2] among others, have studied the justice composition theory, there has been only one very preliminary attempt to test directly the docket composition theory.[3] I say "directly" because considerable attention has been given to testing this theory using surrogate measures of docket composition. For example, Canon and Jaros related social, political, and economic environments of states to supreme court dissent rates.[4] These environmental variables, they hypothesized, affect dissent rate by shaping both docket and justice composition. Docket composition, however, was not actually measured and related to dissent.

Other studies have attempted to measure the relationship between structural changes, particularly the creation of an intermediate court of appeals, and dissent. The theoretical justification here again is that such structural changes modify the docket composition of the supreme court, which in turn increases the dissent rate. Specifically, the dynamic is that supreme courts that are buffered from trial courts by an intermediate court decide proportionally more complex, policy-relevant cases than supreme courts, which must hear all appeals directly from the courts of original jurisdiction. The logic continues that because these complex cases have a higher probability of dissent, the dissent rate will be higher in supreme courts that have an intermediate court than in those without one. Thus, again, the rationale for this hypothesis is that docket composition is affected by structural changes, which affect dissent. Also again, however, there have been no studies that include a direct measure of docket composition.

In previous studies of the docket composition and justice composition theories, cross-sectional, rather than longitudinal, designs have been used. As pointed out by Glick and Pruet in Chapter 9, cross-sectional studies provide the unique opportunity to examine the relationship between a wide variety of legal and social settings and dissent rate. A question that has not been asked, however, is the extent to which the generalizations observed in cross-sectional studies hold when examined from a longitudinal perspective. For example, to what extent can historical changes in dissent rates in state courts be accounted for by changes over time in the composition of dockets and justices. In addition to providing a reliability check for findings generated from cross-sectional designs, longitudinal studies will permit for the first time exploration of the existence of cycles or regular patterns in dissent and also for the impact of specific historical events on dissent rate.

The purpose of this chapter is to test the validity of the docket composition theory using longitudinal data. This will be accomplished in the context of an exploratory study of the Arizona Supreme Court for the years 1913 to 1976.

DATA AND HYPOTHESES

Arizona was the last of the contiguous states to enter the Union in 1912. The state constitution provided for a supreme court with sole appellate jurisdiction over all criminal cases and all but the most minor civil appeals. The court was composed of three members elected for fixed terms by nonpartisan ballot.

To evaluate the ability of the docket composition theory to explain the historical evolution of dissent in Arizona, all cases (including *per curiam* but not memorandum) decided in the sixty-four-year period

Figure 11.1. Dissent Rate in the Arizona Supreme Court, 1913–1976

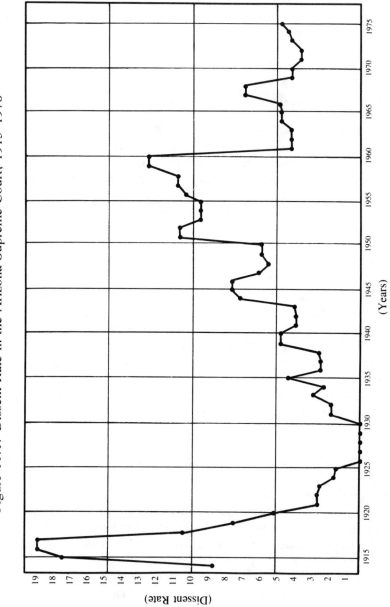

(Years)

(Dissent Rate)

Note: On this and the following figures, no values are shown for 1913 and 1976 because a three year moving average was used.

1913 (first full year of statehood) to 1976 were coded. A total of 8,174 cases as reported in the *Arizona Reports* were so coded as to year decided, litigant types, issues involved, winner, dissent, and court immediately below. For the purposes of this study the dependent variable is yearly dissent rate, which is equal to the number of cases with at least one dissent in a year divided by the total number of cases decided that year. For each year a dissent rate was also calculated for three specific case types: public, criminal, and private law.[5] Additionally, the percent of the docket devoted to each of these case types was calculated for each year.

The operational research question to be explored is the extent to which historical variation in the Arizona dissent rate can be accounted for by variations in docket composition. Specifically, the approach will be to examine the relationship between dissent rate and percent of the docket devoted to private, public, and criminal law issues, the hypothesis being that the higher the percent of cases decided in a year which concern public law matters the higher the dissent rate for that year. This hypothesis is based upon two assumptions. First, it assumes that public law cases contain, on the whole, more controversial legal questions, which are likely to evoke greater dissent than private or criminal law cases. Second, it is assumed that there will be historical variation in the percent of cases devoted to public law issues. This variation may be related to social and political changes, such as the advent of the New Deal, or to structural changes, such as the creation of an intermediate court of appeals.

ANALYSIS

Figure 11.1 presents the time series for dissent rate. The series pictured has been smoothed using a three-year moving average to highlight basic patterns.[6] As can be seen, the dissent rate in Arizona is historically very low: 4.99 percent. This is consistent with previous cross-sectional studies, which have placed Arizona in the low-dissent group of states, as do Glick and Pruet in Chapter 9. As can also be seen, however, the dissent rate fluctuated considerably over time. Particularly noteworthy are the periods of high dissent during the 1910s and 1950s. There also appears to have been a general upward trend in dissent from 1930 to 1960.

What accounts for this variation over time? According to the docket

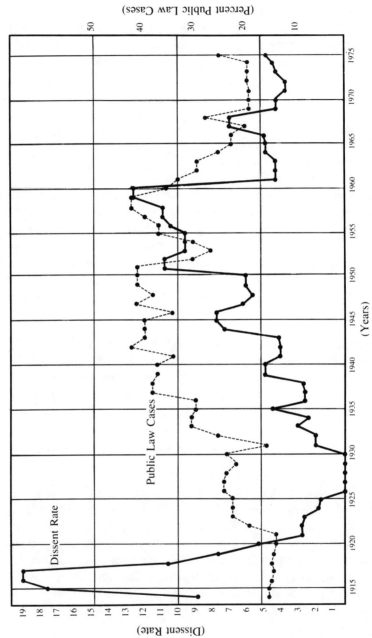

Figure 11.2. Dissent Rate and Percentage of Cases Involving Public Law Issues

Table 11.1. Dissent Rate by Case Type in the Arizona Supreme
Court, 1913-1976

	Criminal	Private	Public[a]	Total
Unanimous	2,163	3,523	2,081	7,766
	(96.82)	(95.97)	(91.67)	(95.01)
Dissent	71	148	189	408
	(3.18)	(4.03)	(8.32)	(4.99)
Total	2,234	3,671	2,270	8,174
	(100)	(100)	(100)	(100)

[a]Excluding criminal cases.

composition theory, the periods of high dissent will also be periods of
high public law litigation. A precondition to the plausibility of this
theory, however, is that the dissent rate is substantially higher for public
law cases than for private or criminal cases. To this point that has simply
been an assumption; it has not been empirically tested. Table 11.1
demonstrates support for that assumption. As can be seen, the dissent
rate for public law cases is twice as great as the rate for either private or
criminal law. The same relationship holds if the data are compared by
decade.

Figure 11.2 presents the same dissent time series as in Figure 11.1
but compares it directly with the proportion of the docket each year
devoted to public law issues (also smoothed by using a three-year
moving median). Visual inspection of this figure provides both support
for and refutation of the docket composition theory. Support is provided
in the apparent covariation of the smoothed dissent and docket series
from 1925 to 1976. We see that both lines experience a long-term
upward trend during the 1930s, 1940s, and 1950s and then drop off in
the 1960s. The data also show that in the first decade of the court there
was a radical disparity between dissent rate and docket composition. In
this period we find the highest dissent rate of any period, juxtaposed
with the lowest percent of public law cases of any time period.

In its simplest form the docket composition theory, as herein
operationalized, may be expressed as follows: dissent rate $(DR) = a +
bX + e$, where a is the intercept and X is the percent of cases formally
decided which involve a public law issue. As might be expected from
Figure 11.2, this form of the theory when applied to the entire sixty-
four-year period has little explanatory power. When the actual values

are calculated, $DR = 5.10 + .0277X + e$. R^2 is equal to less than .05 and b is statistically insignificant. Examination of the residuals confirms the expectation that the radical difference between dissent rate and percent of public law cases in the 1910s caused this low relationship. This is best demonstrated if we limit analysis to the period 1920 to 1976. The equation then becomes $DR = -1.29 + .215X + e$, where $R^2 = .256$ and b is statistically significant at the .01 level.[7]

A more in-depth look at the period 1913 to 1920 may help to explain these findings. This is a period during which the dissent rate in Arizona was very high. The rate for the entire sixty-four years is 4.99 percent, but it is 8.55 percent for this period and 10.8 percent for the subperiod 1913 to 1917. As pointed out earlier, however, counter to the docket composition theory, we find that this was also a period with a very low proportion of public law cases. In fact, only 18.59 percent of the cases decided by the court between 1913 and 1920 involved public law. That is the lowest proportion, by far, of any of the identifiable periods.

Although the docket composition theory seems to fail for this period, the justice composition theory holds some promise. Significantly, the changes in dissent in this period and between this one and the 1921 to 1930 period are directly related to the changing composition of the court. The years 1913 to 1917 constituted the first natural court. The unusually high dissent rate for the court appears to be the result of a single justice. Justice Donnell Cunningham cast thirty-one of the thirty-seven dissenting votes during this period. The other six were in response to his majority opinions. He also accounted for 50 percent of the dissents in the second natural court and 75 percent in the third. His retirement marks the beginning of the fourth natural court in 1921 with its dramatic decline in conflict.

Although justice diversity seems to be the obvious explanation of these facts, background analysis does not offer much help in supporting that explanation. All three of the justices on the first natural court were hand picked by the new Democratic leadership and were extremely similar in backgrounds. All were Democrats, were traditional Protestants, were legally trained out of state, had prosecutorial experience, began their tenure on the court at the same time, and had political experience. The only observed difference was that Justice Henry Ross received his legal training in a medium-quality law school and the other two justices trained in law offices.

Despite the failure of background measures to reveal it, there do appear to have been some fundamental ideological differences among the justices. This is best exemplified by Justices Alfred Franklin and Cunningham, who were delegates to the state constitutional convention in 1910. Even though both men were Democrats, a scalogram analysis of the voting behavior at the convention shows that they were at exactly opposite ends of the scale measuring support for big business.[8] These differences in attitude appear to have persisted on the court.

Another period of discontinuity between dissent rate and docket composition is 1950 to 1961. There was a dramatic increase in the dissent rate in the early 1950s and an even more dramatic downturn in the rate in 1961. This fact appears to be partially a result of changes in docket composition, although the more important variable seems to be court size. In 1949 the supreme court was increased in size from three to five. Social psychological and probability theories suggest that such an expansion should be expected to increase the dissent rate.[9] That the increase in dissent rate is directly related to the expansion of the court is reinforced by the precipitous drop in dissent rate in 1961, the exact year that the supreme court was granted the power to sit in panels of three in most cases. Thus we have a quasi-experimental situation that enables us to observe the dissent rate as court size increased from three members to five and then after eleven years was reduced back to three and a half (the average number of justices sitting on cases in the year 1961). The dissent rate behaves exactly as would be expected.

Taking into account the changes in the size of the court, the docket composition model can be modified to include not only percent of public law cases but also number of justices. Thus the equation becomes $DR = a + bX_1 + bX_2 + e$, where X_1 is the percent of cases containing a public law issue and X_2 is the number of justices on the court.[10] If the period 1913 to 1920 is excluded, the actual values for this equation are $DR = -6.27 + .123X_1 + 2.19X_2 + e$. R^2 is now equal to .564 and both b_1 and b_2 are statistically significant at the .01 level.

Two periods are left unexplored: 1921 to 1949 and 1961 to 1976. The former experienced a slow, gradual growth in the percent of the docket devoted to public law issues and dissent rate. The docket changes are consistent with the increased role of government regulation in American life during this period. The correlation between dissent and percent public law cases is consistent with the predictions of the docket composition theory.

The period 1961 to 1976 witnessed only minor changes in the dissent rate, but it is a significant period for gaining a more complete understanding of the docket composition theory. In 1965 Arizona created an intermediate court of appeals (ICA). With the creation of the ICA the supreme court was granted what appeared to be almost total discretionary access control. The only limit to the supreme court's docket control was a statute stating: "The Court of Appeals shall have: appellate jurisdiction in all actions and proceedings originating in or permitted by law to be appealed from the superior court, except the criminal actions involving crimes punishable by death or life imprisonment."[11]

Although limitation on the supreme court's access control seems minimal, a 1965 court opinion interpreted the statute as requiring the supreme court to hear formally all criminal convictions carrying a possible sentence of death or life imprisonment.[12] Thus all convictions had to be reviewed by the supreme court for the following offenses (among others) regardless of whether the death penalty or life imprisonment was actually given: assault with a deadly weapon by a prisoner, child molestation, murder (first and second degree), sodomy with a child, most drug offenses, and even derailing a train.

This limitation resulted in about 20 percent of the supreme court's filings being criminal cases that had to be formally reviewed. This in turn resulted in more than 50 percent of the court's formal opinions being devoted to such criminal cases, which explains part of the reason why the percent of public law cases was so low during this period. It also partially explains the low dissent rates. Most of these criminal cases were apparently relatively easily resolved first appeals with little merit, thereby resulting in a very low dissent rate. This fact combined with the general explosion of criminal cases in the early 1960s accounts for much of the change in docket composition and arguably for the low dissent rate during this period.

Immediately after the creation of the ICA, there was an increase in the percent of public law cases and a concomitant increase in the dissent rate. For a few years the court was able to use its new-found access control to focus on issues that produced relatively high dissent rates. By 1969, however, the wave of mandatory criminal appeals dominated the court's formal decisions, and the dissent rate again dropped. It is only at the very end of the time series that percent of public law cases and dissent rate increased because in 1974 legislative change modified the court's obligatory jurisdiction in criminal cases to include only those in which the death penalty or life imprisonment was actually given.

This discussion implies that structural changes do have an impact on docket composition and indirectly on dissent rate. It also demonstrates the significance for docket composition and dissent rate of general social and legal movements, such as the increase in criminal appeals generally during the 1960s. Finally, it warns us that we must not merely look at whether a state has an ICA but also must examine relevant statutes, rules, and decisions to understand fully the likely impact on docket composition.

DISCUSSION

The findings presented to this point suggest that changes in docket composition do have an impact on the historical evolution of dissent rate on the Arizona Supreme Court. That conclusion, however, must be tempered by some important caveats. Although percent of cases containing a public law issue and dissent rate do tend to covary over time, there is no necessary causal relationship between them. For example, ideological heterogeneity seems to be a sufficient condition for a relatively high dissent rate, as is demonstrated by the first three natural courts. As to whether a high percent of public law cases is also a sufficient condition for high conflict, we have no answer as yet. Such an answer must await a systematic evaluation of the individual and joint effects of justice composition and docket composition on dissent rate.

The accomplishment of this next step, however, does not appear achievable, at least in the context of Arizona, with a simple background diversity operationalization of justice composition. Apparently growing out of the social homogeneity and one-party domination of Arizona, the twenty-eight justices who have served on the supreme court have had remarkably similar backgrounds. For example, over 95 percent were Democrats from medium-quality schools and had prosecutorial experience. They are almost equally similar on all measures traditionally used for background diversity studies.[13] This fact leads to two conclusions. First, the similarity of justices' characteristics at specific points in time and over time at least partially accounts for the relatively low historical dissent rate in Arizona. Second, however, our discussion of the first natural court suggests that there may have been

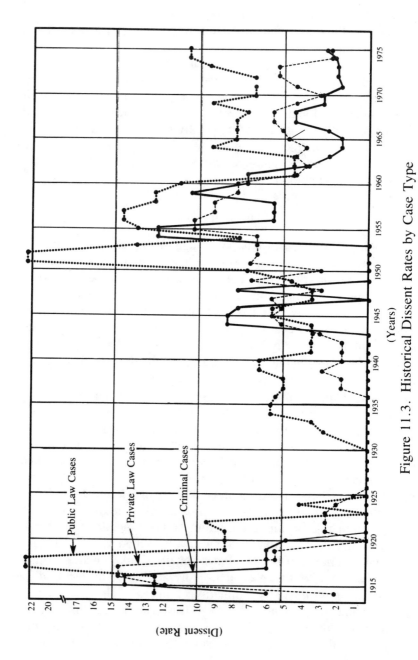

Figure 11.3. Historical Dissent Rates by Case Type

greater ideological diversity than background analysis reveals. A true test of the impact on dissent of justice composition, individually and interactively with docket composition, requires more sensitive measures of ideology. Unfortunately, when dealing with historical analysis, the most obvious solution, questionnaires, is not applicable.

Although not directly measuring justice composition, Figure 11.3 provides some indirect evidence about the relative ability of the justice composition and docket composition theories to account for variations in dissent rate. Figure 11.3 shows the historical evolution of dissent rates calculated individually for public law, criminal law, and private law cases. As can be seen, there is a perceptible degree of covariation in the three series, which is inconsistent with what would be expected if the docket composition theory were wholly explanatory of dissent. Docket composition theory is based on the assumption that dissent rates for particular types of cases are constant over time and that changes in the aggregate dissent rate are therefore a function of changes in docket mix. Although as I have shown, docket mix is significantly related to dissent, Figure 11.3 implies that there is also a causal factor that similarly affects changes in the dissent rates for each type of case and therefore in the aggregate dissent rate. One obvious such factor is ideological diversity.

As a way of concluding, I want to discuss briefly the potential contributions of the approach taken here and suggest needed modifications in future research on appellate court conflict and consensus.

Two incremental improvements in the study of state supreme court conflict and consensus have been suggested and demonstrated in this chapter. These are an explicit test of the docket composition theory and the use of a longitudinal design. The results suggest that docket composition does have an impact on the level of dissent on the Arizona Supreme Court. As we have seen, however, ideological diversity is also related to the level of dissent. Final determination of the relative ability of these two variables to explain historical variations in dissent must await more refined operationalizations of each. For example, my operationalization of docket composition, which classifies cases only into three broad types, clearly does not totally reflect the degree of docket controversy or complexity. Not all public law cases are controversial, complex, or both. Similarly, not all criminal and private law cases are mundane. Some alternative measures worthy of consideration in future research include the percent of cases overturning the lower court, the average number of Shepards Citations per case, and the percent of cases containing constitutional law issues.

Also required is a more refined operationalization of justice composition. Background diversity measures proved unsuccessful for Arizona. As Rathjen and Patterson have shown, however, this is not necessarily the case for other states. Therefore, such measures may provide the necessary operationalization for most states. For states such as Arizona, attempts to measure precourt values, not just backgrounds, may be the best method. This test could entail, as done here, examining the behavior of the justices in other public positions before they came to the court.

This study constitutes the first attempt to study conflict and consensus on a state appellate court using yearly data over a relatively long period of time. The approach appears to justify further exploration. In addition to validating the findings of previous cross-sectional studies, by permitting the use of a quasi-experimental interrupted time-series design, it offers a powerful method of evaluating the impact of such factors as changes in court size, the introduction of an intermediate court of appeals, and modifications in laws and procedures. Therefore, as an overall research strategy, a combination of cross-sectional and longitudinal studies of judicial conflict and consensus seems war-

Finally, in this chapter, as well as others in this volume, a very limited conceptualization and operationalization of conflict and consensus has been used. In each a simple index has been constructed which reflects the percent of cases formally decided in a year with at least one dissent. Such a measure is appropriate, however, only if we take a very limited view of conflict and consensus. It suggests that the only choices for a justice in a particular case are the dichotomous ones of conflict (dissent) or consensus (no dissent). Although these are polar options for a justice, there exists an important middle ground that is ignored: the concurring opinion. A concurrence is not conflict of the magnitude of a dissent, but it implies a significant difference of opinion among justices and as such is a dimension of conflict that should not be overlooked. Because previous research has not included concurring opinions, the level of conflict in state supreme courts and collegial courts more generally has probably been substantially underestimated. Additionally, the correlates of conflict, more broadly defined in this way, may be considerably different. Therefore, further research should explore alternative conceptualization and operationalizations of conflict and consensus.

1. For an overview of the literature on judicial dissent, see Steven A. Peterson, "Dissent on American Courts," *Journal of Politics* 43 (1981): 412-34.

2. John W. Patterson and Gregory J. Rathjen, "Background Diversity and State Supreme Court Dissent Behavior," *Polity* 8 (1976): 610-22; Dean Jaros and Bradley C. Canon, "Dissent on State Supreme Courts: The Differential Significance of Characteristics of Judges," *Midwest Journal of Political Science* 15 (1971): 322-46; Henry Robert Glick and Kenneth N. Vines, *State Court Systems* (Englewood Cliffs, N.J.: Prentice-Hall, 1973).

3. Henry R. Glick and George W. Pruet, Jr., "Dissent in State Supreme Courts: Patterns and Correlates of Conflict," Chapter 9 of this volume.

4. Bradley C. Canon and Dean Jaros, "External Variables, Institutional Structure, and Dissent on State Supreme Courts," *Polity* 3 (1970): 175-200.

5. In conventional uses of the terms, criminal law is included as a type of public law. For our purposes here, however, the two have been separated because it is expected that the degree of complexity and controversy, and therefore dissent rate, will be higher in other public law cases than in criminal cases. In fact, criminal cases will probably have the lowest dissent rate of all cases because of the large number of such cases that are appealed without particular merit.

6. A moving median rather than a moving mean was used to reduce the impact of extreme values.

7. Initial estimation of this equation produced a Durbin-Watson statistic in the undefined region. This means we could not reject the possibility of autocorrelation problems. Therefore, the estimates reported here are those achieved after correcting for autocorrelation, using the Cochrone-Orcutt correlation technique. For a discussion of this technique, see Charles Ostrom, *Time Series Analysis: Regression Techniques* (Beverly Hills: Sage, 1978), pp. 39-44. All other regression estimates in this chapter will also reflect the same correlation.

8. Gordon M. Bakken, "The Arizona Constitutional Convention of 1910," *Arizona State University Law Journal* (1978): 1-30.

9. For example, see Burton M. Atkins and Justin J. Green, "Consensus on the United States Courts of Appeals: Illusion or Reality?" *American Journal of Political Science* 20 (1976): 735-48; Thomas G. Walker, "Behavioral Tendencies in the Three-Judge District Court," *Midwest Journal of Political Science* 17 (1973): 407-13.

10. The number of justices variable was coded as follows: 1913-48, $X_2 = 3$; 1949-60, $X_2 = 5$; 1961-76, $X_2 = 3.5$.

11. *Arizona Revised Statutes*, §12-120.21 (A) (1).

12. *State* v. *Mileham*, 1 Ariz. App. 67 (1965).

13. Patterson and Rathjen, "Background Diversity."

12

Coalition Building on the California Supreme Court: Votes on Access and the Merits

ROBERT L. DUDLEY

Despite the frequent admonition of legal scholars and the official disapproval expressed in Canon 19 of the Canon of Judicial Ethics, conflict continues to be an ever-present reality of appellate court environments. One expression of this conflict—dissent behavior—has, for more than three decades, provided the data bases for a wealth of studies that have constructed and tested increasingly more sophisticated models of judicial decision making.[1] At the same time, scholars have demonstrated that conflict is often present even in unanimous cases.[2]

The vast majority of this work, however, has focused on what S. Sidney Ulmer terms Type I decisions—decisions on the merits.[3] This is, of course, understandable because decisions on the merits are the most visible actions taken by the courts and the votes are a matter of public record. The problem is that votes on the merits represent only a portion of the workload of appellate courts. As David W. Rohde points out, there are "at least four discrete 'decision points' . . . the vote on whether or not to accept a case for decision, the vote on the merits, the assignment of the majority opinion, and the bargaining over the content of the majority opinion."[4]

Of these four "decision points," perhaps the least systematically studied has been "whether or not to accept a case for decision." This is so even though on appellate courts with broad discretionary powers, these decisions are the most numerous. Investigation in the area has been seriously hampered by the paucity of information—especially votes. Until the release of the Burton papers, for example, there had been no direct access to a set of voting records encompassing thousands of review decisions made by the United States Supreme Court. Without this information, court observers were forced to make inferences about review decisions from votes on the merits or rely upon occasional dissents from denial of review[5] and out-of- court remarks by justices and law clerks.[6]

In spite of these difficulties, several scholars have examined the criteria used in the case-selection process. The most often cited of these efforts is the cue theory of Joseph Tanenhaus and associates.[7] Believing that justices of the Supreme Court employed cues as a means of separating petitions worthy of serious consideration from frivolous appeals, the authors hypothesized the existence of four such signals: (1) the federal government as petitioner, (2) the presence of a civil liberties issue, (3) the existence of dissension among judges of the lower court or between two or more courts, and (4) the presence of an economic issue. All but the last appeared to improve significantly the likelihood of a case being granted certiorari. But when Ulmer, with the aid of Justice Burton's papers, reexamined the cue theory he concluded that the only cue significantly related to the decision to grant certiorari was the presence of the federal government as a petitioning party.[8]

Paralleling the work of Ulmer is Doris Marie Provine's comprehensive study of the Burton papers—including the cases "special listed." Like Ulmer, she found the federal government more successful than other petitioners. Nevertheless, she rejected the argument that the presence of the federal government constituted a cue, suggesting instead that the federal government's good fortune was the result of the solicitor general's careful screening of cases, thereby avoiding cases with obvious defects.[9] As a repeat player, the federal government was better situated to exploit the secret decision-making process used by the Court.

Although Provine rejected the relevancy of cue theory, she did note that certain characteristics were associated with cases granted review. In fact, her work demonstrated that five categories accounted for "all but a handful" of the cases granted review: those involving the United States, civil rights and civil liberties, labor disputes, issues of federalism, and criminal cases.[10] These findings suggest that the cues postulated by Tanenhaus and associates may be important determinants of case selection even if they are not cues. They may be, as Stuart H. Teger and Douglas Kosinski argued, merely the surrogates for salient issues—suggesting a policy dimension to case selection.[11]

Donald R. Songer, on the other hand, has argued for the validity of cue theory and has suggested that the policy significance of decisions constitutes a fifth cue.[12] Thus access decisions are not independent of, but are influenced by, the same policy considerations that are characteristic of justices' decisions on the merits. Justices will, according to Songer, vote to grant access when they feel that they can advance desirable policy goals by doing so. This policy theory of access was also articulated by Glendon Schubert in his examination of certiorari petitions of the Federal Employer Liability Act cases in the 1938–49 terms.[13] Using game theory techniques and the voting patterns on the merits, he contended that some justices make case-selection decisions in ways that will maximize their power and realize their policy preferences.

Of course, this policy theory of access contradicts the explanations of the screening decision criteria offered by the courts—most prominently the United States Supreme Court's Rule 17. Official explanations generally stress legalistic criteria such as conflict among lower courts or the existence of important federal questions not previously adjudicated by the Court. Plenary decision making is most often presented as a mechanical and time-consuming process that detracts from the real work of the Court. In language reminiscent of the attacks on early empirical studies of judicial decision making, access decisions are often portrayed as purely nondiscretionary judgments. Nevertheless, either in spite of or because of these explanations, several political scientists have expanded on the implications of cue theory.

The expansion has been necessary because, although cue theory provides valuable insights into the agenda-setting process of appellate courts, it does not furnish an explicit emphasis on the linkage of access and merit decisions. Still, the concentration on policy considerations, similar to those present in merit decisions, is highly suggestive of what such an explanation would be like. Thus with cue theory as the building block, recent research has begun to answer the question posed by Ulmer: "What are the implications of a decision to grant certiorari?"[14]

Ulmer suggested that Supreme Court justices were more likely to vote to grant review when the lower court outcome was contrary to their ideological position; in this case the issue was attitude toward institutionalized government authority.[15] Additional evidence of this relationship was offered by Ulmer in his study of the Supreme Court between 1947 and 1956. By sampling the granted cases during this period and comparing votes on petitions for certiorari with votes on the merits in the same cases, he was able to demonstrate that most of the justices voted to hear cases so they could reverse the lower court decision. Thus Ulmer hypothesized that "the relationship between two successive decisions in the same case is psychologically determined."[16]

Replication by Lawrence Baum and Provine led to similar results. In one study Baum used proximity scales to order justices of the California Supreme Court on the two decision points. Based on the scaling analysis, he concluded that the justices responded to petitions for hearing on the basis of their response to the ideological content of the lower court decision. In a second study Baum directly replicated and confirmed Ulmer's work on the propensity to reverse cases the justices voted to hear. Provine's work also supplied at least limited support for Ulmer's thesis.[17]

The present study explores the linkage between the plenary vote and the vote on the merits for the California Supreme Court. After documenting the extent of disagreement over which cases belong on the agenda, the chapter describes and tests the "error-correction" hypothesis, that is, that judges vote to hear cases so they can reverse lower court "errors."

THE CALIFORNIA SUPREME COURT

The data used in this chapter consist of all cases accepted for review by the California Supreme Court under its discretionary jurisdiction and for which decisions on the merits were rendered between January 1, 1973, and January 1, 1980. During this period eleven justices served on the two natural courts, as defined by the tenure of the chief justice.[18]

This analysis is possible because the California court makes available to the public individual votes on petitions for review.[19] The availability of screening votes is probably sufficient justification for selecting the California Supreme Court, but this court is also attractive for study because it has long been thought to be the most "legally professional" of the state courts,[20] although that reputation may be diminishing.[21] As Glick and Pruet demonstrate in Chapter 9, the California court also has a high rate of dissent, providing numerous nonunanimous cases on which to apply the standard methods.

California's supreme court is a seven-member tribunal composed of justices appointed by the governor and approved by a commission composed of the attorney general, one appellate judge, and the chief

justice of the supreme court. At the first general election after appointment, each justice stands before the electorate on a retention ballot.
Thereafter the justices must seek voter approval at twelve-year intervals.
In the past they have run little risk of defeat. Since 1978, however, the
justices have had considerable difficulty in obtaining voter confirmation. For example, Chief Justice Rose Bird won confirmation in
1978 with a mere 51.7 percent of the vote. The three most recent judges
to seek voter approval also have won by narrow margins.[22]

The jurisdiction of the California Supreme Court includes only a
few classes of mandated cases, such as appeals from death sentences.
Thus most of the court's work involves discretionary jurisdiction over
appeals brought from the five courts of appeal. The criteria for granting
hearings are contained in the court's Rule 29, which is similar to the
United States Supreme Court's Rule 17. In fiscal year 1977–78 just
under three thousand petitions for hearings were filed, of which 7.9
percent were granted.[23]

In some ways, the California Supreme Court's treatment of petitions for hearing resembles the United States Supreme Court's procedures for handling writs of certiorari. Both courts make use of the
"rule of four," although on the seven-member California court, four
votes constitute a majority.[24] Both courts also make use of special
listings, which in California are referred to as the A and B lists.
Additionally, both courts seem to make heavy use of their clerks in the
preparation of a memorandum for each case. California, however, with
its more professionalized staff of clerks, places a greater reliance on the
clerks than does the United States Supreme Court. In criminal cases the
only memorandums prepared for the justices' consideration at the
initial stage are those of the central staff. Civil cases, on the other hand,
are distributed to each of the six associate justices' chambers in rotation. Although this procedure assures a more efficient use of staff, it
also suggests that when they go into the conference the justices will
know the details of only a few petitions.[25]

The United States Supreme Court and the California Supreme
Court also differ in the opinion-assignment procedure. On the California court after a petition for hearing has been granted, the chief justice
assigns one of the seven justices (in civil cases the justice who presented the original memorandum if he voted in the majority to grant),
the task of preparing a "calendar memorandum." These memos, which
are circulated within the court ten days before oral argument, sum-

Table 12.1. Percentage of Cases Reversed by the California Supreme
Court, 1973-1979

Court	All Cases	Criminal Cases	Civil Cases
Combined courts	60.7	60.2	60.8
Wright court	58.7	64.2	55.8
Bird court	65.5	59.1	68.9

marize the facts of the case and highlight the legal issues at stake. Although not officially considered as such, calendar memos are typically first drafts of opinions. The original opinion assignment will be taken from the author of the calendar memorandum only if he or she votes with the minority on disposition.[26]

Finally, as Table 12.1 shows, the reversal rate for the California Supreme Court is similar to that reported by J. Woodford Howard for the United States Supreme Court.[27] The 60.7 percent reversal rate in California is close to the 66 percent rate reported by Howard. There are differences, however, between the Wright and Bird courts. First, the overall reversal rate for the Wright court was only 58.7 percent, whereas the comparable percentage for the Bird court was 65.5. The two courts also differed in their treatment of criminal and civil cases. During the era of Donald Wright's chief justiceship, the court was more likely to reverse criminal than civil cases. But this pattern was reversed for the Bird court. Clearly, then, there are contextual differences to which the analysis must be sensitive.

Taking into consideration the availability of the votes and the California court's similarity with the United States Supreme Court, the data should provide ample opportunity to test ideas developed in work on the United States Supreme Court.

DISSENT IN CASE SELECTION AND ON THE MERITS

As a first step in examining the role of policy considerations in case selection, we can look at the degree of unanimity achieved by the California court on the plenary decisions. The value of doing so was highlighted by Provine, who argued that "if case selection is functionally equivalent to decision making on the merits, most case selection decisions should be nonunanimous, as most decisions on the

Table 12.2. Distribution of Votes for Review on Petitions Granted

Number of Votes	Combined Courts[a]			Wright Court[a]			Bird Court[a]		
	All Cases	Civil Cases	Criminal Cases	All Cases	Civil Cases	Criminal Cases	All Cases	Civil Cases	Criminal Cases
4	38.2	37.5	39.5	24.3	21.4	29.3	54.3	56.5	50.3
5	25.5	23.7	28.2	28.2	25.0	33.1	23.1	20.9	26.6
6	18.1	18.3	17.4	22.7	25.5	18.1	13.1	11.5	15.8
Unanimous[b]	18.1	20.3	14.7	24.3	28.1	19.0	9.3	10.9	6.6

[a]Columns do not add to 100 because of rounding.
[b]Includes all 7-0, 6-0, and 5-0 voting patterns.

merits are."[28] Since 82 percent of the access decisions during the Burton period were unanimously decided, Provine suggested caution in supposing the fungibility of the two decision points.

The point is well taken. Political scientists studying courts need to be reminded from time to time that not every action taken by courts is nonunanimous. There is, however, a danger of making too much of voting unanimity. Specifically, there is no reason to assume that unanimity demonstrates harmony at the first stage any more than it does at the votes-on-the-merits phase.[29] Indeed, given the futility of voting on the losing side at the former decision point, unanimous decisions may be even less meaningful than at the latter stage. Nor does unanimity necessarily indicate a lack of policy commitment. This may simply be an example of Ronald Dworkin's distinction between hard and easy cases.[30]

Nevertheless, Provine provides a framework for comparison with the California Supreme Court since she indicated that nearly one-third of the cases granted review during the Burton period received unanimous approval.[31] As Table 12.2 indicates, the percentage of cases unanimously granted review in California is considerably less than Provine reported for the United States Supreme Court. Unanimously granted hearings occurred on the California court only 18.1 percent of the time. Moreover, as the table shows, the most frequent vote division was the one consisting of four votes for review—the minimum number. The next most frequent occurrence was the grant with five affirmative votes. Apparently, then, there is considerable disagreement over the proper subjects for the court's agenda.

A closer inspection of Table 12.2, however, reveals that the breakdown for the entire period is somewhat misleading in that it disguises

Table 12.3. Distribution of Votes for Cases Decided on the Merits

Number of Votes	Combined Courts[a]			Wright Court[a]			Bird Court[a]		
	All Cases	Civil Cases	Criminal Cases	All Cases	Civil Cases	Criminal Cases	All Cases	Civil Cases	Criminal Cases
4	11.6	13.6	8.5	7.7	7.3	8.3	15.0	18.6	9.2
5	15.5	15.3	16.0	14.4	14.6	14.1	16.3	14.5	19.3
6	8.0	7.0	9.7	6.7	7.8	5.0	9.2	6.2	14.2
Unanimous[b]	6.4	63.9	65.6	71.0	70.1	72.5	59.2	60.6	57.1

[a]Columns do not add to 100 because of rounding.
[b]Includes all 7-0, 6-0, and 5-0 voting patterns.

significant differences between the Wright and Bird courts. Voting divisions on the Wright court were almost equally distributed across categories. Roughly a quarter of the cases granted review received the minimum number of votes, and almost another one-fourth were unanimously accepted. The most frequent occurrence was the five-vote grant, but the difference is slight. In vivid contrast is the breakdown presented for the Bird court. Rather than being equally distributed, the results are clearly skewed in the direction of four-vote grants. Slightly over 50 percent of the grants fell in the four-vote category and just under 10 percent were granted unanimously.

Finally, Table 12.2 reports the percentages for each vote division by the type of case—civil or criminal. Since these cases were the object of dissimilar reversal rates and are handled by different procedures, with the central staff preparing the original memorandum on criminal cases, it seemed possible that they would be subject to different vote distributions. Such, however, was not the case. There were slight differences between civil and criminal cases, with criminal cases less likely to be granted unanimously, but the differences are hardly major.

In marked contrast to the voting divisions on access decisions are those reported in Table 12.3 for determinations on the merits. Table 12.3 reports a high rate of dissent for the California Supreme Court, but the level of dissent on the merits is considerably lower than that evidenced on the gatekeeping decisions. It is of particular importance here that by far the most frequent voting division on the mertis was the unanimous decision. The aggregate data for the entire period demonstrate that 64.6 percent of the cases were decided unanimously and only 11.6 percent received the minimum number of votes.

Again, however, there are differences between the two courts. In the

Wright court, a full 71 percent of the cases were decided unanimously and only 7.7 percent were supported by the minimum winning coalition. During the Bird court years only 59.2 percent of the decisions were unanimous and 15 percent received only four votes. In both courts the second most frequent occurrence, after the unanimous decision, was the disposition with a five-vote majority.

VOTING TO REVIEW AND VOTING TO REVERSE

To date, the strongest evidence available to substantiate a policy or merits-conscious approach to case selection has been the work, previously discussed, of Ulmer, Baum, and Provine. All three authors have substantiated the existence of a policy approach to case selection by demonstrating the use of an error-correction strategy by judges. As Baum described the strategy, judges "might seek to 'correct errors' in the lower courts by voting to grant a hearing whenever a lower court decision departed significantly from their most preferred doctrinal position."[32] Such a strategy is, of course, not the only way that judges can pursue policy goals at the gatekeeping stage, but it is the simplest strategy. Any other approach requires that the judges estimate the likely responses of their colleagues and adjust their behavior accordingly.[33]

To test the hypothesized relationship between the two decision points, Ulmer, Baum, and Provine constructed tables comparing the percentage of times each justice voted to reverse decisions for which he voted to grant review with the percentages of reversals in cases he voted to deny review. Each of the authors then concluded that for some justices supporting an application for hearing was positively associated with sustaining the appellant's claim on full review. Ulmer reported a statistically significant association (using a chi-square test) for eight of the eleven justices, and Baum reported a significant relationship for four of eight judges. Provine did not report any test of significance.[34]

With these previous studies as a model, Table 12.4 was constructed for the California Supreme Court. As the table demonstrates, all eleven judges were more likely to reverse than to affirm in cases they voted to hear, but the differences in the percentages are far from impressive. They are, however, generally higher than those reported by Ulmer.[35] Indeed, two of Ulmer's justices, Burton and Clark, were more likely to affirm than to reverse decisions they voted to review. Additionally, the lowest percentage in the first column of Table 12.4, Frank Richardson

Table 12.4. Votes on Petitions for Hearing and on the Merits of
Accepted Cases, 1973-1979

	Percentage of Votes to Reverse			
Justice	When Judge Voted to Grant	When Judge Voted to Deny	Difference	Chi-Square
Bird[a]	65.6	53.3	12.3	2.34
Wright[a]	61.4	50.0	11.4	.31
Tobriner	64.3	47.3	17.0	5.72[b]
Mosk	61.2	56.1	5.1	.51
Clark	59.9	45.0	14.9	7.30[b]
Richardson	56.8	47.2	9.6	1.90
Newman	60.4	67.3	−6.9	.70
Manuel	66.4	50.0	16.4	2.00
McComb	64.4	36.5	27.9	10.72[b]
Sullivan	57.9	66.7	−8.8	.50
Burke	63.6	25.0	38.6	3.51[c]

[a]Chief justice.
[b]Significant at .01 level.
[c]Significant at .05 level.

at 56.8, is higher than all but four of the analogous computations presented by Ulmer.

Table 12.4 also reports a positive relationship between votes to grant and votes to reverse for nine of the eleven judges, with Frank Newman and Raymond Sullivan the exceptions. But for only four justices was the relationship statistically significant. It is perhaps more important that only two of the eleven judges were as much as 20 percent more likely to vote to reverse when they had voted to hear a case than when they had denied access. Additionally, of the 2,203 pairs of votes, only 61.3 percent were consistent—votes to grant and reverse or deny and affirm. Since the expected cell frequencies would have yielded 55.7 percent, the actual cell frequencies are only a slight improvement.

It would seem then that the hypothesized relationship between access decisions and merit decisions finds little support from this analysis of the California Supreme Court. There is, though, a possibility that such a judgment is premature because, as has been shown, there are some significant differences between the Wright and Bird courts. Possibly the problem with Table 12.4 is that the aggregation cloaks important intercourt differences. Thus Table 12.5 was constructed to control for natural courts.

Table 12.5. Votes on Petitions for Hearing and on the Merits of Accepted Cases, Wright and Bird Courts

	Wright Court				Bird Court			
	Percentage of Votes to Reverse				Percentage of Votes to Reverse			
Judge	When Judge Voted to Grant	When Judge Voted to Deny	Difference	Chi-Square	When Judge Voted to Grant	When Judge Voted to Deny	Difference	Chi-Square
Wright	61.4	50.0	11.4	.31	—	—	—	—
Tobriner	63.4	43.5	19.9	3.2	69.1	48.4	20.7	4.7[a]
Mosk	62.6	52.5	10.1	1.2	62.3	64.3	-2.0	.0
Clark	57.0	47.5	9.5	1.3	67.1	44.9	22.2	7.5[b]
Richardson	61.4	53.8	7.6	.26	55.6	48.2	7.4	.81
McComb	64.4	36.5	27.9	10.7[b]	—	—	—	—
Sullivan	57.9	66.7	-8.8	.47	—	—	—	—
Burke	63.6	25.0	38.6	3.5[a]	—	—	—	—
Bird	—	—	—	—	65.6	53.3	12.3	2.3
Newman	—	—	—	—	60.4	67.3	-6.9	.70
Manuel	—	—	—	—	66.4	50.0	16.4	2.0

[a]Significant at .05 level.
[b]Significant at .01 level.

Table 12.5, which presents the results broken down by natural courts, does nothing to change the aggregated findings. Once again, for only four judges was there a statistically significant relationship. Table 12.5 does, however, show an interesting effect of the aggregation. During the Bird court both Matthew Tobriner and William Clark exhibited a strong relationship between votes to grant and votes to review, yet neither demonstrated a statistically significant relationship in the Wright court. This is understandable regarding Tobriner because his increase, during the Bird court, is quite small, but Clark's behavior is more surprising.

Although the findings with regard to Clark are interesting, they should not obscure the basic conclusion that the relationship between the two votes is weak. Once again, all of the justices were more likely to reverse decisions for which they granted hearings than to affirm them, but most were almost as likely to reverse in cases in which they voted against accepting the writ. Indeed, two justices in the Bird court, Stanley Mosk and Newman, and one in the Wright court, Sullivan, were more likely to reverse when they voted to deny review. Finally, the percentage of vote pairs that are consistent with the error-correction theory are 59.6 and 63.2 for the Wright and Bird courts, respectively. These are compared to the percentages derived by using the expected cell values, 54.9 and 55.8. Obviously, once again, the observed values are only slightly better than those that would be expected if there was no relationship.

Given the limited relationships discussed here, it would seem that the error-correction strategy of gatekeeping decision making is at best unevenly supported by the data. After all, even with controls for natural courts, only four of the eleven judges demonstrated any evidence confirming the strategy. Moreover, in no instance did the percentage of consistent votes—votes to grant and reverse or deny and affirm—for the court as a whole significantly exceed those expected with unrelated variables. Perhaps, then, the official criteria for case selection provide a better explanation for this decision stage than merits consciousness, although if this is true, the pervasive disagreement evidenced in Table 12.2 is perplexing.

Provine, however, suggested one more possibility. It may be that the weak relationships discovered here are at least partly the result of differing conceptions of judicial role. Certainly justices differ in their perceptions of their task, and it may be expected that such differences help to explain individual differences in the strength of the relationships between the two sets of votes.

THE COURT'S ROLE AND ERROR CORRECTION

To explain the imperfect correlations between votes to review and votes to reverse that her data evidenced, Provine developed two purposive role types—review-prone and review-conservative justices. As conceived by Provine, the two role types derived from the expectation that justices will differ somewhat in their perceptions of the proper workload of the court. Specifically, justices may disagree over the extent to which the court, in her case the United States Supreme Court, can and should serve as the court of last resort for disappointed litigants. Illustrative of this argument is Provine's conclusion that Justices Black and Douglas differed from Justices Burton and Frankfurter "less in the types of cases they voted to hear than in the numbers they felt competent to decide on the merits."[36] Justices Black and Douglas seemed to believe that the Court should decide numerous cases with little delay, a position that to some of their colleagues seemed insensitive to the workload of the Court. On the other hand, to review-prone justices such as Black and Douglas, a reluctance to vote for review demonstrated a callous disregard of the petitioner's plight. Thus the differing roles are a product of the tension between providing relief to as many appellants as possible and protecting the institution by reserving review for the important cases.

Recognizing the existence of this tension makes it possible to argue that a justice's votes to reverse in cases he or she voted against reviewing can be explained by his or her belief that although the case was v rongly decided by the lower court, it was not important enough to warrant review. Likewise, a justice's failure to vote for reversal in every case he or she voted to grant review to may mean that the justice simply perceived the issue as too important to ignore. Viewed from this perspective, conflict over case-screening may be the result of divergent gatekeeping norms as well as policy discordance.

Indeed, a comparison of Tables 12.2 and 12.3 offers considerable support for this position. As was noted earlier, the level of conflict at the two stages differed considerably. During both the Wright and Bird courts, the justices were much more likely to disagree on case-screening than on the merits. On the Wright court 81.9 percent of the access decisions were nonunanimous, but only 35.4 percent of the decisions on the merits evidenced dissent. Similarly, for the Bird court the percentages were 90.7 and 40.8, respectively. Of course, these differences are not proof that caseload concerns motivated the justices in their gatekeeping decisions, but they do strongly suggest that the sources of conflict at the two stages differed.

Perhaps, then, the ambiguous evidence of merits consciousness produced above is the result of a failure to account for this alternative source of conflict. To examine this possibility it is necessary to repeat the error-correction analysis controlling for conflict on the merits. Since unanimously decided cases are less likely to be the product of policy disputes, we should expect little evidence of merits consciousness in case selection. Given unanimity on the proper disposition of the case, conflict at the access stage is most likely attributable to forces other than policy considerations—gatekeeping norms. Conversely, those cases decided nonunanimously obviously generated policy conflict, and it is here that merits consciousness in case selection should be most prevalent.

Turning then to the unanimous cases (Table 12.6), it is apparent that merits consciousness played a minor part in the justices' access decisions. For example, of the eight justices who served on the Wright court, only four were more likely to reverse when they voted to grant than when they voted to deny review, and in none of these cases was the difference statistically significant. Moreover, of all the vote pairs cast during the period only 59.8 percent were consistent with the error-correction theory—votes to grant and reverse or deny and affirm. Since the expected cell frequencies would have yielded 55.9 percent, the observed frequencies are a marginal improvement.

Even more striking in their failure to support the error-correction theory are the results reported, again in Table 12.6, for the Bird court. As the table demonstrates, only Justice Tobriner voted to reverse when he granted a hearing more often than when he voted to deny review. The difference, however, is not statistically significant and barely exceeds 10 percent. The other six justices all voted to reverse cases they denied review to more often than those they granted. Not surprisingly, the 52.8 percent of vote pairs consistent with the error-correction theory is actually 2.6 percent less than would be expected if there were no relationship.

Overall, then, the cases unanimously decided on the merits offer no

Table 12.6. Votes on Petitions for Hearing and on the Merits of Cases Decided Unanimously, Wright and Bird Courts

	Wright Court				Bird Court			
	Percentage of Votes to Reverse				Percentage of Votes to Reverse			
Judge	When Judge Voted to Grant	When Judge Voted to Deny	Difference	Chi-Square	When Judge Voted to Grant	When Judge Voted to Deny	Difference	Chi-Square
Wright	58.8	100.0	−41.2	1.38	—	—	—	—
Tobriner	59.2	50.0	9.2	.37	64.7	53.3	11.4	.70
Mosk	61.8	56.0	5.8	.27	57.3	70.0	−12.7	.59
Clark	57.1	60.5	−3.4	.11	62.5	68.1	−5.6	.29
Richardson	63.2	57.1	6.1	.10	54.2	69.0	−14.8	1.86
McComb	63.0	47.1	15.9	2.42	—	—	—	—
Sullivan	56.8	73.3	−16.5	1.45	—	—	—	—
Burke	62.5	0	—	—	—	—	—	—
Bird	—	—	—	—	57.6	68.8	−11.2	1.08
Newman	—	—	—	—	61.8	65.6	−3.8	.12
Manuel	—	—	—	—	61.8	62.5	−.7	.0

support for the error-correction theory of gatekeeping. Furthermore, this weakness of the error-correction theory cannot be attributed to the influence of unanimous access decisions because cases decided unanimously on the merits were not necessarily consensus selections for review. Indeed, 78.6 percent of the unanimous cases were granted review by a divided court.

Mirroring these results are those presented in Table 12.7, which tests the error-correction theory using only nonunanimous cases. Perhaps the first point to notice in Table 12.7 is that, of the eleven judges who served on the California Supreme Court during the period under study, only one, Justice Newman, demonstrated a negative relationship between votes to grant and votes to reverse. The table also reports a statistically significant level of support for the error-correction theory in the case of five of the eight judges on the Wright court. Likewise, during the Bird court years, having supported an application for review was, for six of the seven justices, positively associated with supporting the grantee on full review. In the case of Chief Justice Bird and Justices Tobriner, Clark, Richardson, and Wiley Manuel, moreover, the association was statistically significant. Additionally, not one of these five judges was less than 30 percent more likely to reverse after having voted to hear a case than after having elected to deny review.

In general, Table 12.7 provides support for the error-correction theory by confirming its existence for eight of the eleven judges. Of the three justices for whom the theory is not supported, one case—Justice Sullivan—could have been the result of low cell entries. The same, however, cannot be said of Justices Mosk and Newman or of Justice Richardson in the Wright court.

The association between voting to review and voting to reverse is also evident when controls are added for the size of the majority. This pattern is indicated clearly in Table 12.8, which reports the aggregated results, for the entire period, by the size of the on-the-merits majority. The data reveal that the smaller the majority at the merits stage, the stronger the association between voting to review and voting to reverse. Thus in cases decided by the minimum winning coalition, 66.3 percent of the votes to grant review were followed by votes to reverse. Additionally, 68.9 percent of the vote pairs were consistent with the error-correction theory. Had there been no relationship, we would have expected 53.9 percent of the vote pairs to be consistent with error correction. Furthermore, as the size of the majority grows, so too does the percentage of inconsistent vote pairs.

Table 12.7. Votes on Petitions for Hearing and on the Merits of Cases Decided Nonunanimously, Wright and Bird Courts

| | Wright Court | | | | Bird Court | | | |
| | Percentage of Votes to Reverse | | | | Percentage of Votes to Reverse | | | |
Judge	When Judge Voted to Grant	When Judge Voted to Deny	Difference	Chi-Square	When Judge Voted to Grant	When Judge Voted to Deny	Difference	Chi-Square
Wright	67.4	25.0	42.4	2.85[a]	–	–	–	–
Tobriner	74.4	36.4	38.0	5.51[b]	75.9	43.8	32.1	5.92[b]
Mosk	64.7	46.7	18.0	1.40	68.6	50.0	18.6	.59
Clark	56.7	23.8	32.9	5.43[b]	72.7	9.7	63.0	26.05[b]
Richardson	55.0	50.0	5.0	.04	57.8	25.9	31.9	6.89[b]
McComb	67.9	16.7	51.2	11.50[b]	–	–	–	–
Sullivan	60.0	33.3	26.7	.82	–	–	–	–
Burke	66.7	40.0	26.7	2.34[a]	–	–	–	–
Bird	–	–	–	–	78.4	35.7	42.7	12.08[b]
Newman	–	–	–	–	58.5	69.6	–11.1	.76
Manuel	–	–	–	–	73.9	41.7	32.2	4.49[a]

[a]Significant at .05 level.
[b]Significant at .01 level.

Table 12.8. Aggregation of Votes to Review and Votes to Reverse by
Size of Majority on the Merits

Number of Votes on the Merits	Percentage of Votes to Reverse		Difference	Percentage of Voting Pairs Consistent with Error Correction
	When Judges Voted to Grant	When Judges Voted to Deny		
4	66.3	25.0	41.3	68.9
5	66.2	33.9	32.3	66.2
6	61.4	50.0	11.4	58.3
Unanimous[a]	59.8	61.8	−2.0	55.1

[a]Includes all 7-0, 6-0, and 5-0 voting patterns.

In a political system that stresses the importance of adjudication as a fundamental source of justice, access to courts is of the utmost importance. The decision to decide is most obviously crucial on appellate courts that have discretionary jurisdiction because the refusal to grant a request to appeal is, for most petitioners, the final decision. Yet as John A. Stookey and William Bowen noted, "To date, little has been known about the factors which prompt a state supreme court to accept a case for review."[37] This vitally important gatekeeping process remains largely unexplained.

The evidence presented here suggests that, at least with regard to the California Supreme Court, agenda setting is far from a consensual process. Fewer than 20 percent of the cases granted review between 1973 and 1980 were unanimously accepted, and only 9.3 percent of the Bird court grants were unanimous. Assuming that the existence of dissent serves as a measure of conflict within a court, it must be concluded that the case-screening process on the California Supreme Court was marked by extensive conflict. In fact, the level of conflict was notably higher on access decisions than on the merits.

This analysis also suggests that case selection is not equivalent to decision making on the merits. Decisions on whether to accept cases for hearing in the California Supreme Court were substantially related to decisions on the merits, but only when the data were restricted to nonunanimous decisions on the merits. For this particular subset of cases, the proposition that judges vote to hear cases so as to reverse lower court errors was strongly supported. Moreover, as the number of dissents on the merits increased, so too did the evidence supporting the error-correction theory. The voting patterns in cases decided unanimously on the merits did not, however, provide any support for the error-correction approach. Not one of the eleven justices who served on the California Supreme Court during the period under study demonstrated a statistically significant relationship between the two votes in the unanimous cases.

In the final analysis, then, a great deal of conflict at the agenda-setting stage cannot be explained by merits consciousness alone. It may well be that the case-screening conflict present in unanimously decided cases springs from the differing role conceptions suggested by Provine. Clearly justices can be expected to differ in their perceptions of the proper role for the court, and such differences may well constitute a distinct source of conflict. At the very best, it seems unlikely that future attempts to improve our understanding of the case-screening process can ignore such a consideration.

1. See, e.g., Fred Kort, *A Special and a General Multivariate Theory of Judicial Decisions* (Beverly Hills: Sage, 1977).

2. See Burton M. Atkins and Justin J. Green, "Consensus on the United States Courts of Appeals: Illusion or Reality?" *American Journal of Political Science* 20 (1976): 735-48; Robert J. Sickels, "The Illusion of Judicial Consensus: Zoning Decisions in the Maryland Court of Appeals," *American Political Science Review* 59 (1965): 100-104; Donald R. Songer, "Consensual and Nonconsensual Decisions in Unanimous Opinions of the United States Courts of Appeals," *American Journal of Political Science* 26 (1982): 225-39.

3. S. Sidney Ulmer, "Supreme Court Justices as Strict and Not-So-Strict Constructionists: Some Implications," *Law and Society Review* 8 (1973): 14.

4. David W. Rohde, "Policy Goals and Opinion Coalitions in the Supreme Court," *Midwest Journal of Political Science* 16 (1972): 208.

5. S. Sidney Ulmer and William Nicholls, "The Integration of Dissent Behavior in the United States Supreme Court," *Jurimetrics* 19 (1978): 170.

6. Bob Woodward and Scott Armstrong, *The Brethren: Inside the Supreme Court* (New York: Simon and Schuster, 1979).

7. Joseph Tanenhaus, Marvin Schick, Matthew Muraskin, and Daniel Rosen, "The Supreme Court's Certiorari Jurisdiction: Cue Theory," in Glendon Schubert, ed., *Judicial Decision-Making* (New York: Free Press, 1963), chap. 5.

8. S. Sidney Ulmer, "The Decision to Grant Certiorari as an Indicator to Decision 'On the Merits,' " *Polity* 4 (1972): 429-47.

9. Doris Marie Provine, *Case Selection in the United States Supreme Court* (Chicago: University of Chicago Press, 1980), p. 82.

10. Ibid., p. 83.

11. Stuart H. Teger and Douglas Kosinski, "The Cue Theory of Supreme Court Certiorari Jurisdiction: A Reconsideration," *Journal of Politics* 42 (1980): 834-46.

12. Donald R. Songer, "Concern for Policy Outputs as a Cue for Supreme Court Decisions on Certiorari," *Journal of Politics* 41 (1979): 1185-94.

13. Glendon Schubert, "Policy without Law: An Extension of the Certiorari Game," *Stanford Law Review* 14 (1962): 284-327.

14. Ulmer, "Decision to Grant Certiorari," p. 434.

15. Ulmer, "Supreme Court Justices," p. 20.

16. Ulmer, "Decision to Grant Certiorari," p. 437.

17. Lawrence Baum, "Policy Goals in Judicial Gatekeeping: A Proximity Model of Discretionary Jurisdiction," *American Journal of Political Science* 21 (1977): 13-35; Lawrence Baum, "Judicial Demand-Screening and Decisions on the Merits: A Second Look," *American Politics Quarterly* 7 (1979): 109-19; Provine, *Case Selection,* p. 108.

18. These data are provided in the court's minutes, which are published in the advance copies of the *California Reports.* Users of the minutes will encounter one difficulty because only votes to grant review are published, not votes to deny. Therefore, the minutes for each day were examined to ensure that evidence of participation existed for each justice. If no evidence could be found indicating substantial participation in that day's conference, the justice was coded as not participating.

19. The Wright court as used here runs from January 1, 1973, to February 1, 1977, the date Chief Justice Wright's resignation became official.

20. Henry Robert Glick and Kenneth N. Vines, *State Court Systems* (Englewood Cliffs, N.J.: Prentice-Hall, 1973), pp. 11-12.

21. "No Longer Best or Brightest," *Time,* November 29, 1982, p. 57.

22. Ibid.

23. Judicial Council of California, *Annual Report of the Administrative Office of the California Courts* (San Francisco: Judicial Council of California, 1979), pp. 43-46.

24. See Stanley Mosk, "Foreword: The Rule of Four in California," *California Law Review* 63 (1975): 2-8.

25. Preble Stolz, *Judging Judges: The Investigation of Rose Bird and the California Supreme Court* (New York: Free Press, 1981), pp. 195–96.

26. William M. Goodman and Thom Greenfield Seaton, "Foreword: Ripe for Decision, Internal Workings and Current Concerns of the California Supreme Court," *California Law Review* 63 (1973): 309-64.

27. J. Woodford Howard, Jr., "Litigation Flow in Three United States Courts of Appeals," *Law and Society Review* 8 (1973): 40-41.

28. Doris Marie Provine, "Deciding What to Decide: How the Supreme Court Sets Its Agenda," *Judicature* 64 (1981): 327.

29. See, e.g., Sickels, "Illusion of Judicial Consensus."

30. Ronald Dworkin, *Taking Rights Seriously* (Cambridge, Mass.: Harvard University Press, 1977), pp. 81-130.

31. Provine, *Case Selection,* p. 32.

32. Baum, "Policy Goals," p. 14.

33. Glendon Schubert, *Quantitative Analysis of Judicial Behavior* (Glencoe, Ill.: Free Press, 1959), pp. 173-267; Schubert, "Policy without Law"; Saul Brenner, "The New Certiorari Game," *Journal of Politics* 41 (1979): 649-55.

34. Ulmer, "Decision to Grant Certiorari," p. 440; Baum, "Judicial Demand-Screening," p. 113; Provine, *Case Selection,* p. 108.

35. Ulmer, "Decision to Grant Certiorari," pp. 442-43.

36. Doris Marie Provine, "Case Selection in the United States Supreme Court," paper delivered at the Annual Meeting of the American Political Science Association, August 31-September 3, 1979, Washington, D.C.

37. John A. Stookey and William Bowen, "Discretionary Review of Criminal Cases in the Arizona Supreme Court," *Arizona State University Law Journal* (1978): 755.

Epilogue

SHELDON GOLDMAN
and CHARLES M. LAMB

The purpose of this book was to explore the type, frequency, intensity, and especially the causes and phenomena related to conflict and consensus on American appellate courts. The studies in the preceding chapters have taken several approaches for investigating these concepts. They include examining attitudes and values (or ideology-policy considerations), role conceptions, and small group decision making as well as probing the influence of a number of variables that may be relevant for the analysis of judicial dissent, including caseloads, the complexity of the issues before the court, departure from precedent and reversal of lower courts, and threats to courts from their political environments. Collectively, macro and microlevel analyses have been used to describe, explain, and theorize about the causes of conflict and consensus, in part confirming prior findings, certainly building on prior research, and providing new insights into judicial behavior.

By encouraging the contributors to this volume to examine judicial conflict and consensus in various ways and by including studies of all three major levels of collegial courts, we have hoped that the significance of this volume has gone beyond the findings presented in the individual chapters. Specifically, we believe that collectively the studies not only fill in gaps concerning theories of judicial behavior but also permit us to compare different levels of appellate courts in some useful ways and to suggest some paths to potentially fruitful further research. Let us elaborate on each of these points.

THEORY

Several empirical theories to explain judicial behavior have emerged since the pioneering work of C. Herman Pritchett.[1] The preceding chapters focused on conflict and consensus and relied on voting data to explore judges' decision making. The authors analyzed judges' attitudes and values, selected backgrounds, role perceptions, and small group interactions. First used to test hypotheses involving the behavior of justices on the U.S. Supreme Court, these approaches, with some methodological modifications, are now used to study judges' behavior on the U.S. courts of appeals and state supreme courts. This book suggests that students of the courts of appeals and the state supreme courts have creatively responded to the "upper court myth" criticism of the judicial politics field. Although there is still a strong focus on the U.S. Supreme Court, lower-level appellate courts offer a rich opportunity for testing decision-making hypotheses, as the studies reported in this volume show.[2]

The attitudinal approach is reflected in an impressive body of literature. It has provided a staple means for investigating Supreme Court behavior for some three decades[3] and has been used to an extent regarding the courts of appeals[4] and state supreme courts.[5] Theorizing about the influence of attitudes on judges' decisions is chiefly anchored on the fundamental assumption that empirical regularities in what can be interpreted as distinct patterns of judges' voting behavior can be taken to reflect their attitudes and values[6] or at least that they behave as if they hold such attitudes and values. The examination of opinions may be added to quantitative analysis, however, so as to illuminate even further judicial attitudes, as this volume's study by Spaeth and Altfeld suggests. Bloc analysis and cumulative scaling constitute the two major traditional methods for probing the attitudes of judges, but alternative measurement procedures have been developed.[7]

Because the attitudinal approach has been so clearly and closely associated with research on judicial behavior, its explicit use by some of the contributors to this book is not surprising. Danelski's chapter sheds a great deal of light on how attitudinal and other behavioral approaches may be combined in a multicausal model to produce a fruitful research strategy.[8] After content analysis, he applies scaling in an innovative way to examine activism and restraint role conceptions as they relate to judicial conflict and consensus in civil liberties decisions. Whereas Danelski specifically uses scaling, the chapters by Heck, Spaeth and Altfeld, Wasby, Lamb, and Flango, Ducat, and McKnight rely to varying degrees on quantitative measures of judicial interagreement related to the theory upon which bloc analysis is grounded. That is, bloc analysis is not used in its traditional form in these chapters,[9] but these authors provide different types of analysis demonstrating levels of agreement and disagreement between and among judges in non-unanimous decisions. The studies in this book implicitly or explicitly suggest a crucial point—that diversity of attitudes is related to the dynamics of conflict and consensus on American collegial courts. This is true, as the chapter by Dudley demonstrates, even in a significant portion of access decisions as distinct from decisions on the merits. Data showing the extensiveness of overt dissent on appellate courts are presented in the contribution by Ulmer, which spans the history of the Supreme Court from John Marshall's chief justiceship, Green's chapter, which focuses on all courts of appeals, and the work by Glick and Pruet, who provide longitudinal data on dissent behavior for all fifty state supreme courts. Other chapters also contain valuable findings on dissent behavior as well as unanimous decisions that mask attitudinal conflict.

Inasmuch as individual attitudes and values may be shaped in part by life experiences, a number of studies have sought to test the relationship of judges' attributes or background characteristics to their behavior.[10] Although this empirical research has resulted in mixed conclusions concerning the existence and strength of the relationship, the backgrounds approach continues to be of interest to students of judicial behavior.[11] The theoretical underpinnings of this approach are less sophisticated than those underlying attitudinal analysis. Essentially, theorizing involves the basic notion that personal background traits and related life experiences converge to leave an imprint on judges that may affect their decisions. Background variables most frequently given attention include political party identification, religion, socioeconomic status, and prior judicial or political experience.

Some chapters in this book touch upon the backgrounds approach. Peterson's propositional inventory on dissent in American courts concludes that there is "some confirmation" for the hypothesis that judicial disagreement increases as the diversity of judges' backgrounds increases.[12] Although Glick/Pruet, Flango/Ducat/McKnight, and Stookey allude to the possible relationship between conflict and diverse backgrounds, it is directly addressed in only two chapters, one by Songer and the other by Lamb. Songer specifically tested the hypothesis for party affiliation, as well as ideology and the presence or absence of a district court judge serving on a panel. Songer's data base, it will be recalled, included courts of appeals decisions between 1953 and 1975 which concerned criminal law and labor relations issues. He discovered strongest support for the ideology variable, mixed results for the presence or absence of a district judge, but no significant relationship between dissent and political party identification. Lamb, on the other hand, had a different finding in his study of the D.C. Circuit. Lamb showed that Warren Burger, a Republican Protestant, tended to be in very high conflict in criminal cases with colleagues who were Democrats and either Catholic or Jewish. In light of the checkered findings in the entire body of the backgrounds-behavior literature, however, perhaps it is no surprise that the conclusions of Songer and Lamb are not entirely consistent on the party variable, especially since one study is at the macrolevel and the other is a microanalysis.

Judicial role analysis receives greater attention than background analysis from our contributors.[13] In theory, a judge's view of his or her role may be an important factor influencing the degree to which attitudes, values, and backgrounds affect decision making. The specific role conceptions most often addressed in this book are those of activism and restraint. In general, activist judges are more likely to view their proper role as intervening in the political process to promote policy which they believe to be advantageous to society; restraint-oriented judges are more likely to view their proper role as deferring to the elected branches in making policy and resolving societal problems.[14]

Of the studies in this book, some bear only indirectly on activist-restraint role concepts, such as Dudley's, which suggests that some voting on access decisions may be governed by role considerations. Two chapters, however, both of which focus on the U.S. Supreme Court, directly examine activism versus restraint.[15] Danelski theorizes that expectations of restraint and adherence to precedent tend to limit dissent by avoiding attitudinal and value differences among justices that might otherwise cause conflict in the Court. To test this proposition empirically, he successfully scaled votes in civil liberties cases that, based on content analysis, seemed to turn on activism-restraint expectations and concluded that these role concepts in fact underlay the votes cast in those decisions. Danelski also quantitatively investigated dissenting opinions in those cases, developing activism-restraint scores for justices who articulated those role conceptions. He then used Spearman rank-order correlations to demonstrate that role concepts and values are significantly related, discovering that disparities in commitments to values and role expectations often cause conflict in the Supreme Court. Overall, role concepts are an important part of Danelski's multicausal model. The microlevel analysis of Spaeth and Altfeld, on the other hand, looked at activism-restraint concepts on the Warren Court with a specific focus on Justice Frankfurter.[16] Like Danelski, the authors examined voting behavior in cases amenable to resolution on the basis of exercising restraint but demonstrated that Frankfurter's voting was frequently inconsistent with the restraint role conception. Moreover, their in-depth analysis contains detailed insights into judicial behavior that are not normally possible in macro studies. They probe rates of interagreement between specific justices in four different data sets and demonstrate that voting conflict was markedly less evident in some issues than in others. Spaeth and Altfeld are also the only contributors to this volume who combine voting and opinion analysis to show that although a justice's language in opinions often gives lip service to fundamental notions of restraint, the reasoning used may actually rationalize the casting of activist votes.

Finally, the small group approach has been addressed to varying degrees in this book.[17] Small group theory essentially suggests that it is the group condition, the interactions among judges in the decision-making process, that affects the decisions ultimately reached. As noted in the Prologue, we believe that it is useful for students of judicial behavior to develop quantitative approaches for the analysis of courts as small groups to complement nonquantitative analyses based solely on the private papers of deceased judges. Some contributors to this volume consider small group theory more indirectly than do others. Ulmer's exploratory analysis, for example, suggests that the level of conflict on the Supreme Court is in part a measure of the leadership abilities of chief justices and that their influence in the small group may decline when they dissent and thus relinquish the power to assign majority opinions. Similarly, Heck hints at small group concepts by emphasizing voting alliances and the tendency of the chief justice to remain close to the Court's "center of gravity" so as to exercise leadership opportunities. Wasby's major finding that consensus on the Ninth Circuit is lowest for panels that contain a visiting judge and highest for those containing only Ninth Circuit judges in active service has implications for the dynamics of the small group. Outsiders are by definition not fully socialized into the group and are less subject to group norms and the constraints they may place on dissent behavior. Stookey's research on the Arizona Supreme Court suggests that the size of the court may be related to dissent rate. Glick and Pruet show a positive relationship between size of court and dissent rate on state supreme courts, particularly those systems with intermediate-level courts. Three of this volume's twelve studies are even more directly relevant for small group theory: the chapters by Danelski, Flango/Ducat/McKnight, and Green. The first two focus on the small group concept of leadership, and we discuss them first.

Theory underlying the examination of collegial courts as small groups suggests among other things that personality may determine which judges are most likely to provide leadership on a court.[18] Danelski's chapter is important to this line of inquiry because it seeks to examine quantitatively the Supreme Court's decisional process by exploring the relevance of personality in the exercise of leadership. Specifically, he hypothesized that the adequacy of task and social leadership affects conflict and its resolution and that personality is related to the adequacy of such leadership. After confirming that conflict is more likely to be resolved when task and social leadership are clearly evident, Danelski relies on Justice Douglas's docket books for the 1939, 1940, 1942, and 1943 terms to analyze empirically vote changes between conference and final decisions. The theory behind the investigation is that conflict resolution is manifest when justices initially dissent from the majority in conference but ultimately agree with the majority's final decision.[19] Although several variables might potentially account for the resolution of such conflict, leadership in the small group certainly provides the basis for a partial empirical explanation. Danelski confirms the effective leadership abilities of Chief Justice Hughes and Justice Black by developing leadership scores, that is, the percentage of times a justice's dissenting and pass votes in conference subsequently became majority votes in cases assigned to him for opinion. Of additional theoretical interest is that when a new chief justice is a relatively weak leader, other justices may actively compete for leadership on the Court. Pursuing this hypothesis, Danelski's data show that leadership scores became widely dispersed among Court members when Stone replaced Hughes as chief justice, thereby demonstrating the hypothesized competition. Judicial biographies and other nonquantitative research indicate that the personalities of Hughes, Stone, Black, Frankfurter, and other justices may have affected their ability to provide satisfactory leadership. Danelski goes beyond this literature by empirically comparing justices' acquiescence in majority opinions on the Hughes and Stone courts after they originally cast a dissent in conference. This important comparison shows that acquiescence decreased by more than 25 percent after Stone became chief justice and suggests to Danelski that the personalities of the two chiefs probably accounts for some differences in their leadership abilities. In several ways, then, Danelski has contributed to theoretical approaches for studying leadership on collegial courts and may point toward additional progress in future empirical research addressing the importance of personality in resolving conflict in judicial decision making.

A somewhat different perspective than Danelski's is taken by Flango, Ducat, and McKnight, whose principal objective was to investigate leadership on state supreme courts through analysis of opinion assignments and coalitions in decisions with nonunanimous opinions.[20] A judge, in theory, may provide leadership if he or she regularly attracts colleagues to join his or her opinions, and the exercise of leadership may affect the level of conflict and consensus on a collegial court. Actual or informal leadership may also be distinguished from formal leadership associated with being chief justice. Given this basic theoretical foundation, they quantitatively probe conflictual and consensual voting patterns on the Michigan and Pennsylvania supreme courts to measure leadership via several different methods.[21] They show that leaders on state supreme courts may be potentially identified, for example, by the percentage of a judge's total opinion output that becomes the majority position, by the percentage of times that a judge writes for the court majority when he had an opportunity to do so, by the capacity to speak for the majority relative to the size of the dominant coalition, and by the percentage of colleagues an opinion-writer can attract to his position. In fact, however, after experimenting with these and other potential measures of leadership, it was concluded that some may not be valid indicators of leadership on collegial courts but rather measure other factors such as equitability of opinion assignment or power. The Inter-individual Solidarity Index appeared to be the best indicator of leadership. Finally, Flango, Ducat, and McKnight maintain that judges may exhibit leadership in minority coalitions. This concept of alternative leadership may be manifested in a judge's capacity to attract others to join dissenting opinions—provided, of course, that leadership is not defined as determining what the law will be at a particular time. Indeed, the authors observed that, theoretically, the ability of a dissenting judge to gain the support of his colleagues may be a more accurate indicator of leadership under some circumstances than the degree of support given to the majority opinion-writer.

Green's chapter seeks to penetrate the small group from another angle by updating and expanding the scope of previous empirical research on unanimous and nonunanimous decision making on the U.S. courts of appeals.[22] Because of structural changes, increases in the number of judges on the courts of appeals since 1978, and the expanded use of special judges sitting "by designation,"[23] the decision-making environment on these intermediate appellate courts has changed considerably in recent years. Green theorizes that these changes have altered the nature of the three-judge appeals court work group, that is, the number of possible panel combinations has grown geometrically and the same judges serve together in a three-judge small group less frequently. Comparing data on dissent rates in all three-judge criminal law decisions by the circuits from 1966 to 1970 with the dissent rates for such cases in 1980, no striking changes in the level of appeals court dissensus was found. Dissensus did increase in 1980, however, when unanimous decisions were used to measure disagreement. This finding suggested to Green that all appeals court decisions, not just those in which a dissent is officially registered, must be included in a data base used to examine dissensus on the courts of appeals, and that changes in the nature of the three-judge appeals court work group since 1978 have caused a growth in dissensus on some circuits. Overall, then, because of fundamental structural differences in how most appeals courts decide cases, as compared to the U.S. Supreme Court and the state courts of last resort, Green has generated small group theory quite unlike that developed by Danelski or by Flango, Ducat, and McKnight.

COMPARATIVE INSTITUTIONAL BEHAVIOR

It is fair to observe that students of judicial behavior have not given much attention to comparative institutional behavior.[24] Writing in 1983 about the study of judicial politics, Baum pointed out that "scholars in the field have shown little taste for cross-institutional research even within the judiciary. It is notable, for instance, how little research compares federal and state courts."[25]

To the extent possible, based on the studies in this book, we can suggest some tentative comparative conclusions concerning judicial conflict and consensus. The basic question is whether, if we control for appellate court level, there are regularities of behavioral patterns concerning conflict and consensus that permit us to make generalizations about these phenomena. We must emphasize at the outset, however, that our ability to answer this question is limited because our contributors only occasionally focus on the same causes of conflict and consensus at different levels of appellate courts.

Most fundamentally, all the studies in this book indicate that conflict and consensus in voting patterns vary on the different levels of American appellate courts over time. The chapters by Spaeth and Altfeld, Songer, Lamb, Stookey, and Dudley likewise demonstrate fluctuations in specific issues presented to courts for resolution. Beyond this, Peterson's 1981 propositional inventory on dissent in American courts provides a framework to improve an understanding of comparative institutional behavior.[26] He divides the influences on judicial dissent into four categories: legal culture, organizational and institutional factors, the sociopolitical system, and individual factors. The last of these categories was discussed in the preceding section on theory.

Although an edited volume like this one cannot address all the causes of dissent such as those outlined by Peterson, several interesting patterns nevertheless can be noted. Under the rubric of legal culture as an influence on dissent, Peterson explains that judges and academics alike have "indirectly confirmed" the hypothesis that dissent is generated by difficult questions.[27] The chapters in this volume by Ulmer, Songer, and Stookey are most relevant here. Ulmer suggests that dissent on the U.S. Supreme Court is in part a function of the complexity of issues and that the marked increase of 5–4 decisions since the Taft Court is consistent with the hypothesis that Supreme Court decisions on the merits have become more complex over time. Ulmer then develops a measure of case complexity to test the proposition that when personnel changes occur on the Court, a chief justice can more easily marshal his majorities when cases are less complex. He concludes that, although further research is needed, dissent rates by chief justices have been significantly influenced by case complexity, along with other factors such as frequency of new appointments and the presidents making those appointments. In contrast, Songer approaches the complexity hypothesis from different perspectives regarding the U.S. courts of appeals and reaches a similar tentative conclusion. He first selected criminal cases that would be expected to produce a higher percentage of difficult legal questions but discovered no significant differences in rates of dissent. When Songer hypothesized that the Supreme Court tends to grant review in cases involving more difficult issues and that the rate of appeals court dissent in those cases would be greater than in cases denied review, however, his tentative findings provided moderately strong support for the expectation that complex questions produce greater conflict on federal appeals courts.[28] Overall, these studies of two different levels of federal appellate courts provide support for a complexity-dissent relationship, but both indicate the need for further research. Stookey also tested the hypothesis with the Arizona Supreme Court but reached more mixed conclusions than Ulmer and Songer. Assuming that public law questions in state supreme courts are likely to be more complex and controversial than others, Stookey found that the dissent rate on the Arizona Supreme Court was indeed twice as high as that in private and criminal law cases between 1913 and 1976. When specific time periods were considered, however, he was forced to conclude that his docket composition theory of conflict had limited explanatory power in the context of state supreme court decision making.

Peterson's inventory indicates that there is "some confirmation" for the proposition that dissent increases with the overturning of precedent.[29] The studies in this book do not directly test this hypothesis, but they do analyze whether reversing lower courts seems to increase conflict. Songer proposed that one may indirectly examine appeals court departures from Supreme Court doctrine by determining whether appeals court decisional trends in criminal and labor relations cases were consistent with the Supreme Court's decisional tendencies during the same general time period. After comparing the percentage of prodefendant and prolabor decisions at both federal appellate levels, however, he discovered no support for the proposition that the rate of dissent in appeals courts significantly increases when decisions are contrary to Supreme Court trends. Songer, however, found higher dissent rates when the courts of appeals reversed district court decisions than when they affirmed them. The same result was found by Lamb, whose study of the D.C. Circuit showed that dissent was clearly more likely to emerge when three-judge panels reversed rather than affirmed district court decisions (but this pattern did not hold for *en banc* reversals). Wasby, relying only on three-judge panel decisions for the Ninth Circuit, also found that conflict usually occurred twice as often when the lower court was reversed than when it was affirmed.

In considering organizational and institutional factors that influence dissent, this book's studies shed some light on the relationship between workload and conflict, which Peterson reports has received "indirect confirmation."[30] Contrary to the suggestions or findings of others, including the interviews reported by Wasby, Songer found no statistically significant relationship between appeals court caseload per judge and level of dissent. Nor did he discover a relationship between average caseload per judge and variation in dissent rates across circuits. Similarly, although Green found evidence suggesting that workload suppressed dissents on the courts of appeals between 1966 and 1970, his analysis of dissent rates during 1980 indicated that this relationship no longer existed. Glick and Pruet also hypothesized that less disagreement will be evident on state supreme courts with larger caseloads, and their findings, falsifying the hypothesis, are consistent with those of Songer and Green. Looking at appeals court outputs, Lamb additionally found no relationship between magnitude of dissent, the time taken for judges to reach final decisions, and the total number of decisions announced by the D.C. Circuit. Findings for the courts of appeals and the state supreme courts thus call into question the widely believed "common sense" proposition that the greater the caseload the less incentive a judge has to dissent. The U.S. Supreme Court has had a vastly increased workload over the past two decades compared to a half century ago, but this has not diminished dissent on the Court, as Ulmer's findings indicate. Thus the evidence in this volume can be taken to suggest strongly as a behavioral proposition that dissent on American courts is unrelated to caseload pressures.

Some political scientists have examined the association between high rates of dissent and threat situations to a court, with the findings being mixed.[31] This relationship is analyzed by Ulmer regarding chief justices of the U.S. Supreme Court and by Songer regarding the courts of appeals. Ulmer concludes that fluctuation in dissent rates over time cannot be attributed to congressional pressure on the Supreme Court. Songer similarly finds no significant differences between rates of dissent on the courts of appeals during threat and nonthreat periods.

Insofar as the influence of the sociopolitical system on dissent is concerned, two studies tested whether urbanization was associated with increases in judicial conflict, a hypothesis that has been previously confirmed.[32] Regarding the courts of appeals, Songer developed an urbanism index for each circuit, compared it to dissent rates in each circuit, and found strong support for the hypothesis. Regarding state supreme courts, Glick and Pruet likewise found a relationship between urbanization and dissent, although the correlation was somewhat weaker in recent years than found in prior research. Glick and Pruet also indicated support for previous findings that states with intermediate appellate courts witness higher rates of dissent on their supreme courts, with intermediate courts apparently siphoning off less controversial cases.[33]

Beyond the specific propositions reported by Peterson, the studies in this book suggest other, at times related, causes of conflict. For example, several chapters note that the policy direction of a court's decisions may generate additional conflict among judges—a proposition that is only to be expected. Obviously, if a majority of judges begins to depart substantially from a court's prior policy trends, dissenting members are likely to express their concern. Danelski illustrates this in his analysis of dissenting behavior on the Supreme Court. Heck demonstrates that conflict accompanied policy shifts between the Warren and Burger courts, which was especially prominent in the voting behavior of Justices Brennan and Marshall. By contrast, concerning the courts of appeals, one of the strongest relationships discovered by Songer is that dissent is more likely to emerge in liberal criminal decisions or in conservative labor decisions. Lamb's study additionally indicates that conflict between Burger and his colleagues changed over time because of some policy shifts in specific criminal issues and perhaps because of the ideological composition of certain three-judge panels.

From our brief excursion into comparative institutional behavior, we conclude by emphasizing two points. First, the studies in this book suggest more similarities than differences in the causes of conflict and consensus on American collegial courts. Despite significant differences in the magnitude of dissent on the three major levels of American appellate courts, the degree to which certain variables seem to be related to conflict and consensus is perhaps greater than one would have anticipated. Second, the investigations in this book have helped to confirm some of the propositions identified by Peterson to a greater extent than before.

IMPLICATIONS FOR FUTURE RESEARCH

At least two basic ways exist for suggesting future macro and microlevel examinations of judicial conflict and consensus beyond that which has been alluded to thus far. An obvious way is simply to view the studies in this book in conjunction with Peterson's survey of the judicial dissent literature. From this vantage point, it becomes clear that some hypotheses relating dissent to the legal culture, organizational and institutional factors, the sociopolitical system, and individual factors have been more systematically examined than others. Still deserving greater attention on one or more levels of appellate courts, for example, are hypotheses relating dissent to court professionalism, intercourt relations, coalition formation, and controversial issues on which there is little agreement in society generally.[34] Operationalizing and testing some of these hypotheses may be difficult, which may account in part for the paucity of research to date relating to them. From this book, it also would seem that more research is needed on the courts of appeals and especially on the state supreme courts concerning several of Peterson's hypotheses.

Another way of pointing toward future research is for students of judicial behavior to pursue some lines of inquiry developed by the contributors to this book that have received relatively little previous attention. Although we have mentioned in passing some fruitful lines of future research, several additional illustrations drawn from the studies in this book are appropriate:

- Danelski correctly notes that quantitative measures of personality need to be developed further so as to increase our understanding of the relationship between leadership and conflict, and certainly his conception of policy leadership deserves attention.
- Ulmer's chapter explicitly and implicitly suggests a large number of hypotheses that could be profitably examined regarding dissent by chief justices.
- Heck's concept of center-of-gravity justice deserves further testing.
- Spaeth and Altfeld suggest a line of research deserving attention—whether the discrepancy between a judge's professed role orientation and his or her actual voting behavior affects conflict with colleagues.
- Songer's findings suggest that more detailed analysis of circuits by year is warranted.

• Green's research again underscores the importance of probing conflict in unanimous as well as nonunanimous decisions. The coefficient of variation appears to be a useful methodological tool for accomplishing this task. Green was concerned only with criminal cases. Similar analyses of other issues are needed to determine whether some (and which) issues more readily lend themselves to conflict, overt or masked.

• Wasby's findings for the Ninth Circuit obviously raise the question whether they would hold true for the other circuits.

• Lamb's microanalysis of one judge could serve as a model for examining, for example, circuit judges whose prominence might eventually take them to the Supreme Court. Comparisons of behavior of judges on the Supreme Court with their behavior when they previously served on the circuit bench might also be conducted.

• Glick and Pruet's immensely important finding that dissent rates on the state supreme courts is on the increase suggests that more attention can and should be paid to these courts. At the very least, there is an urgent need to retest Nagel's classic study of the relationship of background characteristics to voting behavior on state supreme courts.[35] Glick and Pruet's finding relating the amount of state expenditures to dissent levels on state supreme courts deserves further examination.

• Flango, Ducat, and McKnight's study of Michigan and Pennsylvania could well be replicated with other state supreme courts, particularly in light of the relatively high dissent rates reported by Glick and Pruet. The use of the Inter-individual Solidarity Index might result in useful analytic payoffs such as were found by the authors.

• Stookey's finding suggesting a relationship between court size and dissent rate deserves further investigation, especially if it can be done longitudinally with other courts whose number of judges has varied. Similarly, analysis of docket composition and dissent rates over time as conducted by Stookey for Arizona could well be undertaken for other states.

• Dudley's analysis comparing votes on access decisions to votes on the merits raises the obvious question whether other state courts with control over their dockets display similar behavior. Dudley's finding that there was greater overt dissent on access decisions than on decisions on the merits begs for similar study of other courts' access decision making.

There is much that we know about conflict and consensus on appellate courts and much that we need to know. A full research agenda is open to anyone who has the imagination, energy, and persistence to follow through. We know more about judicial conflict and consensus than we did twenty years ago. We should know still more twenty years from now if the quality and quantity of research in the field are maintained.

1. For a recent overview of these approaches, see James L. Gibson, "From Simplicity to Complexity: The Development of Theory in the Study of Judicial Behavior," *Political Behavior* 5 (1983): 7-49. See also the survey by Glendon Schubert, "Behavioral Studies of the American Legal System," in Robert J. Janosik, ed., *Encyclopedia of the American Judicial System* (New York: Macmillan-Scribner's, forthcoming). For earlier surveys of the development of these approaches, see, e.g., C. Herman Pritchett, "Public Law and Judicial Behavior," *Journal of Politics* 30 (1968): 480-509; C. Herman Pritchett, "The Development of Judicial Research," in Joel B. Grossman and Joseph Tanenhaus, eds., *Frontiers of Judicial Research* (New York: Wiley, 1969), chap. 2; Glendon Schubert, "Judicial Process and Behavior, 1963-1971," in James A. Robinson, ed., *Political Science Annual,* 3 (Indianapolis: Bobbs-Merrill, 1972), 94-138; Sheldon Goldman, "Behavioral Approaches to Judicial Decision-Making: Toward a Theory of Judicial Voting Behavior," *Jurimetrics Journal* 11 (1971): 142-64.

2. The rich literature on trial courts further underscores our points that research in judicial politics is no longer dominated by a U.S. Supreme Court focus and that in modified form the approaches developed for the study of the Supreme Court are adaptable even for trial court research although, of course, special methods have been devised to meet the special problems of such investigation.

3. See C. Herman Pritchett, *The Roosevelt Court: A Study of Judicial Politics and Values, 1937-1947* (New York: Macmillan, 1948); Glendon Schubert, *The Judicial Mind: The Attitudes and Ideologies of Supreme Court Justices, 1946-1963* (Evanston: Northwestern University Press, 1965), chap. 5. See also the discussion of the attitudinal literature in Sheldon Goldman and Thomas P. Jahnige, *The Federal Courts as a Political System,* 3d ed. (New York: Harper & Row, 1985), pp. 137-46.

4. See, for example, Sheldon Goldman, "Conflict on the U.S. Courts of Appeals 1965-1971: A Quantitative Analysis," *University of Cincinnati Law Review* 42 (1973): 635-58; Burton M. Atkins and Justin J. Green, "Consensus on the United States Courts of Appeals: Illusion or Reality?" *American Journal of Political Science* 20 (1976): 735-48.

5. See, for example, Daryl R. Fair, "Experimental Application of Scalogram Analysis to State Supreme Court Decisions," *Wisconsin Law Review* (1967): 449-67.

6. See Schubert, *Judicial Mind,* pp. 22-37.

7. See C. Neal Tate, "The Methodology of Judicial Behavior Research: A Review and Critique," *Political Behavior* 5 (1983): 65-70.

8. See also David J. Danelski, "Values as Variables in Judicial Decision-Making: Notes toward a Theory," *Vanderbilt Law Review* 19 (1966): 721-40.

9. See Glendon Schubert, *Quantitative Analysis of Judicial Behavior* (Glencoe, Ill.: Free Press, 1959), chap. 3.

10. See, for example, Micheal W. Giles and Thomas G. Walker, "Judicial Policy-Making and Southern School Segregation," *Journal of Politics* 37 (1975): 917-36; Stuart S. Nagel, *The Legal Process from a Behavioral Perspective* (Homewood, Ill.: Dorsey, 1969), chaps. 16-19; S. Sidney Ulmer, "Social Background as an Indicator to Votes of Supreme Court Justices in Criminal Cases: 1947-1956 Terms," *American Journal of Political Science* 17 (1973): 622-30.

11. For leading recent studies see Robert A. Carp and C. K. Rowland, *Policymaking and Politics in the Federal District Courts* (Knoxville: University of Tennessee Press, 1983); C. Neal Tate, "Personal Attribute Models of Voting Behavior of U.S. Supreme Court Justices: Liberalism in Civil Liberties and Economics Decisions, 1946-1978," *American Political Science Review* 75 (1981): 355-67.

12. Steven A. Peterson, "Dissent in American Courts," *Journal of Politics* 43 (1981): 424.

13. For an overview of the role literature, see Goldman and Jahnige, *Federal Courts*, pp. 162-67 and the research cited therein.

14. See the studies in Stephen C. Halpern and Charles M. Lamb, eds., *Supreme Court Activism and Restraint* (Lexington, Mass.: Lexington Books, 1982); Mary Cornelia Porter and G. Alan Tarr, eds., *State Supreme Courts: Policymakers in the Federal System* (Westport, Conn.: Greenwood Press, 1982).

15. Although none of this volume's chapters directly tests for the saliency of role conceptions on the courts of appeals and the state supreme courts, other literature is available. See Henry Robert Glick, *Supreme Courts in State Politics: An Investigation of the Judicial Role* (New York: Basic Books, 1971); J. Woodford Howard, Jr., *Courts of Appeals in the Federal Judicial System: A Study of the Second, Fifth, and District of Columbia Circuits* (Princeton: Princeton University Press, 1981).

16. This chapter is related to earlier work on Frankfurter by Spaeth. See Harold J. Spaeth, "The Judicial Restraint of Mr. Justice Frankfurter—Myth or Reality," *Midwest Journal of Political Science* 8 (1964): 22-38; Harold J. Spaeth, *Supreme Court Policy Making: Explanation and Prediction* (San Francisco: W. H. Freeman, 1979), pp. 78-80.

17. To be sure, a number of facets of small group research have not been examined in detail by this book's contributors although some may be inferred from various analyses. For a general survey of the small group literature see, for example, Goldman and Jahnige, *Federal Courts*, pp. 149-58 and the research cited therein.

18. See David J. Danelski, "Conflict and Its Resolution in the Supreme Court," *Journal of Conflict Resolution* 11 (1967): 82-84; David J. Danelski, "The Influence of the Chief Justice in the Decisional Process of the Supreme Court," in Sheldon Goldman and Austin Sarat, eds., *American Court Systems: Readings in Judicial Process and*

Behavior (San Francisco: W. H. Freeman, 1978), pp. 506-18. A similar concept emerges from a number of in-depth works on individual justices. See, for example, H. N. Hirsch, *The Enigma of Felix Frankfurter* (New York: Basic Books, 1981); Alpheus T. Mason, *Harlan Fiske Stone: Pillar of the Law* (New York: Viking, 1956).

19. Also relevant to this line of inquiry is the literature on issue fluidity. See, for example, Saul Brenner, "Fluidity on the Supreme Court: 1956-1967," *American Journal of Political Science* 26 (1982): 388-90.

20. Although opinion assignment on the U.S. Supreme Court is not systematically analyzed in any chapter in this book, it is occasionally referred to in some of them. See Harold J. Spaeth and Michael F. Altfeld, "Felix Frankfurter, Judicial Activism, and Voting Conflict on the Warren Court," Chapter 4 of this volume. For more systematic research on this subject, see the sources cited in Peterson, "Dissent in American Courts," p. 418, n. 30.

21. See also the related work of S. Sidney Ulmer, "Leadership in the Michigan Supreme Court," in Glendon Schubert, ed., *Judicial Decision-Making* (Glencoe, Ill.: Free Press, 1963), pp. 13-28.

22. Atkins and Green, "Consensus on the United States Courts of Appeals."

23. See also Stephen L. Wasby, "Of Judges, Hobgoblins, and Small Minds: Dimensions of Disagreement in the Ninth Circuit," Chapter 7 of this volume.

24. For some exceptions, see Edward N. Beiser, "A Comparative Analysis of State and Federal Judicial Behavior: The Reapportionment Cases," *American Political Science Review* 62 (1968): 788-95; Werner F. Grunbaum and Lettie M. Wenner, "Comparing Environmental Litigation in State and Federal Courts," *Publius* 10 (1980): 129-42; Kenneth C. Haas, "The Comparative Study of State and Federal Judicial Behavior Revisited," *Journal of Politics* 44 (1982): 721-46.

25. Lawrence Baum, "Judicial Politics: Still a Distinctive Field," in Ada W. Finifter, ed., *Political Science: The State of the Discipline* (Washington, D.C.: American Political Science Association, 1983), p. 205.

26. Peterson, "Dissent in American Courts."

27. Ibid., pp. 413-14, 424.

28. Songer finds some support for the hypothesis that constitutional issues are more likely to be accompanied by dissent than nonconstitutional issues, but Green's chapter finds little support for this hypothesis.

29. Peterson, "Dissent in American Courts," p. 414.

30. See ibid., pp. 415-16, 424. Other potential organizational and institutional factors listed by Peterson, such as diversity of background characteristics and the exercise of leadership, were discussed in the preceding theory section.

31. See ibid., pp. 419-20; Nagel, *Legal Process,* chap. 21.

32. See Peterson, "Dissent in American Courts," pp. 420, 424.

33. See ibid., p. 419.

34. See ibid., pp. 415, 418-20.

35. Nagel, *Legal Process,* chaps. 14, 17, and 18.

Contributors

Michael F. Altfeld is Associate Professor of Political Science at Michigan State University. He has published in the fields of international relations, defense policy, methodology, and formal theory, in addition to judicial politics. His articles have appeared in such journals as the *International Studies Quarterly,* the *Journal of Conflict Resolution, Political Methodology,* and the *Western Political Quarterly.*

David J. Danelski is Cecil H. and Louise Gamble Professor of Political Science, Dean of the Faculty, and Vice-President for Academic Affairs at Occidental College. His books include *A Supreme Court Justice Is Appointed* (1964), *Comparative Judicial Behavior* (1969), *The Autobiographical Notes of Charles Evans Hughes* (1973), among others. The author of numerous articles and chapters, he has served on the editorial boards of several professional journals, including *Law and Society Review, Political Behavior,* and *Teaching Political Science.*

Craig R. Ducat is Professor of Political Science at Northern Illinois University. He is co-author with Victor E. Flango of *Leadership on State Supreme Courts: The Roles of the Chief Justice* (1976). His many other books include *Constitutional Interpretation* (1974, 1979, 1983), *Corwin's The Constitution and What It Means Today* (1973, 1978), *Modes of Constitutional Interpretation* (1978), and *The Right to Privacy* (1976).

Robert L. Dudley is Assistant Professor of Political Science at Colorado State University. He is the author of book chapters and professional journal articles. His books in progress include *Taking the Constitution Seriously* and *Setting the Appellate Agenda.*

Victor E. Flango is Senior Staff Associate at the National Center for State Courts and previously taught at Northern Illinois University. Among his numerous publications are articles in the *American Journal of Political Science, Comparative Politics,* the *Journal of Politics, Judicature,* the *Justice System Journal,* the *Public Administration Review,* the *State Court Journal,* and the *Urban Affairs Quarterly.*

Henry R. Glick is Professor of Political Science at Florida State University. His books include *Supreme Courts in State Politics* (1971), *State Court Systems* (1972), and *Courts, Politics, and Justice* (1983). His articles have appeared in the *American Political Science Review,* the *American Journal of Political Science,* the *American Politics Quarterly,* the *Journal of Politics, Law and Society Review,* and *Polity.*

Sheldon Goldman is Professor of Political Science at the University of Massachusetts, Amherst. His books include *The Federal Courts as a Political System* (1971, 1976, 1985), *Constitutional Law and Supreme Court Decision-Making* (1982), *American Court Systems* (1978), and *The Federal Judicial System* (1968). The author of many articles in political science and law journals, he has served on the editorial boards of the *American Political Science Review* and the *American Journal of Political Science.*

Justin J. Green is Associate Professor of Government and Associate Dean of the College of Arts and Sciences at the University of San Francisco. Formerly the Associate Editor of the *Journal of Politics,* his articles have appeared in the *Administrative Science Quarterly,* the *American Journal of Political Science, Judicature,* and the *Western Political Quarterly.*

Edward V. Heck is Associate Professor of Political Science at San Diego State University. He is co-editor of *Political Ideas and Institutions* (1983), and his articles have been published in the *Journal of Politics, Judicature, Law and Policy Quarterly,* the *Social Science Quarterly,* and the *Western Political Quarterly.*

Charles M. Lamb is Associate Professor of Political Science at the State University of New York at Buffalo. He is the co-editor of *Supreme Court Activism and Restraint* (1982) and *Implementation of Civil Rights Policy* (1984) and author of many journal articles. Currently he is a member of the Executive Committee of the APSA Section on Law, Courts, and Judicial Process and President of the New York State Political Science Association.

R. Neal McKnight is Assistant Professor of Political Science at Northwest Missouri State University. His articles have appeared in *Judicature,* the *Social Science Quarterly,* and *Teaching Political Science,* among other forums.

George W. Pruet, Jr., is Assistant Professor of Political Science at the University of Akron. He previously taught at Florida State University and the University of New Orleans and has presented several papers at political science conventions.

Donald R. Songer is Associate Professor of Political Science at Oklahoma Baptist University. His articles have appeared in the *American Journal of Political Science,* the *Journal of Politics, Law and Society Review, Polity,* the *Social Science Quarterly,* and the *Western Political Quarterly,* as well as other journals.

Harold J. Spaeth is Professor of Political Science at Michigan State

University and a member of the Michigan bar. His books include *The Warren Court* (1966), *An Introduction to Supreme Court Decision Making* (1972), *Supreme Court Decision Making* (1976), and *Supreme Court Policy Making* (1979). His numerous articles have been published in the *American Journal of Political Science,* the *Journal of Politics,* and the *Western Political Quarterly,* among many other forums. Currently he is working on an NSF-funded project for a comprehensive data base covering the Warren and Burger Courts.

John A. Stookey is Associate Professor of Political Science at Arizona State University. His research has appeared in several books and in such journals as *Judicature* and the *Public Opinion Quarterly.* He is currently working on an NSF-funded project addressing the impact of economic cycles on trial court litigation and behavior.

S. Sidney Ulmer is Alumni Professor in the Department of Political Science at the University of Kentucky. His books include *Political Decision Making* (1970), *Military Justice and the Right to Counsel* (1970), *Courts, Law and Judicial Processes* (1981), and *Supreme Court Policy Making and Constitutional Law* (1985). The author of numerous political science journal articles and book chapters, he has served as President of the Southern Political Science Association and on the Board of Editors of the *American Journal of Political Science,* the *Journal of Politics,* and the *Midwest Journal of Political Science.*

Stephen L. Wasby is Professor of Political Science at the State University of New York at Albany. His books include *The Supreme Court in the Federal Judicial System* (1978, 1984), *Continuity and Change: From the Warren Court to the Burger Court* (1976), and *The Impact of the United States Supreme Court* (1970), among others. His articles on the U.S. courts of appeals have appeared in such journals as *Judicature, Law and Society Review,* the *Vanderbilt Law Review,* and the *Washington University Law Quarterly.* Currently he serves on the editorial boards of the *Justice System Journal* and *Law and Policy.*

Index